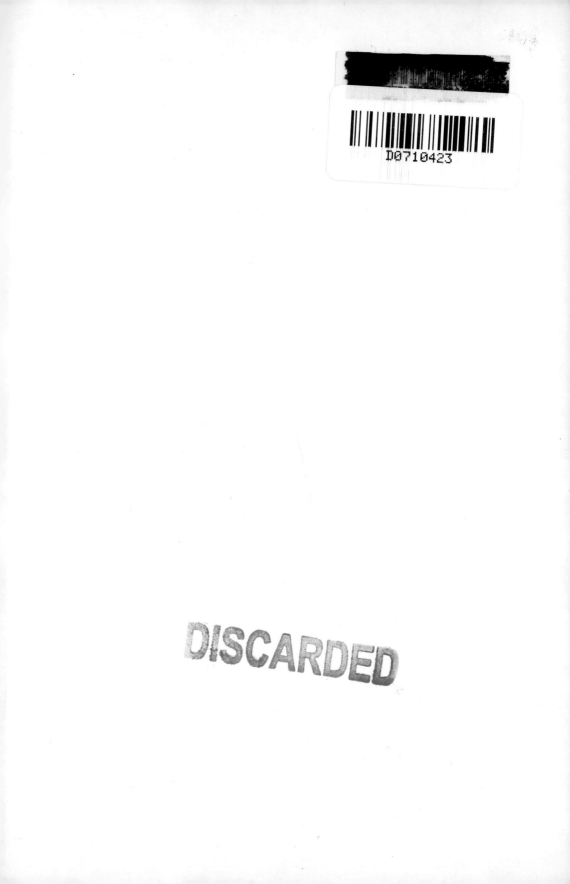

Books by Adam Zamoyski

PADEREWSKI   1982

THE BATTLE FOR THE MARCHLANDS   1981

CHOPIN   1980

PADEREWSKI

PADEREWSKI

Adam Zamoyski

Atheneum

NEW YORK

1982

Library of Congress Cataloging in Publication Data

Zamoyski, Adam.
    Paderewski.

    Includes index.
        1. Paderewski, Ignace Jan, 1860–1941.
    2. Musicians—Poland—Biography. I. Title.
    ML410.P114Z3   786.1'092'4 [B]   81–69136
    ISBN 0–689–11248–3   AACR2

Composed by American–Stratford Graphic Services, Inc., Brattleboro, Vermont
Manufactured by American Book–Stratford Press,
Saddle Brook, New Jersey
Designed by Harry Ford
First Edition

Introduction

Paderewski's name was a household word to several generations. To people who knew nothing about music he was the archetype of the pianist; to those who knew nothing of Poland, he was the epitome of the flamboyant Pole; to those who had no clear idea of his political career he was a Mosaic leader of his people. He was the celebrity par excellence: the public could see and hear him in the concert hall and in the cinema, and they could read about him endlessly in the press, but in fact they knew nothing, or very little, about him. He sprang from a past of which little could be gleaned and lived in a closely knit world of his own creation. The press pried and invented, painting a fabulous image. Paderewski and his entourage countered with another, which they threw up like a smoke-screen to hide him from public scrutiny.

To find the real Paderewski has been no easy task, and the search has held something of the detective story. He was secretive and confided in very few people; they have confided in nobody. He hated writing letters, and many of those he did write have not survived two world wars. Of those that have, the most personal are guarded by people to whom he was a sort of god. His own memoirs and the two biographies published, with his blessing, during his lifetime provide an "official version," which tells us very little about the man himself and invites a degree of scepticism. The figure which emerges is dull, conventional and lifeless—and Paderewski was certainly none of these.

Since this could not possibly be the whole story, I found myself wondering what was being held back, and why. His own version of his political career is both ill-informed and distorted by subjectivity, but this is not unusual in such cases, nor is it particularly difficult to rectify. It became obvious that his role had been less important than he liked to think in some respects, more so in others. The accepted assessment of Paderewski the musician was vague, almost played down. He himself repeatedly insisted that his success was the product of hard work, not of any inspiration or particular approach to music. He gave no inkling of what he was trying to achieve in his compositions and how far he felt he had achieved it, except in very specific terms. It was as though he wished to avoid wider discussion of the subject.

It was, not surprisingly, in the area of his private life that I felt things were being concealed. A typical example is the bland way in which his marriage is represented as suddenly taking place, without much warning, to a recently divorced woman he had known for years. The discovery of a correspondence in Warsaw supplied me with both the truth and the reason for its suppression: Paderewski had in fact been the woman's lover for at least ten years before her divorce. Similarly, I was puzzled by the fact that there was hardly a mention in his memoirs of the Princess de Brancovan, to whom he had dedicated some of his best compositions. Again, archives in Poland yielded the key to this reticence.

But prurience has not been a primary motive in writing this book. What intrigued me above all was to find out whether the polite conventions of contemporary biography were in fact helping to keep up the façade of a nonentity or obscuring a character of real interest. Was the great Paderewski, hailed far and wide as a genius, just a rather dull man whose feet of clay were being kept out of sight, or was he a fascinating man with a crop of emotions and problems too intimate to reveal?

Difficult as it was, my quest has been rewarding, and I should like to take this opportunity to thank those who helped me on my way. I owe a debt of gratitude to those who opened their libraries and archives to me, including: Professor Bohdan Kroll of the Archiwum Akt Nowych, Professor Witold Stankiewicz of the Biblioteka Narodowa and Dr. E. Paderewska-Chroscicka in Warsaw;

Dr. Zdzislaw Jagodzinski of the Polish Library and Captain Waclaw Milewski of the Polish Institute and Sikorski Museum in London; Professor Richard Staar of the Hoover Institution at Stanford University; Helena Liibke in Los Angeles; the staff of the Pilsudski Institute of New York; Richard Belanger of the Conservatory Library at the University of Missouri; Sir Robin Mackworth-Young of the Royal Library, Windsor Castle; Jean Pierre Filipinetti, Edouard Weygand and John H. Steinway.

I have received gracious assistance on matters of detail from: Elizabeth Cuthbert, Malgorzata Perkowska, Elizabeth Wansbrough, Charles Cox, Richard Dorment, Marian Drozdowski, Heinrich Fraenkel, Werner Fuchss, Ignace La Grange, Gerrold Northrop-Moore, Andrzej Piber and Andrzej Rottermund, to all of whom I am deeply grateful. Finally, I extend my warmest thanks to those who knew Paderewski and helped me to know him better, particularly Mrs. Louis Appleton, Mme. Jan Ciechanowski, Halina Zelenska, Dr. Roman Jasinski, Count Zygmunt Mycielski and Count Raczynski.

Contents

Illustrations

xi

ILLUSTRATIONS

MAPS

(PAGES XIV AND XV)

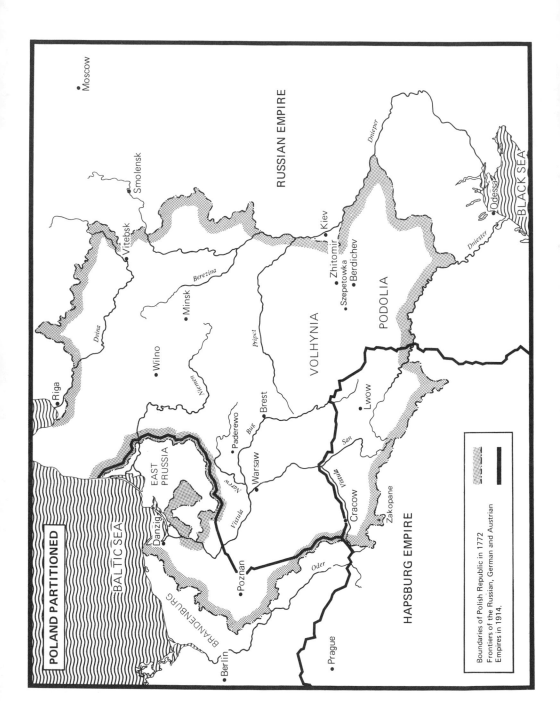

POLAND PARTITIONED

RUSSIAN EMPIRE

HAPSBURG EMPIRE

BALTIC SEA

BLACK SEA

BRANDENBURG

EAST PRUSSIA

VOLHYNIA

PODOLIA

Moscow

Smolensk

Vitebsk

Minsk

Wilno

Riga

Kiev

Zhitomir

Szepetowka

Berdichev

Odessa

Lwow

Brest

Paderewo

Warsaw

Danzig

Poznan

Berlin

Prague

Cracow

Zakopane

Dnieper

Dniester

Berezina

Drina

Pripet

Niemen

Narew

Bug

San

Vistula

Vistula

Oder

Boundaries of Polish Republic in 1772
Frontiers of the Russian, German and Austrian
Empires in 1914.

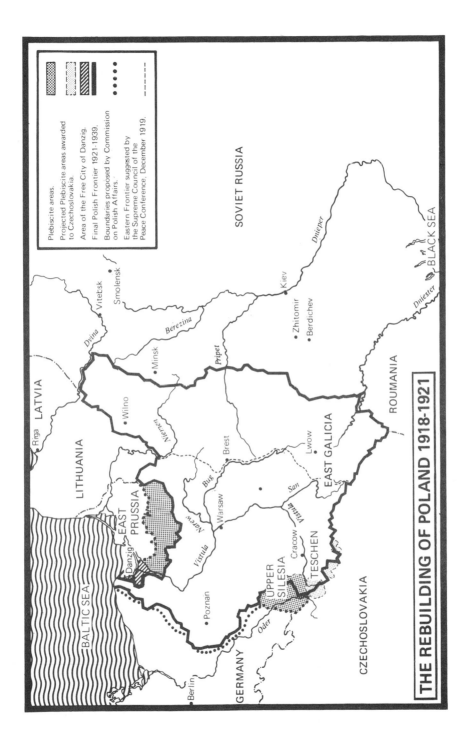

THE REBUILDING OF POLAND 1918-1921

Legend:
Plebiscite areas.
Projected Plebiscite areas awarded to Czechoslovakia.
Area of the Free City of Danzig.
Final Polish Frontier 1921-1939.
Boundaries proposed by Commission on Polish Affairs.
Eastern Frontier suggested by the Supreme Council of the Peace Conference, December 1919.

SOVIET RUSSIA

BLACK SEA

Dnieper

Kiev

Zhitomir
Berdichev

Berezina

Smolensk
Vitebsk

Dvina

Pripet

Dniester

ROUMANIA

Minsk

Wilno

RIGA
LATVIA

LITHUANIA

EAST PRUSSIA

Danzig

BALTIC SEA

GERMANY

Berlin

Poznan

Narew

Warsaw

Vistula

Brest

Bug

Lwow

San

EAST GALICIA

Vistula

Cracow

Oder

UPPER SILESIA

TESCHEN

CZECHOSLOVAKIA

PADEREWSKI

CHAPTER I

A Poor Start

At nine o'clock in the evening of Saturday, 3 March 1888, an unknown Polish pianist ascended the stage of the Salle Erard. He was nervous—frightened, in fact; it was his first recital in Paris, and his performances in Warsaw and Vienna had met with little more than mitigated indifference. He was so shy of his audience that he had begged the manager to turn the gas lights down as low as possible, but even in the murky gloom they thrilled at the sight of him. He wore a modest black frock-coat and a white shirt whose soft collar was folded down over a loosely tied white bow. From this collar emerged a long neck supporting a head immediately and intensely striking by its broad forehead, high cheekbones, strong nose and narrow eyes, but most of all by the red-gold hair which seemed to glow all around it like a halo. He was not, strictly speaking, beautiful, but the composition of the features emitted a harmony which those gathered there drank in as if they had unexpectedly come upon a long-sought perfection.

The young man walked on softly, bowed gracefully and sat down at the keyboard. Suddenly he struck several chords very hard, almost viciously, as though to dispel the tension. That he was nervous could be sensed from the halting yet aggressive way in which he played the first number on the programme, Beethoven's C minor Variations. As he played, however, his fear evaporated and his touch grew more delicate; with one of Schubert's *Moments Musicaux* he beguiled his listeners; with Chopin he subjugated them; with four short pieces

3

written by himself he titillated them; and with a galloping Liszt Rhapsody he swept them on to their feet in frenzied applause.

"I felt that I should like to kiss the hands that had awakened a new world of music for me," was one lady's reaction, and it was not an isolated one.[1] The audience was overwhelmed by what a piano student, Alfred Cortot, was to describe as "that flash of lightning, that dazzling irruption into our hearts and minds of the magnetic personality of this grand seigneur drawn from legend."[2] Even the elders were taken aback—the short, fat, balding Saint-Saëns; Chopin's pupil Camille Dubois; the sombre, moustachioed Peter Tchaikovsky; and the patriarchal Charles Gounod, who shouted, "Bravo, Paderewski! Bravo!"[3]

The pianist felt that he had played "rather acceptably," but he was utterly unprepared for the delirious enthusiasm he had provoked. As he was forced to play encore after encore, his bewilderment turned to alarm. When he tried to leave the stage, "there was a rush to the platfrom and he was dragged back to the piano," in the words of an English lady. "The public refused to leave the hall that night."[4]

After playing a dozen encores he eventually made good his retreat and staggered towards the dressing room longing for a drink and a cigarette, dogged by ecstatic admirers. The prestigious conductor Lamoureux was at his elbow, diary in hand, trying to book him for a concert; but even he was thrust aside as a terrific French duchess charged the cowering pianist, shrieking: "Maestro! It was sublime! Now that I have heard you, you can die!"[5]

Paderewski in fact lived on for another fifty-three years. By the end of the next ten he was the most popular pianist there has ever been; a decade later he was an international institution; ten years after that he was Premier of Poland and a political figure admired by everyone from Lloyd George to Woodrow Wilson, from Mussolini to Herbert Hoover. What had happened that night in Paris was that a curious compound of talent and personality had offered itself to an audience which was avid for that very mixture. All at once, the idol and his public had found each other. This bond of love between him and a congregation which came to embrace millions throughout the world was to be dissolved only by his death—but

4

when that dissolution came, it left a void into which his real personality and his achievements have sunk almost without trace.

Paderewski was a unique phenomenon, the recipient of well-nigh hysterical love from the masses and of fantastic tribute from the discriminating. His popular appeal did not prevent him from being taken seriously, and his name was repeatedly coupled with those of such as Einstein and Mahatma Gandhi, for he was generally held to be one of the transcendent geniuses of the age. Yet the duchess' words were curiously apt. While he was billed for immortality in his lifetime, his fame died with those who knew him; he turned out to be, after all, only a transient immortal.

By its processes, its trappings and its stigmata, Paderewski's career belongs firmly in the twentieth century. He was the first real "star," and he helped to set the pattern which so many musicians and actors have followed since: a pattern of mutual exploitation between artist, manager and public, based on the theme of the rise to fame and the struggle to survive. His life, as well as his performances, became a public spectacle, a progress in which thousands of admirers throughout the world wanted to share. Like many a modern idol, he thrived on the popular need for vicarious sensation. When he triumphed, his admirers exulted; when he stumbled, they suffered. The link between them was the press, which elaborated on the image projected by the artist and his managers, and built him up into the superhuman figure the masses would like. At the same time the press took pains to remind them just how human and originally humble he was—gods descend from heaven, but idols are made of human clay.

Humble origins provide a poetically appropriate start to the long struggle for fame and fortune, but they also, more relevantly, often supply the spur to ambition needed to go through with it. Paderewski was no exception to this. Although his origins were not exactly humble, his ambition was indeed born of poverty and political rejection, for his family and their country had fallen on hard times.

The Paderewskis were one of those numerous Polish families which lived through the centuries according to a code of chivalry long forgotten elsewhere. They amassed honour and distinction in the spirit of the questing knights of legend, but while their blazon shone forth, their purses remained light and their family nests—whose principal architectural features, pointed out with pride, were often the traces of Tatar arrows or Swedish cannon-balls—unimpressive.

The senior branch of the family held on to the ancestral manor of Paderewo on the river Bug in central Poland until the 1580s, but younger sons had long before started moving off into the wild, underpopulated plains of the Ukraine. They went to take land and cultivate it, but they also went to establish an outpost for Christendom against the hordes of the East. Polish colonization brought prosperity to these lands: castles, palaces and fine towns sprang up, and hundreds of thousands of Jews expelled from other countries settled in them to trade.

Towards the end of the eighteenth century, however, the sprawling Royal Republic of Poland declined in power so dramatically that it was gradually swallowed up by its three voracious neighbours, Russia, Prussia and Austria. The Ukrainian lands were incorporated into the Russian Empire, which felt no urge to promote their prosperity, but ruthlessly strove to Russify their population. These attempts were met with dogged resistance on the part of the Poles, who occasionally took up arms in rebellion, as in 1794, 1812, 1830 and 1863, but in each case repression was savage and ruinous, plunging the area into deeper gloom. The Ruthenian peasants groaned under their servitude, the Jews grew steadily poorer and retreated even further into mysticism, while the Poles, mostly minor gentry, clung fiercely to their Catholicism, their pride and the values of their vanished country. They brought up their sons and daughters as dissenters for whom a continuous struggle, often culminating in death or the mines of Siberia, was preferable to peaceful subjection.

Jan Paderewski, a strong, handsome man, hard-working and religious, was a perfect example of his class, the huge warrior caste which defined the Polish gentry. His branch of the family had become completely impoverished, and he therefore worked as a land agent. His employer was Dionizy Iwanowski, the uncle of the Caroline Iwanowska who married Prince Sayn-Wittgenstein and later ran away from him in order to live with Liszt. Mr. Iwanowski was rich and so was his wife. But, apart from being cultivated and, as one local gossip put it, "rather modern," Mrs. Iwaowska had also been too patriotic, as a result of which she had been exiled to Kursk in Russia, whither her husband and daughters followed her.[6] As soon as they were allowed to leave Kursk, the whole family went to live in France, entrusting their estate to the management of Jan Paderewski.

He married Poliksena Nowicka, a young woman from a background similar to his own. Her father had been professor of law at the University of Wilno until 1831, when, in the aftermath of the uprising, he and his pregnant wife had been thrown into jail and then exiled to Russia. It was there that Poliksena was born. In 1858 she bore Jan Paderewski a daughter, Antonina, and two years later, on 6 November 1860, a son who was christened Ignacy Jan. Poliksena died of an infection a few months later.

The Iwanowskis had lived in a stately neo-classical country house, but their agent Jan Paderewski and his two children inhabited a much smaller manor—probably wooden and single-storeyed— just outside the little village of Kurylowka, not far from Zhitomir. This was an old town, one of the largest in the province of Podolia; but now only the great Renaissance synagogue, the baroque churches and the peeling seventeenth-century market square testified to past glory in the face of the muddy backwardness of the present. It was a peculiar backwardness. Judged by the symbols of nineteenth-century progress—railways, metalled roads and commercial development— this part of Europe was primitive indeed. Yet it was rich in fine architecture, scattered with magnificent country houses containing good collections of pictures and books, and inhabited by a cultivated upper class. The whole area had simply been avoided by progress since the end of the eighteenth century, and this gave it an atmosphere all of its own; physically it was remote from the rest of Europe, culturally it remained in close communion with it.

It was a beautiful part of the world. Joseph Conrad, who was born there, remembered with affection "the great unfenced fields— not a flat and severe plain, but a kindly, bread-giving land of low rounded ridges."[7] This intense fertility was one of the things which Ignacy Paderewski remembered in later years, for he spent much of his childhood scrambling through the acres of fragrant orchard, gorging himself on the fruit or just climbing the trees, much to the horror of his father, who could ill afford to keep replacing the boy's torn clothes. The great open spaces also thrilled him; he was from an early age allowed to roam them on his pony, reliving in his mind the tales told by his father of battles fought to defend them by generations of Poles.

The little boy was early made aware of the predicament of his people, and not just through his father's words. Jan Paderewski played his part in the insurrection which broke out in 1863, apparently by hiding arms and supplies for insurgent detachments. His little son was too young to notice or make anything of the comings and goings, the muted conversations with strangers, but at four years he was just old enough to take in an event which was to remain in his mind for the rest of his life. One day when playing in front of the house, he looked up and was instantly struck with terror; there were horsemen riding towards him from all sides. Cossacks—a whole squadron of them—were rapidly encircling the house. A group of them dismounted and entered, brushing aside the terrified child with a lash of the knout. Instinctively fearing for his father, the boy rushed after them and started pestering the one who seemed to be in charge. The soldiers seized Jan Paderewski and, after ransacking the house, dragged him off in chains. The little Ignacy trailed after the officer, pleading for his father, but he was shaken off with a few more lashes of the Cossack whip. The men remounted and rode off, leaving the two children suddenly orphaned.

Ignacy and his sister Antonina were sent into the care of an aunt who lived a hundred miles away to the north. Fortunately, they were not orphaned for long; the Russians kept Jan Paderewski in prison in Kiev for questioning, but could presumably prove nothing against him, since they released him after a year. He had in the meantime lost his job and the house that went with it, so he joined his children and stayed with his sister for the time being.

Three years later, in 1867, he found new employment as agent to another rich Polish family who had an estate further south. Jan Paderewski took his children and his ageing father, Jozefat, with him to his new abode, the little town of Sudylkow, four miles from

Szepetowka. Sudylkow itself was one of those predominantly Jewish towns which had sprung up like mushrooms all over eastern Poland in the sixteenth and seventeenth centuries. As Ignacy later explained, "It was a sad place to live in, very sad." Their house stood on a hill just outside the town and overlooked the Jewish cemetery. "At least twice a week I had to see from our little garden the funerals of those poor Jews and hear the laments. It was terrible. . . . There was no bier, no coffin. The body was simply wrapped in a large black cloth and one saw it carried thus on the shoulders of the bearers to the grave. . . ."[8]

Ignacy was an impressionable boy, and he was beginning to grow melancholy under these conditions. He missed not having a mother, and his father's spell in prison had deepened his fear of being left alone. As he grew older he became aware of the poverty and hardship around him, and began to appreciate how hard his father had to work in order to keep his family at a certain standard. They lived well, though frugally, and no effort was spared to give the children an education worthy of their social, if not their economic, standing.

Soon after moving to Sudylkow, Jan Paderewski married again. His bride was Anna Tankowska, a widow with children slightly older than Ignacy and Antonina. In addition, she brought with her a couple of relatives and her old father, Florian Tankowski, whom she installed in a nearby house. This swelling of the family circle may have added warmth to life, and Ignacy got on quite well with his new step-mother, but it did not succeed in lifting the mood of despondency which had taken hold of him.

In the following year, however, a new arrival transformed the eight-year-old boy's life. Michal Babianski, a distant relative who had fought in the 1830 insurrection and subsequently spent thirty years in exile in Paris, wished to end his days in Poland, and was taken in by the Paderewskis on condition that he acted as tutor to the children. He was an educated man and he had not wasted his years in Paris, so his intrusion into the household was most welcome.

He took an immediate liking to Ignacy, who gradually allowed himself to be drawn out. "He was in entire sympathy with me," the boy later wrote, "and he understood my childish ideas about things." Babianski realized that the boy was full of bottled-up aspirations and he carefully fostered these; the "childish ideas" were confessed to the new-found friend, and turned out to be nothing other than a burning ambition "to become *somebody*" and "to help Poland," in the boy's own words.[9]

Such sentiments are not surprising even at Ignacy's age. Patriotism of this sort was endemic to the Polish gentry, and to the boy it must have seemed that everything that was wrong about life stemmed from the fact that Poland had been enslaved. To "become somebody" is the ambition of many a proud child born into conditions of humiliation and poverty; to help Poland in this case was equivalent to helping everyone he knew. But there were very few ways in which a Polish boy could rise within the framework of the Russian Empire unless he reneged his background and went over to Russian Orthodoxy. The only obvious way was through the arts, and that was why every effort had been made to encourage Ignacy to cultivate the musical talent he had shown from a very early age.

Almost as soon as he could walk, the child had gravitated towards the battered piano standing in the drawing room at Kurylowka. "With one finger I was always seeking, always trying to find the melodies," he remembered.[10] Jan Paderewski had forthwith engaged the services of the only musician he could afford, an old violinist called Runowski, who was kind to the children but not much good at his job. He taught Ignacy and Antonina, who also showed talent, a number of simple pieces for four hands which they quickly mastered, and everyone was delighted—the father because his children could play the piano, the children because they found it so easy.

During the father's imprisonment, their aunt was determined not to neglect the children's talent, and she found another teacher, Piotr Sowinski, a brother of the Wojciech Sowinski in Paris whom Chopin thought so little of. Sowinski lived fifty miles away and could therefore come only once a week, but this did not matter since, in Ignacy's words, "these lessons proved not very important after all, because he was not a *real* piano teacher, but just a poor musician who was giving lessons to the children of the nobility."[11]

The new teacher employed the same methods as the old. He put the siblings through a number of pieces for four hands, mostly arrangements of themes culled from operas by Rossini and Donizetti, but he did not attempt to teach them any theory or pay much attention to developing their fingerwork. The music bored them and they alleviated the monotony by fighting with their elbows and kicking each other while they played, with the result that their duets were "very often more acrobatic than musical."[12]

When they moved to Sudylkow, Sowinski could come only once a month, which meant that the boy spent more time by himself at the old piano with its weak tone and hoarse sound. "I preferred always to improvise rather than practise," he explained. "I did not know *how* to practise. I did not get even the first rudiments of piano technique. . . . But, fortunately, I had that so-called *inborn technique*. I could play anything—not perfectly, of course, but I could overcome certain technical difficulties with comparative ease."[13]

Although he later bemoaned it, the fact of being left so much to his own devices suited him quite well at the time. There was no exacting teacher imposing laborious discipline, no tedious playing of scales and exercises, yet he could play a small repertoire quite acceptably and he could hold the family circle spellbound with his improvisations. He was convinced that he was on the road to becoming a great artist.

He was soon encouraged to write down the results of his improvisations, and for a birthday his father gave him a beautifully bound empty music book inscribed on the cover: *Compositions of Ignacy Jan Paderewski*. But instead of writing down the melodies which came into his head while he was improvising, Ignacy set to work from a different angle, as he explains: "What interested me most when I started composing was that the calligraphic part of the composition should be beautiful. Sound, I did not attach much importance to, then. . . . I did not write music instinctively. I did it by *comparison* when looking at the piano music which I played myself."[14] The book was quickly filled—not with musical ideas or melodies, but with what could have been little more than a series of borrowed clichés strung together in a way that looked elegant to the boy. It is curious to find someone in his position shying away from the instinctive fertility of his imagination, and revelling rather in an almost clerical exercise. It can to some extent be explained by lack of confidence, based on ignorance of even the most elementary rules and practices of composition. It also reveals a tendency which was to surface in his later work with nefarious results, a tendency to glory in the actual verbiage of composition and orchestration, often at the expense of the original musical idea.

At the time, however, Ignacy and his family had every reason to be proud of his achievements, and he was treated with growing respect. This was not, unfortunately, proof against all eventualities, and he occasionally fell foul of parental discipline.

Jan Paderewski was beginning to have trouble with his eyes, so Ignacy was often called upon to read aloud to him. As he was the only one who could read Russian fluently—and only Russian newspapers were allowed in this part of the world—Ignacy would regularly read out the news to the whole family. When the Franco-Prussian War broke out in 1870 these readings assumed importance: throughout the nineteenth century, Poles looked to France as the only great power friendly to their cause, while Prussia was one of the three predators. Babianski and Florian Tankowski could both remember in 1812 seeing the first Napoleon, in whom the Poles had laid such hopes; now they all—including Szmul, the Jewish barber who came to make compresses for Jan Paderewski's eyes—wished his namesake well and prayed for French victory. This put Ignacy in a difficult position; the moment he glanced at the newspapers he could see that things were going poorly for the French, and that the eagerly expectant old men would be sorely grieved. "What was I to do?" he wrote. "I had not the courage to read them what was really happening. I felt that it would break their hearts. . . . There was only one thing to do. . . . I turned all the bad news into good! . . . I sent all the French victorious to the Rhine! And then there was such enthusiasm! Such happiness!"[15]

Having started in this vein, he had to continue, even though he soon realized that things were going to turn out badly. The next time Jan Paderewski had to go to town to see a doctor he made a fool of himself by talking gleefully about the French victories to people who knew better. When he returned home he berated his son and started thrashing him, but was stayed by Szmul the barber, who pleaded that the boy had been guilty only of an excess of kindness.

Ignacy described his father as being equitable, as well as cheerful and even artistic in his tastes, but although they spent much time together, particularly when the father's illness made it necessary for the son to read or play to him or otherwise amuse him, no real intimacy sprang up between them. The fault lay not with the father; Ignacy had of late become reserved and farouche. He had outgrown the silly games he used to play with his sister; he no longer enjoyed climbing trees; one day his pony turned on him and kicked him unconscious while he was feeding it cakes, and he felt so betrayed and offended that he never rode again.

Music could not compensate for his loneliness, and only added to his sense of frustration. It had by now dawned on Ignacy that he was making no real progress, principally because of the shortcomings of his teacher, and he felt stymied by lack of opportunity. His consequent lack of achievement spawned a feeling of inadequacy with regard to music, and shyness, even secretiveness, with regard to the people around him. Left without any outlet, his childish ambition turned in on itself and rankled.

CHAPTER II

Warsaw

One day in 1871 Ignacy and his sister were asked to take part in a concert for charity in the neighbourhood. The audience was delighted by the joint performance of the golden-haired siblings, but it was Ignacy's effortless solo performance which had them all wondering whether a new Chopin had not been born. He was invited to take part in other local concerts and to play at soirées given by wealthy noblemen. The eleven-year-old boy had a limited repertoire: he found it difficult to get hold of music and therefore played the salon pieces he had studied with Sowinski, some Chopin and, above all, his own improvisations. It was these, and the little tricks he had learnt—playing pieces with one hand, or through a towel laid on the keyboard—which went down particularly well in the drawing-rooms of the Podolian country houses.

The boy did not like playing in public, but it seemed a good way of furthering his career as a musician. His instinct was proved right, for he was eventually noticed by the aristocratic Chodkiewicz family, who offered to take him to Kiev for a week that winter. Ignacy jumped at the opportunity and had no difficulty in persuading his father to let him go. Although relegated to the rank of a mere provincial capital, Kiev remained the social and artistic centre of the whole of south-western Russia, and the atmosphere which struck the young boy was that of a great city. He was taken to the theatre, the opera and to a couple of concerts—for the first time in his life he heard an orchestra and saw real musicians.

The experience was thrilling and awakened in the young Ignacy longings for greater things than could be found in the boundless expanses of the Ukraine. But as he nestled under the furs in the sleigh carrying him home to Sudylkow, his eyes fixed on the stars and his thoughts on the Paris Opéra, reality asserted itself in a brutal and nearly fatal manner. The two sleighs—one carrying Ignacy and an agent of the Chodkiewicz family, the other the luggage and fodder—were gliding by night through a remote stretch of snow-covered plain when they were set upon by a howling pack of wolves. The tired horses could not outrun the hungry wolves, and guns proved useless in view of the numbers. Only the quick thinking of the agent saved their lives—he stopped the sleighs, unharnessed the horses from the second one and, while the drivers held off the wolves, made a bonfire of it. While the angry howling went on all around them, the terrified Ignacy ran to and fro tending the fire until daybreak eventually sent the wolves skulking back to their lairs.

Visions of concerts and operas must have seemed remoter than ever to the boy as he finally reached Sudylkow, but at least Jan Paderewski had decided to launch his son on a musical career. The boy would go to Warsaw, where he could study seriously. No arrangements were made in advance, but a few months later, in the summer of 1872, father and son set off. The journey was a considerable undertaking in itself, involving a two-day drive to the nearest railway station, one day of trundling along a branch line in a cattle truck, and finally a slow train ride in the comparative luxury of a second-class carriage.

In Warsaw, Jan Paderewski took his son to the Institute of Music. The old Conservatoire where Chopin studied had been closed down, like so many other institutions, after the 1830 insurrection. It was not until 1860 that a replacement had been founded, by Apolinary Katski, to whom the boy was now introduced.

The director of the Institute was a forbidding personality, and his severe, piercing look might have cowed a boy less precocious than the twelve-year-old Ignacy. He played a few pieces on the piano and, after a short interview, heard Katski tell his father: "We'll take this boy immediately, without any examination."[1]

Jan Paderewski felt proud of his son and delighted that the problem of his schooling had been so simply resolved. Next he set

15

out in search of accommodation for Ignacy and also a piano to rent for him. His quest took them to Kerntopf, the best piano-manufacturer in Warsaw. While Ignacy was trying out some of the instruments in the shop, Jan Paderewski fell into conversation with Edward Kerntopf, the eldest son of the family. He was in his early thirties and ran the business with his father. As he talked to Jan Paderewski and listened to Ignacy play, he took an instant liking to the boy and decided to take a hand in the matter. He said it was absurd that Jan Paderewski should ruin himself on lodgings and pianos; the Kerntopfs would take Ignacy into their family, and he would be able to practise on any of the pianos in the shop and warehouse. Jan Paderewski was delighted not only to spare expense, but also to be able to leave his son in such good hands. He agreed, and a few days later left Warsaw highly contented with the arrangement.

The Kerntopf factory, shop and living-quarters occupied some twenty rooms in an old house in the centre of Warsaw. It was by no means luxurious, and Ignacy had to share a bedroom with the three youngest Kerntopf boys, but the house was comfortable and reassuring. He took a little time to get used to the other children, but soon found a new pleasure in having companionship of his own age.

The very fact of being in Warsaw excited him. It was not Paris or Vienna, but it was a large, teeming, modern city with proper trams, gas lights, and possessed a fine example of that ultimate nineteenth-century status-symbol—the grand opera house. Life had suddenly become varied and interesting, and appeared to Ignacy to hold great promise—in the shape of the Institute of Music. It all seemed very simple: he would be shown how to play the piano and how to work at becoming a great musician. "It had never occurred to me that I should meet disappointments there," he later wrote, and at the time he looked forward to his first lesson "with an eagerness that would be impossible to describe."[2]

An unpleasant surprise lay in store for him. The piano teacher at the Institute listened to him play and then declared that he had no technique, no aptitude and entirely the wrong hands for the piano. At his own request, the boy was transferred to another teacher, Julian Janotha, who instantly recognized talent in his new pupil and assured him that he had "a real and natural gift." This was very gratifying, but it turned out to be just as frustrating as the first teacher's reaction. Paderewski wanted to be taken back to the very beginning and be shown the rudiments of fingering, touch and other fundamentals. But Janotha felt that he was talented enough to dispense with these, and simply put him through a series of studies and encouraged him to play more.

Things went much better in the realm of theory, particularly in studies of harmony and counterpoint, taught by Gustaw Roguski, a pupil of Berlioz to whom Paderewski took a liking. Roguski found him alert and intelligent; he made such rapid progress that it soon became accepted at the Institute that he would be a composer. In spite of his lingering ambition to be a pianist, the boy was happy to go along with this, since the study of harmony and counterpoint gave him pleasure and satisfaction.

Students of composition were encouraged to take up various instruments, and Paderewski decided to try the flute. This was a mistake. "I could never become a flute-player, I was told, because my lips were too thick," he explains, so he decided to try the oboe or clarinet.[3] However, the teacher of these two instruments told him he would never be good at either. Paderewski then tried the bassoon and the horn, with which he had little more success. Having got thus far, he decided that he might as well try all the other instruments, for then at least he would have an acquaintance with the whole orchestra. He moved on to the trumpet, and eventually the trombone, and here he met with unexpected success. After a few lessons the trombone teacher said to him: "Now, my dear boy, listen to me. You are always trying to play *piano*. But why? Piano is useless for you—you have no future with the piano; your future is here, playing the trombone! You are really remarkably gifted for it, and you will earn your livelihood with the trombone, not with the piano."[4] The consequence was that Paderewski became first trombone in the Institute's orchestra.

After a year and a half at the Institute, his ambition had still found no real outlet. He had been thwarted in his desire to become a pianist and fobbed off with the trombone. The satisfaction he gained from his theoretical studies could in no way compensate for this disappointment. Nor could the musical life of Warsaw, which had at first seemed rich and varied to the boy from the country. Moniuszko and the other good composers of the middle of the century had died, and by the early 1870s the musical climate was stagnant with sub-Chopinesque folksiness and the most dubious foreign imports.

Paderewski was not one to be crushed by disappointments. On the contrary, he grew more determined in their face. By the time he was fifteen he was a strong-willed and precocious boy. He had also lost much of the shyness of his childhood and developed an effervescent sense of humour and a line in jokes that delighted his classmates. His crop of chaotic and almost red hair had earned him the nickname of "squirrel," and he had a reputation for mischief with the masters at the Institute. In the summer of 1875 he refused to go to the orchestra's rehearsals, since he was preparing for his exams, and this started a regular mutiny as other boys followed his example. Katski was furious and, seeing Paderewski as the ringleader, expelled him from the Institute. He was, however, prevailed upon to take him back almost immediately.

During the summer holidays Paderewski and two of his friends decided to go on a small tour, hoping to make some money and possibly even gather a few provincial laurels. They set off into the eastern parts of Poland and Lithuania, giving concerts which brought in so little money that the eldest of the trio, the cellist Biernacki, soon went back to Warsaw. Paderewski and the violinist Cielewicz carried on, hoping their luck would change. It did, but for the worse. The Russian police soon grew suspicious of the two young men wandering from town to town—students in this part of the world were viewed as potential disseminators of forbidden ideas or literature—and arrested them both. Jan Paderewski was notified of his son's position and had to come from the Ukraine to secure his release. Thus ended Paderewski's first concert tour.

His next year at the Institute was a difficult one. While he worked hard at his studies of theory and even at his trombone, he refused to give up the notion of becoming a pianist. He toiled at the keyboard, but, in his own words, "did not know *how* to work." He tried all the teachers the Institute could suggest, but they either humoured him and taught him nothing, or else they dismissed him as being without aptitude. Typical was a teacher who refused to give him any more lessons, saying: "Now, I'll give you some good advice—do not try to play the piano, because you will *never* be a pianist. Never."[5]

His playing must have been very strange. It revealed a lack of proper technique and lacunae of fundamental education which horrified the more formal teachers. At the same time he could play even difficult pieces quite acceptably and with, as he put it himself, "certain accents and emotions that betrayed a natural talent."[6] Through the haze of poor timing, uneven touch and clumsy fingerwork, a few rays of genius were discernible to many people. Another quality which was appreciated, particularly by visiting musicians who often used him as an accompanist, was his ability instantly to grasp not only the notes but also the mood of an entirely unfamiliar piece.[7]

Although Paderewski knew his own weaknesses better than anyone else, no one was more conscious than he of his exceptional talent. This is why he remained imperturbably set on his course and determined to master the art of playing. He was growing used to encountering damning judgements and even ill-will. When a new row over the rehearsals of the Institute's orchestra blew up, with Paderewski at its centre, resulting in his repeated expulsion from the Institute, he was not too concerned. If the Institute could not teach him what he wanted to know, then he would find it elsewhere—he was convinced that all he needed was a teacher who would reveal to him the technical secrets. His will and his talent would do the rest.

The almost Napoleonic determination of the fifteen-year-old boy was based on a mixture of the consciousness of his own musical worth and the ambition he nourished of becoming "somebody." Expelled from the Institute, he now faced with courage the prospect of having to earn his living. People rallied round with offers of financial help, but he would accept this only from his friend Edward Kerntopf, whom he knew he could repay some day. "Even if he had not helped me," Paderewski later wrote, "I know I would have helped myself—I am convinced of that."[8]

He gave lessons to poor students and to children, and he sometimes played at soirées. He soon decided to try his luck as a performer once again, and since his friend the violinist Cielewicz had finished his course at the Institute, they set off together. Again they went east, this time deeper into Russia. "We met with the greatest difficulties," explained Paderewski, "but just when we were in the blackest despair, quite of a sudden would come a little success, which was most unfortunate because we would be so encouraged again, that we would proceed a little further!"[9]

They would arrive in a town, visit the local musicians or the most important people, and ask permission to borrow a piano and give a concert. It was by no means easy in some of the little Russian towns they visited to find even an upright piano, and Paderewski would as often as not have to spend the afternoon tuning it himself. Then came the concert, usually in some smelly town hall or school building, or else in the cramped drawing-room of a local dignitary—to audiences reminiscent of Gogol's vignettes of Russian provincial life.

Paderewski's repertoire was limited mainly to pieces by Liszt and Chopin, but this was of little consequence, since the provincial audiences were on the whole drawn by the event rather than its essence. Often the audiences were tiny and the takings correspondingly insignificant, so the two musicians rarely had much money in their pockets. Winter caught up with them in Novgorod, and they suffered cruelly. Paderewski's boots cracked in the snow, so he had to play with a muddy toe sticking out, and their wretched clothes were not suited to the conditions they had to live in—the travel in open carts and the cheap hotels. They had to stuff crumpled newspapers under their shirts in order to ward off the cold, which affected them all the more as they were often hungry. For two weeks they lived only on bread and tea, and on a couple of occasions all but starved to death.

They grew steadily weaker, and eventually Paderewski came down with scarlet fever at a miserable inn in the middle of nowhere. With their last kopeks they dispatched a plea for help to Jan Paderewski at Sudylkow. A hundred roubles came by return of post, which permitted them to procure food, medicine and heat. When Paderewski had recovered a little, they went to St. Petersburg. There a confidence trickster managed to relieve Paderewski of all the money he had, and now the poor pianist, left on his own by the departure of Cielewicz to Warsaw, was in total despair. Miraculously, another hundred roubles arrived from his father, who had had a vivid dream that his son was in need. With this money Paderewski made straight for Sudylkow. He was accepted into the family without reproach, but his father managed to persuade him to try and finish his studies.

He wrote a humble application to be readmitted to the Institute of Music. Roguski, the counterpoint teacher, interceded on his behalf, and the prodigal was allowed to resume his studies where he had left off. He applied himself to the work with determination, and in the summer of the following year, 1878, he took his exams and graduated. Jan Paderewski came all the way to Warsaw to be present at the public ceremony in which every graduate gave a performance before collecting his diploma. His son played Grieg's Piano Concerto with the orchestra of the Institute before being handed his diploma by Katski. "A step forward at last!" the young Paderewski said to himself as he took the piece of paper;[10] father and son felt that something had been achieved—but in fact it was very little.

CHAPTER III

The Quest for Virtuosity

There was no question of Paderewski making a living as a performing musician at this stage, whatever his gifts. He therefore fell back on the resort to which so many had been driven—giving piano lessons. He taught students in the middle year of the Institute and any other pupils he could find in Warsaw. Money was scarce, so he supplemented his income by playing at soirées and taking part in concerts wherever he could. Neither of these afforded him much satisfaction, as an unknown pianist was often hardly listened to and there sometimes seemed little point in playing at all.

One Polish diarist records a musical evening in Lwow where the guests listened like lambs to the celebrated one-armed pianist Count Zichy but sighed with relief when he had finished, longing to attack the buffet. At that moment the hostess announced the promising young pianist from Warsaw, Ignacy Paderewski, whereupon the guests sank back into their seats with a groan.[1]

Concerts could be just as bad. The primitiveness of the conditions and the audiences, particularly in the provinces, is neatly captured in a story Paderewski often told. He was to give a concert in a remote watering-place, but when he arrived he found that there was only an old upright piano whose hammers were so stiff and warped that they failed to fall back after striking the string. He practised for some time, thinking the instrument might loosen up, but it was no good. Just as he was about to give up, a young student who had come with him offered to stand over the piano and flick the hammers down with a switch. The plan worked well enough, although it was a nerve-racking race between the two and, in Paderewski's words, "the piano always came out victor." He was so intrigued to know what the audience had made of the strange exhibition that he slipped into the hall after the performance and eavesdropped. "And how," one person asked a friend, "did you like that young pianist?" "Oh, very well," answered the friend, "he was all right, but the other one, you know, the second pianist who was playing at the back of the piano, he was the best, I think, and he worked much harder than the other! He was the *real* artist, make no mistake!"[2]

The lack of recognition with which he had met so consistently since entering the Institute was beginning to tell on his ambition to become a pianist, which gradually became little more than a latent dream. On the other hand, he was being encouraged to compose, and he worked hard at this.

He often had recourse to the guidance of Roguski, to whom his earliest extant piece, the *Valse Mignonne,* is dedicated. In his last year at the Institute he had written several similar pieces. There was an Impromptu, a Prelude, a Minuet and other works of no great merit or individuality. Throughout 1878 and 1879 he carried on in this vein, adding a Waltz, a Gavotte and two Intermezzi to his oeuvre. At the end of 1879, however, he embarked on a new and much more ambitious project: a Sonata for Piano and Violin.

Although he had never tried his hand at a work of this length, and had no previous experience of writing for anything other than the piano, he completed the Sonata within a few months, and the result is unexpectedly competent and even sophisticated. It is elegant and, in parts, highly imaginative. While the second and third movements show the unmistakable influence of the music of Brahms, Liszt and even Dvorak, the first is striking by its individuality. From the opening bars one is conscious of a strong resemblance to the scherzo of Ravel's String Quartet, written twenty years later, principally due to Paderewski's frequent use of dissonant chords, the impressionistic treatment and the juxtaposition of a busy piano part with a slow, lyrical theme for the violin. The writing is in many places reminiscent of similar works by Saint-Saëns and Fauré, although it lacks their sensuality. The Sonata has its faults—one of them being its length—but as the first major work of a young composer, it announces talent of a very high order. When Brahms heard it five years later, he thought it "very effective, very fine," and was astonished that Paderewski should want to study any more.[3] In 1879, however, there was no such authoritative praise forthcoming, and Paderewski had little hope of ever meeting Brahms.

Although he certainly resented the fact of not being able to travel abroad, it would be wrong to think of Paderewski as being unhappy in Warsaw. The Kerntopf boys having grown up, conditions in the house had become cramped, and as a result he moved out. He went to live instead with the family of two friends from his class at the Institute, Timothy and Joseph Adamowski. One was a violinist and the other a cellist, which meant that the three of them could make music together, and they did so often.

His relations with Edward Kerntopf were by no means severed by this move. Apart from the feelings of friendship between them, Paderewski was ever conscious of the gratitude he owed his avuncular friend, while Kerntopf held to his first impression of Paderewski as an exceptional personality and musical talent. Kerntopf was a businessman rather than an artist by nature, but he had decided that the young man was worth all the support he could give him.

There were various other musical circles in which Paderewski was in evidence, but a curious aspect of his life in Warsaw is that he was not taken up and cosseted by the aristocracy, as usually happens in these cases. This may have been because he refused to be patronised, but it was more probably because he was still something of a rough diamond; engrossed in his ambitious plans and yet lacking in self-assurance, he was in no fit state to shine or parade his gifts in public.

The only salon which he did frequent, that of Mrs. Helena Gorska, was directly connected with the musical establishment, through her husband. Wladyslaw Gorski was a good violinist and a not so good composer; as he was convivial by nature and had married well, he cut a figure amongst other musicians. He often asked Paderewski to take part in his concerts, and the two became friends. It was Gorski's wife, however, who really befriended the young man and took him under her wing.

Helena Gorska was well-born; more than that, she was interestingly born. Her father, Baron Rozen, was descended from an ancient German Baltic family which had become Polonized over the centuries. He had served as an officer in the Russian army and been wounded during the Crimean War. While convalescing on the island of Corfu he fell in love with a Greek lady, whom he married. She died in the following year, giving birth to a daughter, Helena, to whom she bequeathed striking looks. When Paderewski met her, Helena Gorska was in her early twenties. She had grown into the ideal beauty of the period; rich black hair enveloped the regular, noble features of her face, with its Greek nose, large eyes and small mouth; the full lines of her body gathered in a thin waist and ended in small hands and feet. With languid grace she ruled over her small literary and artistic salon, the principal adornment of which were her two *soupirants,* the poet Adam Asnyk and the academic painter Siemiradzki.

Helena Gorska could hardly fail to take an interest in the eighteen-year-old Paderewski. He had grown into a strangely beautiful young man with, as the visiting violinist Leopold Auer noted, "a remarkable head, two eyes which glowed with the most pronounced intelligence, though he said not a word, and a great mane of blond hair which completely framed his face."[4] Helena Gorska was fascinated and also felt a motherly concern for him; she lavished praise and advice on him, strove to build up his self-confidence, introduced him to people of interest and opened up to the young man a world of which he had been oblivious.

From the age of twelve, when he entered the Institute, Paderewski had studied nothing but music, and he realized with horror that he was entirely ignorant in many other fields. He now taught himself Latin, mathematics, history and Polish literature, devouring anything that came to his notice with such an appetite that he soon more than filled the gaps in his education, and carried on into other subjects. He had a good memory, and years of hard study at the piano had trained it to store facts, figures and quotations as well as musical phrases. The result was that his mind became a repository of the most catholic mixture of knowledge, to which he went on ravenously adding over the years. As in his musical studies, he felt that he knew nothing, that there was still so much to be learnt, so much to be mastered.

The feeling of inadequacy persisted despite all the efforts of people like Helena Gorska, particularly where the piano was concerned. He had become convinced that without the panacea of a course of serious study with a great teacher he would always be stumbling in the dark—and the possibility of finding the right teacher seemed to recede. It had receded so far, in fact, that Paderewski now took a step which nobody aspiring to become a performing musician would dream of taking, precluding as it did all possibility of travelling abroad.

He had fallen in love with one of his pupils at the Institute, Antonina Korsak. She was four years older than he, a pretty, blonde girl from a noble family somewhat less impoverished than his own. Paderewski was twenty years old, so this was probably not his first love, but it was the first time he felt strongly enough to want to possess a woman. He had temporarily forgotten his dreams of travel and study, and wanted security and comfort. "I wanted a home," he wrote, "a personal life of my own—a place and someone that belonged to me."[5] They married at the very beginning of the year 1880. The months passed in a cloud of happiness; even their relative poverty was exciting as they organized their pathetic household. As spring turned to summer, Paderewski's pride and exuberance knew no bounds—Antonina was with child. The child, a son, was born on 1 October, but after nine days of suffering the mother died. Paderewski was shattered. He had scaled heights of happiness and plumbed depths of misery in the space of a few months, and he wondered at the injustice of it all. Though not a particularly devout Catholic, he accepted his fate with godly resignation. He was no rebel, and his uncomplicated mind was ready to bow to divine wisdom.

For the time being he was spared an additional blow which hung over him: the son his beloved Antonina had died bringing into the world was born a cripple, but this did not become apparent for some time. Paderewski put the remainder of his wife's meagre dowry into a trust fund for the little Alfred, as he had been christened, and left him in the care of Antonina's mother.

He worked hard over the next couple of months, writing a whole set of short pieces for piano, later published under the collective title of *Chants du Voyageur*. They betray neither passion nor despair, merely gentle melancholy. It is also significant that they are dedicated to Helena Gorska. She was both mother and sister to him, as well as artistic Egeria, and it was she who guided him from despair to fortitude. He was free once again, free to follow his musical ambition, which reasserted itself gradually as the shock of his wife's death wore off. He started saving up money and giving extra lessons. He would go abroad and study under the best teachers; he would find out how to compose—for it was composition that Helena Gorska had persuaded him to give himself up to—and then he would be able to write grand works.

He set his sights on Berlin, where he would study composition under Professor Friedrich Kiel, of whom he had heard from other Poles. He made his final arrangements and set off in January 1882. Kiel received him well and agreed to teach him, but Paderewski was discouraged by the first few lessons, which revealed to him how little he knew. The terrible feeling of inadequacy welled up, inciting him to work. He pushed himself so far, working ten or twelve hours a day, that he made himself ill and eventually had a nervous breakdown. But he recovered from this rapidly, and continued his course with Kiel, who was beginning to look on him as a star pupil, and also encouraged him to work at the piano, for which he said Paderewski had a remarkable talent.

Paderewski needed little prompting; his customary single-mindedness was impervious to the seductions of the Prussian capital. He did not like Berlin. He felt the Germans looked down on him for being Polish, and was frightened by the jingoistic atmosphere and the militarism. He found Berlin "a city of life and excitement, but little real gaiety," and his only respite from work was in the company of musicians.[6]

On his arrival, he had called on Moritz Moszkowski, a Polish composer who had settled in Berlin, where he was highly regarded. He introduced his young fellow-countryman to several musicians and to the music publisher Hugo Bock. Bock liked not only Paderewski but his music as well, and instantly set about publishing some of it.

Paderewski would spend his evenings with the Bock family; they kept open house for musicians and enjoyed the company of the young Pole. At their house he met the violinist Joachim, with whom he gave some recitals of chamber music, and later Pablo de Sarasate, whom he judged superior to Joachim. He felt spontaneous affection for the Spanish violinist as well as great admiration for his talent, and he dedicated his Sonata for Piano and Violin to him.

At Bock's he also met the tiny Scottish-born pianist Eugène d'Albert, the favourite pupil of Liszt, who used to call him "Albertus Magnus." Paderewski was impressed by his playing and showed his appreciation by dedicating to him the set of Variations (op. 11) which he had just written. Another frequent visitor to the Bock household was Richard Strauss. In the evenings Paderewski and he would play the piano together to amuse the Bock children. The grimaces Strauss made while playing were so ridiculous that they made Paderewski self-conscious enough to go home and look in the mirror as he played himself. He found that he made faces too, so he started a rigorous routine of doing all his practising for the next few months facing a mirror, to make sure that all unwonted expression was banished.

The crucial moment of his stay in Berlin was his meeting with Anton Rubinstein, who was universally acknowledged as the greatest living pianist and the heir of Liszt—although his striking resemblance to Beethoven was the source of a widely held belief that he must be the great composer's illegitimate son. He was a Herculean figure who thundered his way through long and noisy programmes, literally demolishing instruments as he went. His colossal power was matched by his endurance, and he thought nothing of adding an entire sonata to his programme as an encore—provided the piano was still up to it at that stage. Having founded the St. Petersburg Conservatoire, he was one of the fathers of the nineteenth-century musical flowering in his native Russia, but he was known throughout the world, having toured even America—earning the record sum of $200 for a concert. His importance lies in that fact that he was the first, and one of the greatest, of an entirely new breed of musicians: the pianist who was above all an interpreter of others' works rather than an exponent of his own—the virtuoso par excellence.

Paderewski did not in fact hear him play. It was the grand old man who asked to hear the young Pole. When Paderewski had played various things, including his new Variations, Rubinstein exclaimed: "You have a brilliant future. You should compose more . . . more for the piano."[7] Rubinstein later said to Zygmunt Stojowski that he had listened to Paderewski as a composer, and not as a pianist. According to another source, he had reproached Paderewski with playing "like a composer" and exhorted him to develop his technique.[8] Paderewski himself noted that Rubinstein had said: "You have an inborn technique and you could have, I am sure, a splendid pianistic career."[9]

The oracle had spoken, or so it seemed to Paderewski as he returned to Warsaw in August. At last somebody whose opinion was unimpeachable had offered encouragement to the slumbering ambition of the would-be virtuoso. The determination to become a pianist reasserted itself with force. He resumed his work as piano-teacher and carried on writing, but he also laboured with obsessive purpose to improve his technique. Just how hard he worked is illustrated in a story told by the Adamowskis. They had arranged to take him to the country for a weekend, but he declined at the last moment, saying that he must work on a piece he was trying to master, so they went without him. When they returned on the Sunday evening, they found him lying unconscious on the floor by the piano, having neither eaten nor slept but practiced literally until he dropped.[10] If it killed him, he would be a great pianist.

He returned to Berlin once in December 1882 in order to give a concert of his own works with Gorski, and again a year later, at the beginning of 1884. The purpose of this last visit was to pursue his studies in orchestration. Since Professor Kiel had died in the interim, Paderewski took a course of lessons from Heinrich Urban which lasted several months and at the end of which he felt his education as a composer was complete.

He had been writing continuously during these years, but the promise held out by the Sonata did not materialize; he produced only short works for piano of varying degrees of banality. The reason for turning out these salon pieces, usually published in sets under collective titles such as *Album de Mai* and *Chants du Voyageur,* was largely financial: as they are generally pretty and not too difficult, they sold well—staggeringly well in some cases. The famous Minuet (op. 14, no. 1) sold in its millions and was transcribed for everything from the flute to a full orchestra. By the mid-1880s he was reaping a respectable income from them.

Some of the pieces are very pretty, like the *Andantino Gracioso* from the *Chants du Voyageur,* written in 1882. Many contain a novel idea or an interesting turn of phrase which is, however, rarely developed. An exception to this, and probably the best of these early works, is the *Cracovienne Fantastique* (op. 14, no. 6), which is clever, original and contains a pleasant dash of humour. But the well-known Minuet from the same collection is more representative of the majority; it is an occasionally sparkling pastiche in which accents of Mozart, Schubert, Polish folk music and Lisztian gypsy music are jumbled together in a manner which brings to mind images of Viennese tea-rooms.

On the whole, Paderewski was not writing for virtuoso effect in these pieces, and the stress is rather on song and cadence. They were written not as vehicles for showing off the professional pianist's skill, but as elegant trifles for home consumption by amateurs—hence their popularity. Whatever their merits, they are disappointing. They lack inspiration and any sense of direction, and in this they vividly reflect the composer's state of mind at the time.

After taking his leave from Professor Urban, Paderewski returned to Poland, to spend the summer at Zakopane in the Tatra mountains. This mountain village, nestled in a valley overlooked by the highest peaks of the Tatras, had over the years become a fashionable resort with a distinctly artistic flavour, since it had been discovered that the air was good for people suffering from elegant complaints. The nineteenth-century love of alpine prospects was in this case combined with a growing interest in the rugged but civilized mountain people—noble savages if ever such were—and their distinctive lore.

Paderewski had arranged to meet Helena Gorska in Zakopane. They were by now in the throes of an *amitié amoureuse,* more passionate on her side, more sentimental on his. They went for long walks in the mountains, enthused over the scenery and listened to the curious music made by the mountain people in their becoming costumes of heavily embroidered white wool. When the time came for Helena to leave, she was disconsolate, as she revealed to a lady on her way to Zakopane whose carriage she crossed on the mountain road. "I envy your going to Zakopane; you are going to see one of the most extraordinary young men you ever met," said

Helena wistfully. Then she sighed and added, lower: "And I must go away. I must."[11]

The lady in question was one of the queens of Zakopane society, the actress Helena Modrzejewska, who, under the simplified name of Modjeska, had earned a dazzling reputation, particularly in the United States, with her interpretations of Shakespearean roles. She was a beautiful woman of forty-four, at the height of her fame and success. The success had been financial as well as artistic; she divided her time between Arden, her magnificent estate in California, and her spacious wooden villa at Zakopane, built in the local style.

She did meet Paderewski, and she was struck by him. Now that Helena Gorska was gone, the young man spent most of his time with her namesake. "It was impossible to keep him away from the piano," she wrote. "Sometimes he played long after midnight, and had to be taken from the instrument by force when the refreshments were announced." She was no musician, yet she found something exceptional in Paderewski's playing. "He seemed so deeply wrapped up in his music that this intensity was almost hypnotic," she noted. "He also phrased with so much clearness and meaning that his playing made an effect of something new and quite unconventional."[12] Already present in his playing and noticed here for the first time were two elements which, reinforced and exaggerated, were to make him into the most popular pianist of all time.

A successful performer herself, Modrzejewska had instantly spotted star material in Paderewski. "You must start your career as a pianist," she urged him, "you must not wait any longer."[13] He explained to her that he was not ready, that he needed to study under some great teacher first, but she cut him short and asked which teacher. He named the renowned Leschetitzky of Vienna, in the same breath pointing out that he could never dream of scraping together enough money to go and study under him. Like most successful people, Modrzejewska had adopted the point of view that there is no such thing as an insurmountable obstacle, and she galvanized Paderewski with stories of her own victories. He must make the money he needed, at once, by giving a concert in nearby

Cracow. She would appear and recite some poetry in between his playing, and that would guarantee a full house. It did, for, as Paderewski explained, "her name on the programme was magic."[14] Apart from filling the house, she also attracted attention to the young pianist, and the evening was a success. The takings were considerable, and Modrzejewska refused to accept any of them. She merely pressed Paderewski to take the money and go to Vienna, study as long as he must, and then go out into the world as a pianist. She made it out to be his duty to himself and to his country to make his mark. Her words expressed the very thoughts that had been animating Paderewski since childhood.

He took the money and in October went to Vienna, where he forthwith called on Leschetitzky. Theodor Leschetitzky is the subject of the most confusingly contradictory opinions. He was born in 1830 at the magnificent castle of Lancut, where his father was resident piano-teacher to the Potocki family. His father was of Slovak extraction, but his mother, Teresa von Ullman, was Polish. Leschetitzky himself was sent to Vienna as a boy to study under Czerny, and later taught the piano in St. Petersburg before finally settling in Vienna. He soon acquired a world-wide reputation, and aspiring pupils, especially women, flocked to him from as far afield as America.

The powerfully built Leschetitzky was a formidable despot, but always ended by striking up some kind of spiritual relationship with his pupils. No fewer than four of them married him, and more would have willingly. "Yes, Leschetitzky is awful to study with," moaned one lady pupil, "but, were he to kick me down the front steps, I would crawl to him again up the back steps."[15] She described him as "a never-ending source of inspiration."[16] Even Paderewski noticed that there was "a great deal of magnetism about him."[17]

While they maintained a certain individuality, Leschetitzky's pupils were all marked by a grand style of playing that was instantly recognizable. They made much noise and their playing occasionally appeared insensitive and even ham. Their style was certainly exceptional, and it aroused widespread interest in the "Leschetitzky method." He himself would have none of it, however. "I *have* no method and *will have* no method," he told one new pupil. "Write over your music-room door the motto: NO METHOD!" To another he said: "To make a pupil play three notes on the piano expressively and with variety of touch, that is my method." One pupil explained that he practised "the method of common sense," while others maintained that he helped them form their own individual style without imposing his own, that he allowed them to work out their own fingering, their own interpretation of a piece, and even to change the notes to suit them.[18]

Paderewski's account is more explicit: Leschetitzky imposed high standards of finger dexterity, putting pupils through monumental labours in order to achieve this, and thereafter concentrated on teaching them "to evoke a fine tone from the instrument and to make music not noise." Once the pupil had achieved perfect deftness and command over the force and character of his touch, he was "treated according to the nature of his talent."[19]

Leschetitzky was somewhat put out when Paderewski called on him. The young man had studied widely, written music, given concerts and even taught others, yet now he wanted to go back to the beginning and learn the rudiments himself. Leschetitzky did not like the idea of teaching someone who, by virtue of his extensive studies and evidently strong character, would be a good deal less malleable than most of his other pupils.

After listening to Paderewski play, he told him he had many qualities, including "natural technique" and "the *principal* quality —tone." He was astonished by his pedalling, which was novel and effective, but he could see that the young man's fingers lacked "discipline," and muttered that he had a lot to learn, shaking his great white head.[20] "It is too late! Too late!" he complained. "You cannot become a great pianist because you have wasted your time in studying perhaps more pleasant things for yourself, such as counterpoint, orchestration, and so on."[21]

Nevertheless, he was finally prevailed upon by Paderewski. Over the next four months he gave him a course of nine or ten lessons, all free of charge. Paderewski found them very tedious to begin with, and both teacher and pupil were discouraged after the first two. "I was at that time twenty-four and I had to start from the beginning—

finger exercises!" he exclaimed indignantly. "I had to make up for all the years when nobody showed me how to work. I was already dancing without having learned to walk."[22]

Leschetitzky soon began to appreciate certain qualities in his pupil. He was greatly surprised to find such receptiveness in an already mature young man. "There was no remark so insignificant, no detail so small, as to deserve less than his whole passionate attention," he told a friend.[23] The other aspect of Paderewski which impressed him was his determination. "A great heart, a great head, and an immeasurably strong will" manifested themselves, and "beside his work he saw and knew no other aims."[24]

While he implacably put his new pupil through the most arduous exercises, Leschetitzky also took great pains to explain things to him, and he was an intelligent man. "He opened up another world to me," writes Paderewski; "after those groping, struggling years, even in a few lessons things became clear."[25] From the exercises they moved on to greater things. "After technique," explained Leschetitzky, "we worked at developing style, which in my view means reaching a compromise between the individuality of the virtuoso and the intentions of the composer."[26] Paderewski learnt one of the Saint-Saëns Piano Concertos, a Beethoven Sonata and various works by Brahms and Schumann.

Paderewski thought Leschetitzky "the greatest teacher of his generation." He admired his playing, particularly his singing tone and his attention to rhythm, but it was the master's particular blend of the laboured and the instinctive which enthralled the young man. He felt that if he could only acquire the teacher's technique in matters of touch and fingering, he would have found the perfect vehicle for his own gifts of interpretation. Leschetitzky seemed the one man who could show him how to bring his natural talents to fruition. Above all, Leschetitzky encouraged him to put his own personality forward. Paderewski was so diffident and possessed by such a sense of inadequacy that he was afraid of letting himself go, unless playing to a circle of intimate friends. It needed a man of stature and authority to draw him out.

After giving one of his lessons, Leschetitzky would send the young man off to work on his own and to study specific details under the guidance of his second wife, Annette Essipov. She was a good pianist who had graduated from the St. Petersburg Conservatoire and subsequently given concerts in many countries. Paderewski had met her in Warsaw in the previous year, and they were on cordial, and perhaps intimate, terms. He had dedicated a couple of his works to her, and she often played some of his shorter pieces at her recitals. "She was an intelligent woman with evident culture, attractive to look at, and with a very pleasing personality," runs Paderewski's guarded description of her in his discreet memoirs.[27] In fact, at thirty-three she was still young in spirit, extremely independent in her attitude to her husband and very pretty.

They spent much of their time together, and it was she who introduced him to the pleasures of Vienna. He adored the place from the beginning: "There was a charm and sparkle in the very atmosphere there—a charm in the people, charm in everything!" he wrote. "It is the city of my heart."[28] Vienna had none of the stiffness of Berlin, and the atmosphere was refreshingly cosmopolitan and carefree. Paderewski did not feel like a foreigner there, and he ran into other Poles at every step. There was an artistic coterie which met regularly at the Café Central in the old city, and several Polish aristocratic houses, such as those of Prince Czartoryski and Countess Angèle Potocka, where he was always welcome.

Paderewski blossomed in this atmosphere. For so long he had struggled with all his will and his energy, to no avail. He had worked himself to exasperation and illness in his attempts to master the piano, and his failure had gnawed at him for years, making him introspective, tense and almost bitter. Thanks to Leschetitzky, this boundless energy and tempered will were now being channelled in the proper way, and he felt he was getting somewhere; the tension relaxed and the bitterness of thwarted ambition was dissipated. He could now enjoy life around him as never before. The poverty, the drudgery and the disappointments had left their mark; his innate determination had been tried but not broken, and it emerged the stronger; his precocity had digested his experience and made him mature and wise. At twenty-four he was "a young man of wide culture, of witty, sometimes biting tongue, a man wide awake to all matters of personal interest, who knew and understood the world," in the words of Helena Modrzejewska.[29]

He began to look upon his youth as having been spent in a valley of gloom and sadness; the slight exaggeration was the product of his desire to shake himself free of these memories. As he emerged into what he felt was the sunshine of the plain beyond, he rejected sadness and sought gaiety. He developed a dislike for the colour black, for gloomy people, for anything that could remind him of death or suffering. Over the years this grew into something more than a taste and became almost obsessive. In literature, he disliked Tolstoy and Dostoevsky, preferring Turgenev to them. His favourite reading was Shakespeare, Molière and Gogol. In music too, he professed an aversion to the Russian composers, declaring their music to be too melancholy. It was almost as though he feared being beset by Slavic soul-searching—perhaps there had been in his earlier life fits of depression of which nothing is known.

Paderewski hated to see sadness in others as much as he avoided it in himself; he wanted people happy around him and often went out of his way to make them so. "He was what might almost be called a genius for devising impromptu amusements," Countess Potocka writes, "and when a number of young people were assembled at the house, he and Annette Essipov were always the life of the party, entering into the spirit of the games with childish enjoyment."[30] It was not just by his own gaiety that he cheered people: he employed every means at his disposal to give pleasure, and when he had money, he gave. Countess Potocka saw him just before Christmas go into a shop and come out with his arms full of cakes and sweetmeats, which he distributed to the urchins hanging about outside. Similar stories abound.

The physical beauty of the young man flowered simultaneously. He had been handsome as a boy, and his face had always been striking, but he now shed the tortured, hungry-student look, and his features relaxed into a more harmonious expression, while his hair was allowed to do what it would. Not tall but tall enough, sinewy yet delicate, he combined something of a wild animal with a suave gentleness, a strong masculine rigidity with an almost feminine softness of manner. The softness was enhanced by the barely perceptible lisp in his speech, and by the shimmering copper-gold halo which attenuated the almost savage features.

Paderewski lived in small rooms on the Währing Heights, slightly above and away from the old city. Leschetitzky lived around the corner, Countess Potocka not far away, and the musical Prince Czartoryski but a little further in his palace at Weinhaus. He grew to love those rooms with their fine view of the Kahlenberg Heights, which remind every Pole of King John Sobieski's victory over the Turks. He kept them on for many years and even, much later, wanted to buy them in order to capture forever the memories they held. One of the memories was that of a little creature which had inhabited them during those first four months in Vienna.

One day, while playing one of Chopin's Etudes, Paderewski noticed a little spider sail down from the ceiling and hang just above the piano in front of him. The spider remained motionless as though absorbed by the music. But the moment he started on another Etude, in different time, it shot back up to the ceiling. Perplexed, he stopped and started again on the previous Etude, and, sure enough, the tiny creature came down again. From then on, whenever he played that particular Etude, the spider would come down and hang just above the piano, but all other music sent it angrily scuttling back.

Vienna was an endless source of musical enjoyment to Paderewski. He thought the Philharmonic Orchestra the best in the world and the opera magnificent. He met many musicians, most notably Brahms, whom he found friendly and accessible. He thought Brahms looked like "a caricature of Jupiter" and was surprisingly unimpressed by the man and his work. "Brahms was not such a genius, he was a great master," he patronizingly wrote later.[31] He was nevertheless flattered by Brahms' praise for his own Sonata for Piano and Violin, and he asked the ageing composer to give him some lessons in composition. This he presumably did without the knowledge of Leschetitzky, for the two were consistently rude to each other. Brahms told Leschetitzky his compositions were suitable only for sixteen-year-old girls, to which the other retorted that Brahms' piano works were unfit for anyone under ninety.[32]

In February 1885 Paderewski was back in Warsaw. On 9 April he gave the first concert of his own works, including the Sonata, which he played with Gorski, and many of the short pieces. The hall was full, but the judgements in the press were mixed. One of the most prominent critics, Kleczynski, wrote that Paderewski showed promise as a composer, but he found the works immature;

he could not make out whether they were mere "sketches" or "silhouettes; very finished, but enclosed in narrow margins."[33]

Whatever interest had been aroused by the concert was soon eclipsed by the arrival in Warsaw of Anton Rubinstein. He gave a number of concerts, four of which Paderewski attended. It was the first time he heard the great virtuoso, and the effect was "overwhelming—impossible to describe!" But he was quick to spot unevenness in the man's playing and pointed out that while he was magnificent and poetic in some pieces, he was sloppy and barbaric in others: "It could be dreadful—dreadful!"[34]

Paderewski had no wish to linger in Warsaw, and he had asked Leschetitzky to find him a job somewhere more stimulating. In July 1885 a vacancy for the post of piano teacher at the Strasbourg Conservatoire came up, and the old man wrote a letter of recommendation which secured it for him. The salary was low, but the requirements were not great; he had to give twenty-four hours of lessons per week and in addition take part in a number of concerts in the city. The advantages included a richer musical life than was to be had in Warsaw, and plenty of free time for composing.

Paderewski spent most of this time struggling with the Piano Concerto he had begun in Vienna in the previous year. This first attempt at writing for orchestra gave him a good deal of trouble, and the work dragged on for a couple more years. "How is the concerto getting on?" wrote Leschetitzky in December 1885. "I hope that you will not make it too long, too *recherché,* but attractive and brilliant."[35]

He did make it too long, particularly the first movement, a splendidly bombastic piece of writing showing the influence of Liszt's Piano Concertos but lacking their vigour and freshness. The second movement, however, is in complete contrast. Paderewski takes a beautiful lyrical theme which he develops with the utmost restraint and perfect delicacy, and achieves a hauntingly romantic effect which guaranteed the concerto tremendous popularity and ranks amongst the great examples of unashamedly sentimental music. The third movement takes up elements of the same theme, but the treatment is entirely different; it is written for virtuoso effect, with original and brilliant passages for the piano well to the fore.

38

The Concerto marks a welcome break with Paderewski's work of the previous four years, and the same is true of some of the shorter pieces he wrote during his Strasbourg year. He started work on a set of Variations—soon abandoned and not finished until twenty years later—which show inventiveness and individuality, as well as a new familiarity with the possibilities of the piano, as though Leschetitzky really had opened the doors for him. Just as impressive are some of the short pieces published under the title *Miscellanea pour Piano*. The ferociously difficult and somewhat weird Variations in A major, the romantic Nocturne in B flat major and the beautiful Minuet in A major show Paderewski at his best as a composer of salon pieces, and the Nocturne stands out in all his early work.

The Strasbourg period helped Paderewski because it distanced him from the influence of composers such as Liszt, Schumann, Brahms and others who dominated the musical scene in Central Europe. His lack of self-confidence tended to make him imitative, and much of the music he had written over the previous four years had been cast in the mould of late German Romanticism, which neither suited his temperament nor stimulated his own ideas, such as they were. Both of these were closer to the spirit of French music, to which he was now more exposed, and they flourished as a result.

The time spent in Strasbourg was also beneficial to Paderewski because he was encouraged as a pianist. The concerts he was obliged to give in the city were successful, and he was asked to give more. They also brought him engagements to play in various Alsatian towns, with the result that he became quite well known locally. His prestige at the Conservatoire was enhanced when Rubinstein, who was on his way to give a series of concerts in Paris, cabled Franz Stockhausen, the director, asking him to bring Paderewski for a quick lunch at the station hotel during the two-hour stopover between trains.

Rubinstein urged Paderewski to come to Paris for the concerts— a whole course of them in which the great virtuoso spanned the history of music—and the young man immediately started saving up for the trip. He even denied himself a new pair of shoes, which meant that he went to the Conservatoire in his carpet slippers for a time. Having managed to scrape together the money, he went to Paris. He had lunch with Rubinstein, presented him with a box of cigars and then asked if he might have some tickets for the concerts, which were heavily booked. Rubinstein told him to ask his manager, a man by the name of Wolff; but when Paderewski did so, he was told there were no free tickets for musicians. He never got to a single one of the concerts, which was one of the greatest disappointments in his life, and he vowed to himself that if he ever became a successful pianist, he would never refuse to let musicians in, even if it meant they would have to sit on the stage. He never forgot either the meanness of Wolff or his own pledge.

For all its advantages, the job at the Strasbourg Conservatoire could not satisfy him. Apart from the drudgery of teaching and the low pay, it led nowhere. He was twenty-five years old and, as he put it himself: "If I failed now to establish myself as a pianist and carry out my convictions, it would be too late."[36] Everyone urged him to launch his career in earnest; the French friends he had made in Strasbourg, including the President of the French Chamber of Deputies, Charles Flocquet, insisted that he go to Paris, where his success would be assured. Annette Essipov gave him the same advice when he saw her. The Gorskis, who had moved from Warsaw to Paris in the previous year, supported it with enthusiasm.

Still Paderewski hesitated. He gave up the job in Strasbourg and spent the summer of 1886 in Poland; he gave a couple of concerts in Warsaw which were mildly successful, but he still did not feel "educated enough," and saw enormous faults in his own playing. He longed to take his troubles to Leschetitzky, and, finally, at the beginning of 1887, he left for Vienna once more.

Leschetitzky was delighted to see him again, and he was happy to be in his beloved Vienna once more. He worked hard over the next year, taking some sixteen lessons from Leschetitzky and studying with Annette Essipov the rest of the time. He strove to develop his technique, laboriously exercising his hands with hour upon hour of scales and exercises by Czerny and Clementi, and at the same time he put together a concert repertoire. Leschetitzky was pleased with the progress his pupil had made, and felt that the time was ripe for him to launch his career. As he told a music critic one day, "You will soon have to hear a great deal about this young man."[37]

40

CHAPTER IV

The Lion of Paris

Paderewski felt ready at last, and in the beginning of 1888 he went to Paris. Annette Essipov, who was on a concert tour of France, arranged for him to meet Albert Blondel, the director of the house of Erard, the piano-makers. Blondel liked the young man's playing and booked him for a recital at the Salle Erard on 3 March. Annette Essipov spread word of the event in musical circles, the Gorskis mobilized the Paris Poles and all their French friends, and Paderewski's own acquaintances, such as Charles Flocquet, brought whom they could, with the result that when the day came the hall was well filled.

The recital was immensely successful. Five days later Paderewski gave a recital of his own works, with Gorski joining him in the Sonata for Piano and Violin, and this was repeated ten days later. Very soon afterwards he took part in one of the famous Lamoureux concerts at the Cirque d'Eté, where he gave a performance of Saint-Saëns' Fourth Piano Concerto.

Paderewski could hardly believe his own success. Saint-Saëns sent him his photograph with an inscription thanking him for his performance at the Lamoureux concert. Audiences showed unheard-of enthusiasm, and the critics echoed this. "Monsieur Paderewski is a great artist," ran a piece in *Le Monde Artiste;* "not only does he simply make light of technical difficulties—that is the least valuable attribute of the virtuoso—but he phrases beautifully and renders all nuances with great simplicity; he keeps time with rigorous accuracy, but is neither dry nor stiff. He has beautiful tone." The *Annales du Théâtre et de la Musique* summed him up as having "the soul of an artist and the talent of a virtuoso of high class," which was more to the point, since it was largely the man's artistic soul which was wreaking havoc in his audiences. Even the Paris correspondent of London *Daily Telegraph* felt it incumbent to report the furore caused by "the lion of Paris," as he dubbed him.[1]

"This is not heaven; it's hell!" Paderewski said to himself as the bookings poured in; his repertoire was so limited that he could not possibly follow up his success unless he played pieces he had not studied thoroughly enough, and that was something he hated to do. But he was determined to exploit the situation, so he shut himself away and in the space of three weeks prepared a whole new programme. "It was not perfect academically," he admitted, "but I got it into shape."[2] He then proceeded to fulfil every engagement he was offered, and passed up no opportunity of making money, playing as far afield as Lyon and Brussels.

This frantic desire to make money was based on sound sense. Arthur de Greff, a well-established pianist, warned him as they sat on a café terrace that he would never earn a living as a pianist. This was not jealousy or alarmist talk, as Paderewski well knew; there were too many musicians about, and most of them were living in poverty. In Berlin, for instance, there were often as many as fifty concerts by different pianists in one week, and it was by no means uncommon for a performer not to sell a single seat, his only audience being those to whom he had given tickets and the critics who could be bothered to come.

Furthermore, Paderewski was not convinced of his own merit; he felt he did not deserve the homage he was receiving, for he knew his own shortcomings as well as anybody. If the Parisians had taken to him so suddenly and inexplicably, they might turn from him just as brusquely, he felt. He certainly failed to understand what had happened and what was responsible for his meteoric rise to popularity. Only with hindsight does it seem clear.

The rule that aristocratic society, when it finds itself cut off from the sources of power which created it, reaches out to the world of art in an attempt to justify its continued existence and to palliate its downfall is perfectly illustrated through Paris in the closing decades of the last century. Society *needed* and anticipated artists of one sort or another. Bearing this in mind, the sudden appearance of the tousled Pole could hardly fail to have an impact, particularly in view of the special nature of his talent.

One thing which stands out from all accounts of Paderewski's playing is that his reading of a given work was intellectually satisfying, and that consequently his retailing of it to the audience, through clear phrasing and a wealth of nuance, was immediately intelligible. A public jaded by hearing musicians play works it did not really understand was thrilled when this young man quite simply brought the music to life. Suddenly a recital was no longer a tedious, albeit edifying, way of spending an evening—it was an immensely exciting experience. There seemed little point in discussing his faults or his merits when he had brought them music in a way that so many gifted and accomplished musicians had utterly failed to do. The public would leave the hall feeling that only a true artist could have brought them so close to the essence of music. His person too appealed to the taste of the time—the subtle violence, the refined savagery, the effete masculinity of his looks, his princely bearing, all combined with obscure and exotic, almost Eastern origins, were a cocktail bound to prove irresistible to the Parisians of the nineties.

Annette Essipov vied with Helena Gorska to show off their young friend and introduce him to French society; it was she who brought him to the Avenue Hoche, to the salon of Princess Rachel de Brancovan, a recently widowed, still young lady with two little daughters. She was half-Turkish, being the daughter of Musurus Pacha, one-time Turkish ambassador in London, and her mother was of ancient Greek lineage. She was the widow of Prince Gregory de Bassaraba de Brancovan, the descendant of the Hospodars of Wallachia and a Roumanian subject.

Princess Rachel was a talented pianist who had been taught by Camille O'Meara Dubois, one of Chopin's most talented pupils. She kept one of the eminent artistic and musical salons of Paris, and it was thither Paderewski directed his steps late one April afternoon. As he ascended the staircase, he was watched from a hiding-place by a twelve-year-old girl, the Princess' daughter Anna, the future poet and friend of Proust, who even then fell in love with him:

43

I saw a sort of archangel with red hair and blue eyes, pure, hard, searching and defiant, turned towards the soul. The strong florid neck was revealed by a collar folded down, from which flowed the tails of a foulard tie of sad white, the cloudy whiteness of fruit-blossom. His slender body betrayed its slimness in a black frock-coat of modest cloth which contrasted with the extreme pride in the face, outlined by a short moustache of gold, which also glowed on his strong chin. . . . How I immediately loved that air of the vagabond of noble and proud race who seemed to have come slowly, day after day, from that Poland of kings, where everything that is marked with superiority arrogates to itself, with simplicity and bonhomie, the right to supreme self-respect!

It seemed to me that this strange young man, foreseeing our tenderness, had come to us along the roads of Podolia and Lithuania, wearing his elastic-sided bottines out in the hot dust or the cold winter that kills even the birds. . . . Coiffed with light, his eyes attuned with the stars, a magus came to us; we loved him.[3]

Princess Hélène Bibesco, a cousin of the late Prince Gregory de Brancovan, also a young widow, who had a salon on the Rue de Courcelles, loved him no less. She too was a keen pianist, but not everyone was convinced of her talent. The Comte de Montesquiou, Proust's Baron de Charlus, claimed that she even "made the echo beg for mercy," and thought in terms of her riding into battle astride her piano like some Valkyrie. "She has killed an incalculable number of pianos under her," he wrote in mock alarm; "ladies and gentlemen have been seen to die of boredom under the effluvia of her arpeggios."[4]

Princess Bibesco was so taken with Paderewski that she never stopped inviting him to come and see her. He became the recipient of a fantastic cascade of letters, often with little flowers painted in the margin by her, in which Art, God and Love are stirred into an alarming verbal soup. She swooned so much in his presence and sighed so deeply whenever his name was mentioned that by the autumn of 1888 everyone in Paris was convinced they were having a grand affair.[5]

His affections, however, lay elsewhere—with Helena Gorska. He had not seen her for some three years—he had been in Vienna and Strasbourg and she had been in Paris since 1885—but they had kept up a correspondence throughout. In Poland his feelings for her had been sentimental rather than passionate, but much had changed in the three years since they had last been together. Her marriage to Gorski had begun to break down, and her former serenity was giving way to fits of depression as a result. Formerly she had been a support to Paderewski; now she was herself in need of comfort. He gave it.

It was symptomatic of his state of mind that at the very moment everything was opening up before him, when any woman in Paris could have been his, he recoiled, or at least embraced the most comfortingly familiar. The same was true of the social and intellectual attractions of Paris; he would not bask in his success, for, in his own words, he was "not ready to enjoy it and not ripe enough to deserve it."[6] He was so aware of the limitations of his repertoire that it was almost as though he was afraid of being found out and exposed; at the same time he was keen to exploit his success to the full, for, as he put it, "I was not yet thirty and every hour was precious."[7] The only thing to do, he felt, was to go back to Leschetitzky in Vienna and rapidly learn a whole new repertoire.

He left Paris towards the end of October, after a tussle with Helena, who was in despair at seeing him go. "You have left, my dear child, and once again all is emptiness and sadness," she wrote after him. "I want to thank you with all my heart for the moments of happiness you gave me, those moments of consolation and respite which you brought me. . . . You were not only a lover to me but also the best of friends, who drew me back with chivalry from the abyss over which I stood."[8]

Leschetitzky was away from Vienna, so Paderewski got down to work on his own in his rooms on the Währing Heights. On 10 November he gave a concert with the singer Pauline Lucca, and some time later he gave his first recital in Vienna, in the Bösendorfer Hall. In his own words, it was "an immense, an immediate success."[9] By this time Leschetitzky had returned, and he agreed to give his pupil more lessons. "I found I could still learn something," wrote Paderewski. There was now a hint of friction between the two, as the young man had gained in self-assurance, while the teacher resented the fact that, like some sort of mechanic, he was merely being required to help his pupil with a few technical details. Nevertheless, relations remained good, and Leschetitzky arranged for Hans Richter, the head of the Vienna Court Orchestra and director of the Bayreuth Festival, to conduct the première of Paderewski's now finished Piano Concerto, in which Annette Essipov insisted on being the soloist.

Paderewski could not be present at the première, but the acclaim with which his work was greeted reached him in Paris, to which he had returned in the spring of 1889. It was the year of the Exposition Universelle, and there was a musical season to match: there were singers, dancers and orchestras from Africa, Arabia, the Far East, Scandinavia and Russia. Paderewski gave concerts sandwiched between Javanese Bedaya dancers, Roumanian Laouters and African tribal dancers. He had persuaded Edward Kerntopf to send one of his pianos to the Exposition, and by performing on it himself he managed to win a gold medal for the house of Kerntopf—a small but typical example of the way in which he repaid his debts.

After the end of the Paris season he toured Belgium, the Netherlands and the French provinces. He also went to Germany, Hungary, Bohemia and, finally, Poland, towards the end of that year. The German tour was one of the most gratifying experiences for him, as it was the country where audiences were least likely to be impressed by anything which was not of a high standard; and they were impressed. The *Leipziger Zeitung* reported that "not since Liszt has a pianist been received as Herr Paderewski was last night." The *Leipziger Tageblatt* commented that "the public did not applaud, it raved."[10] In Hamburg there was "enthusiasm bordering on intoxication," according to the local paper, while the *Allgemeine Zeitung* of Munich described him as "a poet of the pianoforte . . . a Chopin infinitely enlarged, a Chopin for the many."[11]

It was also gratifying for him to be able to return to Cracow like a conquering hero in October 1889 and give two concerts which were attended by the most distinguished figures of his country. At one of them the front row was made up of the Bishop of Cracow; Count Tarnowski, the great historian and rector of the Jagiellonian

University; the painter Jan Matejko; the poet Adam Asnyk; and Princess Marcelina Czartoryska, Chopin's favourite pupil. Again there were scenes of wild enthusiasm.[12] When he returned to Paris at the end of the year, he was able to feel that he really had sealed his extraordinary over-night success with the approval of most of Europe.

Paderewski loved Paris. He took rooms there on a permanent basis, in the Avenue Victor Hugo, and he decided to bring his little son over from Poland. The nine-year-old Alfred had recently had to leave his grandfather's house at Zhitomir, as the old man was getting too ill to look after him. The boy had gone to live with the Kerntopfs, and in Warsaw various doctors had decreed that his mysterious ailment was a disease of the bones which might possibly be curable. The best thing to do would be to get him to Paris, where he could have access to the most eminent specialists. Helena agreed to take him in with her own son, Wacio Gorski, who was a few years older, and this turned out to be an ideal arrangement. At last Paderewski was able to see something of his son.

In spite of the fact that this brought him into even closer communion with Helena Gorska, Paderewski still found time to frequent the other people he knew in Paris. He tended to ignore the hand-painted invitations from Princess Bibesco, who in an attempt to lure him even took to sending him the menus of the dinner she would serve, at which everything was à la Polonaise or de Podolie. He did, however, see a great deal of her cousin Princess Rachel.

The arrangement of the Brancovan residence on the Avenue Hoche was contrived to make as much as possible of the Princess' exotic Eastern origins. The smoking room, draped in Turkish hangings, was a den of low divans, cushions, poufs, incense-burners and harem lamps. There was a long gallery full of portraits of Hospodars of Wallachia, and beyond that a boudoir arranged like an Eastern kiosk, with stained-glass windows illuminating the incense-laden atmosphere. The music room was an oasis, or so it seemed from the number of palm trees and hibiscus growing in it. The only concession to place and time was the drawing room, lined in blue plush, with a tapestry of Boucher's *Toilette de Vénus* covering one wall.

The atmosphere was one of heavy luxury, and there was nothing restrained about the household—not even the dinners, to which Paderewski seems to have done justice. As the Princess' daughter Anna noticed, "Paderewski, the ascetic pilgrim, who would have fasted in order to render the slightest service to his native country, suddenly became, at dinner-time, a young Lord of the North, just as one might imagine him through the mist of centuries, stalwart, loquacious, insouciant, as he takes possession of his kingdom at a table groaning with venison offered to his appetite by the opaque forests harried to the sound of the horn, and holds in his strong fist a heavy goblet."[13]

The Princess' hospitality attracted some of the most fascinating people in Paris, amongst them the "marmorean and lofty" Leconte de Lisle, the "delicate, profound and gentle" Sully Prudhomme and the "perfect, impeccable and exotic" de Heredia, as Paderewski described them.[14] There, too, he came across the poet of the Midi, Mistral, of whose speech he could barely grasp a word. Painters who frequented the Brancovan salon included Bonnat and Puvis de Chavannes; other regulars were Sarah Bernhardt and, a couple of years later, Marcel Proust, who used the hostess as the model for Mme. de Cambremer in *A la recherche du temps perdu*.

In Rachel de Brancovan, Paderewski found not only an intelligent friend but also an attractive and passionate woman, and by May 1890 they had become lovers. "How happy one feels to love and be loved," she enthused in notes signed "she who finds that nothing is worth anything without you."[15] Hundreds of *petits bleus* flew between the Avenue Victor Hugo and the Avenue Hoche arranging assignations or, if there were to be others at dinner, urging him to come early, "before the others, before the hours of pretence," and not to leave until long after their last light collation of oysters and pink champagne.[16] The following morning he would usually find a note from her beginning with a cheerful *"Bonjour Chéri!"* and describing her feelings on waking, having dreamt only of still being in his arms.[17]

How Paderewski managed to keep both affairs secret and separate remains a mystery. Helena Gorska needed to be discreet, and he had endless excuses for visiting her at all hours, either to see his son or to call on Gorski, with whom he still occasionally played. But Princess Rachel, who was, incidentally, on cordial terms with

Helena, might easily have enjoyed letting slip a few hints in order to make her conquest known.

Absorbing as they must have been, these affairs did not take up all of Paderewski's time. He spent much of it with members of the Polish colony in Paris, amongst others with the sculptor Cyprien Godebski and Maria Sklodowska, the future Marie Curie, who had just arrived from Poland in order to begin her studies at the Sorbonne and lived in a small apartment in the Rue d'Allemagne with her sister and brother-in-law. As an occasional relief from being lionized by the *gratin,* the homely evenings spent with his own people in the Rue d'Allemagne were a source of great pleasure to him.

Most of all, Paderewski delighted in the opportunity to meet other musicians. Through Princess Rachel he had met the seventy-year-old Gounod—"very stately, with a beautiful white beard, wonderfully expressive eyes, and with a facility of speech that was perhaps a little ecclesiastical at times, because it was so unctuous."[18] Massenet, d'Indy, Widor, Lalo and Fauré were others he came across during this period, and he later met Debussy, but the one for whom he developed the greatest feeling was Camille Saint-Saëns. Paderewski found him easily approached and "unfailingly kind." Musically they had much in common, and this became the basis of a lifelong friendship and mutual esteem. Saint-Saëns was probably the only one of these musicians who valued the young Pole as a composer.

Paderewski had little thought for composing at this point; he was far too obsessed with the necessity of driving home his success as a pianist. The years of struggle and failure had succeeded in making this ambition absolutely central to his life, and at the same time in making him increasingly prone to self-doubt. Paris had acclaimed him, and so had Germany; but still he wondered whether he had achieved an enduring recognition, and this mainly because he doubted whether he had attained the degree of excellence which people saw in him. Even if he had, there was no room, in his view, for relaxation. It had been years of application and practising which had got him where he was, and only continued hard work, he knew, could keep him there. "I was always struggling for perfection, pushing on and on to that ever-receding faraway peak of attainment," he wrote, linking the question of his merit with his success.[19] A dangerous confusion had arisen in his mind. He was beginning to feed on success as though it were evidence of his excellence, and the moment he felt he had conquered Paris, he cast his eyes across the Channel in search of a new challenge. "A London success would mean far more to me in a solid sense than any success in either Paris or Germany," he explained, and he made his arrangements accordingly.[20] In April 1890 he gave two final recitals in Paris—one entirely of Chopin's works, the other dedicated to contemporary French music by Fauré, Saint-Saëns, Lalo and Delibes—and, braced by these triumphs, he set off for London.

CHAPTER V

The Conquest of London

"My experience was my armour and technical skill my weapons," Paderewski wrote, "so I approached London with confidence and a great eagerness and hope."[1] His disappointment was all the greater when his first recital there, in the Jacobethan splendour of St. James's Hall on 8 May 1890, turned out to be an unmitigated flop, with the place virtually empty and the receipts totaling £10.

Paderewski's introduction to London had been totally mismanaged. Through Blondel he had written to Chappell, who was far too great a personage not to find this impudent and therefore passed the matter on to Daniel Mayer, who had only just become an impresario. Mayer had heard of Paderewski and immediately sensed that there were possibilities here, but he went about the arrangements in the wrong way. He billed Paderewski everywhere as "The Lion of Paris," a phrase borrowed from the *Daily Telegraph's* review of the previous Paris season; and this absurd cognomen, coupled with the fact that nobody in London had so much as heard of the Polish pianist, virtually ensured complete lack of interest. The kind of interest needed to fill a hall can be gauged from the fact that during the three months of the 1890 season, over seventy pianists performed in the West End.[2] Twenty years later Arthur Rubinstein was to note that "The English were known for being slow to accept young newcomers."[3]

The atmosphere was all wrong for Paderewski. As one critic explained: "A more coldly critical assemblage perhaps it would have been impossible to find. Not a soupçon of magnetic current was in the air. . . . When M. Paderewski appeared on the platform there was a mild round of applause accompanied by an undercurrent of whispering and suppressed murmurs that had evident reference to his unwonted picturesqueness of aspect. The deep golden tinge of his hair seemed to accentuate the intense pallor of his countenance. One could plainly see that he was nervous."[4]

The reviews were, on the whole, disastrous. "He had not been many minutes at the keyboard before it was evident that we had to do with an executant whose chief claim to attention was his ability to astonish rather than to charm," noted the critic of the *Musical Times* drily.[5] "His loudest tones were by no means always beautiful," wrote Fuller Maitland of *The Times*,[6] while the *Morning Post* pointed out that his playing "was by no means conventional, nor was it always artistic."[7] "Much noise, little music," was the *Evening Standard*'s comment.[8] It was the critic of the *Daily Telegraph* who put the lid on the reviews; he termed Paderewski "a monstrously powerful pianist" who played "with clang and jangle of metal and with such confusion of sound that trying to follow the working of the parts resembled looking at moving machinery through a fog," and compared his playing to "the march of an abnormally active mammoth across the keyboard." The review pointed out that "the result of his labours may be marvellous, but it is not music," and just in case anyone might still be in doubt, it stressed that "plainly, we do not like Mr. Paderewski."[9]

Paderewski could not believe it. "Oh! I cannot play at all!" he sobbed as he broke down in Mayer's arms and prepared to return to Paris at once.[10] He cannot have been entirely surprised; granted the English critics' scepticism towards "the Lion of Paris" and their horror of noisy and emotional playing, the extremely wounding and dismissive phrases of their reviews suggest that all was not well with his performance that night. It may have been nerves, exhaustion, the emptiness of the hall or something else, but clearly something had taken his playing, which they could at worst have dubbed as "sensational," over the brink into sloppiness and aggressivity. Some of the critics had noticed this and been more cautious in forming judgements.

Klein of the *Sunday Times* and Fuller Maitland of *The Times* were on the whole willing to concede that Paderewski had more to offer than just noise, and they awaited the next recital with interest. One critic stood out as being particularly objective from the start, prepared to give credit where credit was due. His notices appeared in *The Star* under the pseudonym of "Corno di Bassetto," which denoted none other than Bernard Shaw. "He plays as clearly as von Bülow—or as nearly so as is desirable, and he is much more accurate," wrote Shaw. "His charm lies in his pleasant spirit and his dash of humour: he carries his genius and his mission almost jauntily. . . ." Here at least was an admission of genius; and the review ended with the words: "his Parisian vogue is not to be wondered at: he makes a recital as little oppressive as it is in the nature of such a thing to be."[11]

The second concert was better attended. Some of the musicians who had gone to the first had been impressed—rapturously so in the case of the young Henry Wood. He relayed his admiration for Paderewski to his piano-teacher at the Royal College of Music, and was so angry at the man's dismissive reply that he left his class.[12] The result was that a small crowd of music students and teachers came to the second recital. Some people had been intrigued, too, by the extreme nature of the reviews of the first recital; others had been mobilized by Paderewski's society friends. These included Lady Randolph Churchill and his two "godmothers" in English society—Mrs. Dallas-Yorke, the mother of the Duchess of Portland and a friend of the Princesses Bibesco and Brancovan, and her sister Lady Barrington, whose husband, Sir Eric, was secretary to the Prime Minister, Lord Salisbury. These people managed to create a certain amount of interest in the controversial pianist, and this was reflected in the size of the audience.

Paderewski gave a much better performance at the second recital and this was appreciated in the reviews. As Klein of the *Sunday Times* recalls, "The 'barometer' began to rise. At his third recital his fine performances of Beethoven's Sonata in A flat, op. 110, and Schumann's 'Carnival' carried the mercury from 'change' to 'fair.'"[13] This seems a conservative estimate, as the *Monthly Musical Record* of 1 June, reviewing Paderewski's first three appearances, wrote that "a still greater artist appeared in the person of the Pole, Paderewski, who, by a combination of marvellous technique and almost unparalleled powers of expression—genuine poetry in music—took his audience by storm," and described scenes of "extraordinary enthusiasm."[14] A couple of weeks later, Shaw acidly noted: "By the time I reached Paderewski's concert on Tuesday last week, his concerto was over, the audience in wild enthusiasm, and the pianoforte a wreck."[15] Reviewing Paderewski's third recital, Shaw had written that he was a man of moods who had been "alert, humorous, delightful at his first recital; sensational, empty, vulgar and violent at his second; and dignified, intelligent, almost sympathetic at his third."[16] Now he was again cross with Paderewski. "Regarded as an immensely spirited young harmonious blacksmith, who puts a concerto upon the piano as upon an anvil, and hammers it out with exuberant enjoyment of the swing and strength of the proceeding, Paderewski is at least exhilarating; and his hammer-play is not without variety, some of it being feathery, if not delicate. But his touch, light or heavy, is the touch that hurts; and the glory of his playing is the glory that attends murder on a large scale when impetuously done . . . a brutal fantasia on the theme of the survival of the fittest."[17]

The critic of the *Monthly Musical Record* echoed more widespread sentiments when he wrote in his review of the same concert: "Paderewski plays fewer wrong notes (if any) than some of the foremost so-called 'correct,' i.e. somnolent and somniferous, players." He also praised the compositions of his own that Paderewski had played, saying that the Concerto was very fine, and the shorter pieces "amongst the best of their kind." The audience seemed to agree, as the same critic remarked: "The enthusiasm evoked by this truly phenomenal artist throughout his performance was such as is rarely witnessed in our concert-rooms."[18] One thing which had never been witnessed before was the strange repetition of what had happened in Paris. At the third recital in St. James's Hall, some of the audience, mainly women, rushed up to the stage, throwing flowers at Paderewski and trying to kiss his hands and touch him.

Some of the success had to do with his looks. "I saw his head coming up on the stage in St. James's Hall, and never forgot it," writes Harold Bauer, then studying to be a violinist in London. On the way out Bauer heard one lady say to another, "I don't like his playing as well as Stavenhagen's, but I never saw such an *interesting* man."[19] In London, Paderewski's looks made an even greater impression than in Paris; he had the perfect Pre-Raphaelite head, even down to the colour of his hair.

One day in May 1890 Paderewski and Burne-Jones crossed in the street, and each noticed the other. Paderewski thought the stranger looked like one of the Disciples, while Burne-Jones went about telling everyone that he had seen an archangel in the street. The following week George Henschel, who was wont to spend his Sundays playing the organ in Burne-Jones' studio, took Paderewski, who was at a loose end, along with him. When the painter opened the door to them, he exclaimed, "My archangel!" He dragged the astonished Paderewski into the studio and insisted on drawing him there and then.[20]

For two hours he drew "rapidly, even violently,"[21] while Henschel played the organ, "which was good for the emotions, but bad for the drawing," according to the artist, although the drawing is magnificent.

Later that day Burne-Jones wrote to a friend:

> There is a beautiful fellow in London named Paderewski —and I want to have a face like him and look like him, and I can't—there's trouble. He looks so like Swinburne looked when he was 20 that I could cry over past things, and has his ways too—the pretty ways of him—courteous little tricks and low bows and a hand that clings in shaking hands, and a face very like Swinburne's, only in better drawing, but the expressions the same, and little turns and looks and jerks so like the thing I remember that it makes me fairly jump.

"He looks glorious," Burne-Jones enthused. "I praised Allah for making him and felt a poor thing for several hours. Have got over it now." Lady Burne-Jones later wrote that "they were very much attracted to each other, but the chances of life never allowed of an intimacy."[22]

Burne-Jones was not the only artist to respond to Paderewski's looks. Lawrence Alma-Tadema drew him, as did his wife; while the painter's little daughter, Laurence, promptly fell in love with him, an infatuation that was to last, without the slightest encouragement, until the end of her life. Paderewski liked Alma-Tadema. "He was a person of the most refined taste and very sure judgement," he wrote. "It was always something very extraordinary to me how he understood music and how he spoke about it."[23] The painter prided himself on the somewhat *outré* musical evenings he held at his fantastic house in Grove End Road, St. John's Wood. There would be a slightly pompous dinner, after which more guests would arrive; then followed a solemn piano recital by some well-known artist. Alma-Tadema had had a special piano built for these occasions—a vast grand intricately decorated and inset with parchment panels framed in silver which artists who had played on it signed. Paderewski signed, but refused to play the monster, and when he was the star of the Tuesday evenings, a van from Erard's would call in the afternoon with an upright piano.

Another artist who set to work immortalizing Paderewski was the sculptor Gilbert, who was commissioned to do a bust by Lady Lewis, wife of the eminent lawyer and herself a great patroness of artists and writers. Her house in Portland Place was, according to some, the grandest and most amusing salon in London. It was there that Paderewski met Beerbohm Tree and Henry Irving, Charles Hallé and the Moscheleses, Arthur Sullivan, Ellen Terry and John Singer Sargent. Paderewski particularly befriended Irving and often went to his after-theatre dinners at the Beefsteak Room. At one of these they even discussed the possibility of his writing some incidental music for one of Irving's productions.

Paderewski played for money at several private soirées, something he, in common with many other musicians, detested doing. "I used to feel that they just engaged the artists to permit the company to talk," he writes.[24] This was often very true, particularly in England. One of Saint-Saëns' favourite stories was that of the London hostess who always looked for "singers without too much voice, lest they drown the conversation."[25] When people started talking, Paderewski would often stop playing and beg their pardon for making so much noise. While this method silenced most people, the hardened talkers never even noticed he had stopped.

Quite apart from the irritation of playing to people who did not want to listen, Paderewski found the whole basis of paid soirées embarrassing. There was no getting round the socially false position of being both guest and tradesman at the same time, and this became particularly glaring when hostesses started haggling, as they often did. There are plenty of stories on the theme of whether the wretched tradesman was going to be asked to dinner or not —Chopin pleading that he had only eaten very little, Sarasate pointing out that his Stradivarius did not dine—but Paderewski's brush with an English duchess is worth adding to the list. Shocked by the amount of money he had demanded for playing to her guests after dinner, the duchess decided to snub him gently and wrote: "Dear Maestro, accept my regrets for not inviting you to dinner. As a *professional* artist you will be more at ease in a nice room where you can rest before the concert." To which the unbashed Paderewski replied: "Dear Duchess, thank you for your letter. As you so kindly inform me that I am not obliged to be present at your dinner, I shall be satisfied with half of my fee."[26]

That summer, at the end of the London season, he set off on a tour of the provinces. He visited several cities, including Liverpool and Manchester, where he played under the baton of Charles Hallé. In November he was back in London and gave a final series of concerts. This time even the critics were won over. Of his performance of the Schumann Concerto, Shaw wrote: "Not a single point was missed throughout: Paderewski varied his touch and treatment with the clearest artistic intelligence for every mood and phase of the work, which could not have been more exhaustively interpreted."[27]

The forty-odd appearances in England had netted Paderewski little money, but he felt pleased with himself as he sailed for France towards the end of November. "The London season left me with a greater security—security in myself and my art," he wrote. "The ground was stronger and firmer under my feet. . . . I had, to a certain extent, conquered London."[28]

He did not spend much time in Paris on his return. Almost immediately he set off on a German tour, which was to be something of an ordeal. On 5 December he played at Frankfurt, where the programme included his own Concerto as well as pieces by Chopin and Liszt. Clara Schumann, now a very old lady, was in the audience. "She was sitting conspicuously in the first row, and I remember that she was very interested in my concerto and applauded me loudly," he wrote. But, on the contrary, when I came to play my solo, and I had selected as a second number Liszt's Fantaisie based upon *Don Juan,* she could not refrain from showing her deep disapproval, and even, I might say, her disgust! . . . She shrugged her shoulders and turned to the lady next to her, talking and expressing with her face her contempt!"[29]

On 8 December he was giving the first of four concerts in Berlin. He played his own Concerto again, this time under Bülow's baton, and the effect was stunning. The audience gave him an ovation, the critics lavished praise on him and on the next day Wolff, the grandest impresario in Europe, came to see him and did him the honour of offering to become his agent. They had had two previous encounters, something which Wolff either did not or chose not to remember. The first time was when Paderewski had gone from Strasbourg to Paris to hear Rubinstein. The second was when, after his first Paris triumphs in the previous year, Paderewski had decided to tour Germany and, swallowing his pride, had asked Wolff to be his agent. He had again been rejected. Now he haughtily told Wolff that he did not need his services. The agent left, warning him that he would regret his decision.

The next day, when Paderewski arrived for the second of his concerts, Bülow was rude to him, conducted badly, and ostentatiously left the platform in the middle of his solo, making as much noise as he could, while the orchestra ruined the performance of the Concerto. It was, in Paderewski's words, "a perfect fiasco."[30] He still had two concerts to give according to his contract and each was greeted by withering reviews, some of which declared that it was quite obvious Poles could not play the piano. When he left, Paderewski vowed never to set foot in the place again, and he was as good as his word.

In Hamburg, where he again had to play under Bülow's baton, not a word was said about anything that had happened in Berlin, and the conductor was charming and full of consideration for him. The tour took him meandering through Germany, where he played to Grand Duchesses of Schwerin and Princesses of Saxony, down to Bucharest, where he gave a command performance for the Queen of Roumania, and finally back to Paris. On New

Year's Day he dined with Rachel de Brancovan; her fondness for him was unimpaired by his long absence.

The way of life he had been leading, however, brought concern and even strictures from Helena Gorska. She felt that he was becoming dominated by his pursuit of fame and fortune to the detriment of his artistic integrity. She wanted to see him play less and "look after and care for those darling little paws" more; she also wanted to see him spend more time composing.[31] To his objections that he must provide himself with greater financial security, she answered: "Live for the present, my child—do not look at the future."[32] This was the one thing he seemed incapable of doing; he had begun to chase a phantom goal, a position of security in which he would at last be able to relax—failing to see that by their nature such pursuits must be tantalizing. Inevitably, he was often prone to fits of discouragement, even despair, but he pressed on with grim determination, while Helena could only lament: "Your lack of energy in the face of minor setbacks hurts me deeply—the despondency which you should not be allowed to feel also hurts me—this pursuit of money hurts me."[33] Her complaints, however, could not deter him from his purpose or dispel his financial insecurity, which seemed to grow as he earned more money.

His receipts tended to get swallowed up by his expenses. He did not have it in him to stay in mean hotels when he was all nerves and exhaustion. He could not bear not to give presents and flowers; he was by nature a gentleman, and he behaved like one. He had found it necessary to take on a private secretary, Hugo Goerlitz, as he could not deal with the arrangements and minutiae of touring. His natural generosity impelled him to help people and give money to anyone who asked for it. In London he had met the eleven-year-old Mark Hambourg and was so impressed by the boy's talent that he immediately gave him the money to go to Vienna and study with Leschetitzky. Even good takings vanished under this regime.

Paderewski was supporting not only his son, but his father as well. He had dreamt of buying a small estate in Poland which his father could live on and administrate, but by the time he had collected enough money his father was too old and suffering from recurring attacks of paralysis. So Jan Paderewski was given a small house outside Zhitomir to live in, and there he vegetated, writing frequent and sad letters to his son, whom he was pining to see. They never did see each other again, and Jan Paderewski died in 1894 after a long illness.[34]

Paderewski himself wanted to settle down in Paris and compose; but instead of trusting to the odd concert and the income from his works to keep him while he did so, he decided that he would work intensively at making money for a year or two and then retire without a care. It was not long before his thoughts focussed on America as the potential gold-mine, but before he could exploit this, he had to consolidate his reputation in Europe.

After playing in the Paris season of 1891, he returned to London in June. This time everything went brilliantly from the start. "The public was now beginning to scent a veritable musical 'lion,'" wrote Klein of the *Sunday Times*. "I used to receive letters from women readers asking all sorts of questions about the Polish pianist and begging for particulars that in no way concerned them. . . . The very existence of such curiosity told a tale. There would be no more 'meagre audiences' when Paderewski played."[35] The prophecy was accurate; both inside and outside the concert hall Paderewski had become an object of fascination.

"Very soon there was hardly an evening reception or a garden-party, or other social function at which the fascinating Pole could not be seen, the centre of attraction, surrounded by a host of admirers of both sexes," wrote Sir George Henschel.[36] His daughter later reminisced: "Paderewski was the glittering centre of musical life in London whenever he went there. Apart from his genius and physical beauty, he carried with him—even to my childish perception—a compelling atmosphere of inward nobility and dignity which alone would have marked him as a being apart. But that there were beings impervious to these atmospheric emanations is also certain. One famous lawyer created a frightful consternation, and sent himself to Coventry for some time, by describing Paderewski as 'a cheery little chap.' That, of course, is true, too. Paderewski was often very cheery and he was by no means a tall man. But as a description of 'the darling of the Gods,' the lawyer's summing up was not a success!"[37]

The lawyer in question was Sir George Lewis, whose wife had

introduced Paderewski to many of the artists of London and commissioned Gilbert to do a bust of him. Lady Lewis' dinner-party book gives an interesting picture of the people he met in her circle. The eminent Victorian artists and musicians are there, but so are the younger generation—Beerbohm, Wilde and Beardsley. What the aesthetes thought of Paderewski is not hard to guess. An article on him in *The Dome,* one of those monthlies so common at the time whose principal *raison d'être* often seems to have been to indulge the contributors, starts off by explaining that "As you would write of Grieg in silver, of Maeterlinck in chrysophase, and good old Omar in ruby, so I would write of Paderewski in ivory."[38] To be coupled with "good old Omar" Khayyam in the 1890s was an accolade indeed.

Paderewski's ubiquity in London life at this period is extraordinary. One moment he was having dinner with Asquith, the next he was talking to Henry James, whom he had met through Lady Barrington. "I liked Henry James immensely from the moment I met him," he writes. "We talked about everything under the sun, as Henry James was interested in everything."[39] The next moment he was at the Alma-Tademas' in St. John's Wood, satisfying all those queuing up to paint him. On one occasion he sat surrounded by Alma-Tadema, his wife, Burne-Jones and Princess Louise, Duchess of Argyll, all wielding their brushes, while Miss Laurence Alma-Tadema sat at his feet doing her embroidery. "It was an amazing ordeal; it was not sitting, it was moving all the time," Paderewski explained, for each wanted him to face him or her a little more.[40] Nor did he escape the attentions of Violet Granby, later Duchess of Rutland, whose charming pencil drawings provide such a broad iconography of the period.

Through Jennie Churchill he was introduced to the Princess of Wales—the future Queen Alexandra—whom he thought the most beautiful woman he had ever seen. And his London season was finally crowned when, on 2 July, he was summoned to Windsor. He found the atmosphere of Windsor "rather solemn, if not austere," and it was with some trepidation that he waited in the Green Drawing Room, into which he had been ushered. Eventually, the Queen entered and quickly dispelled his nerves: 'She addressed me in beautiful French and impressed me as being a queen in every sense of that often misused word. There was such majesty about that little woman. . . ."[41]

Paderewski played "quite marvellously," according to Victoria. "Such power, and such tender feeling. I really think he is quite equal to Rubinstein," she wrote in her diary.[42] He played some Haydn, Schumann, Liszt, Chopin, Schubert and, no doubt aware of Victoria's weakness, Mendelssohn, apart from a few of his own works. Afterwards they exchanged a few words. "I was surprised to find that she knew so much about music," wrote Paderewski. "Whatever she said was just to the point."[43] After the Queen had gone to bed, Paderewski was entertained by Princesses Louise, Christina and Beatrice, and played some more for them. A few days later the usual token gift, in this case a tie pin, found its way to him.

On 11 July Paderewski gave the last recital of this London season, which was a triumph. It was a matinee on a beautiful sunny Saturday afternoon, and with the season in full swing, it had to compete with a great military review before the Emperor of Germany at Wimbledon and the Eton-Harrow cricket match at Lords. Yet St. James's Hall was more crowded than it had been since the momentous farewell concert of the great Rubinstein. The exclusively Chopin programme was greeted with "one of the wildest scenes of enthusiasm that has ever taken place in St. James's Hall," according to one paper. "A remarkable public manifestation," commented the *Daily Chronicle* on Monday, 13 July, "the brilliant player was literally mobbed."[44]

A few days later, just as he was preparing to return to Paris, Paderewski could read with satisfaction, in the *World* of 15 July, Bernard Shaw's summing up of his playing that season: "He has shown himself proof against hero-worship, never relaxing the steadiest concentration on his business as an artist, so that however you may differ with him occasionally, you have nothing to reproach him with."[45] He certainly did occasionally differ with Paderewski, particularly when the latter was playing his own music, which Shaw detested, as can be seen from his review of a concert a couple of weeks earlier, which ran: "There was a tremendous crush at the Philharmonic to hear, or possibly to see, Paderewski. Gangways were abolished and narrow benches substituted for wide ones to make the most of the available space. Paderewski took advantage of the occasion to bring forward, for the second time, his own concerto, which is a very bad one. No doubt it was 'frightfully thrilling' to Paderewski himself to fly up and down the keyboard, playing the piccolo and the cymbals and the big drum, and every instrument except the pianoforte on it, and driving the band along, in spite of Dr. Mackenzie, as if it were a coach-and-seventy thundering down a steep mountain road; but to me it was simply a waste of the talent I wanted to hear applied to some true masterpiece of pianoforte music. I could see that he felt like a Titan when he was threshing out those fortissimos with the full band; but he had the advantage of me, for he could hear what he was doing, whereas he might just as well have been addressing postcards for all that reached me through the din of the orchestra. I do not want ever to hear that concerto again."[46] This sort of broadside made Paderewski nervous and unhappy, so it was comforting that Shaw's final verdict was so sympathetic. Even without Shaw's approval and that of the other critics, Paderewski knew that he had made his mark when, walking in South Kensington, he saw a brass plaque on a door bearing the inscription: "Mrs. Simpson, Piano-Teacher, PUPIL OF PADE-REWSKI."[47]

Paderewski spent that summer, or what remained of it, partly with Rachel de Brancovan at her villa on Lake Geneva, and partly in Paris with Helena Gorska. But all the time he was working exceedingly hard.

His London agent, Daniel Mayer, had managed to obtain a contract for him with the piano firm of Steinway. Steinway had been looking for someone to promote its pianos by touring the United States, but it was not easy to find a pianist with a strong European reputation to do this. Those who had gone before—Thalberg, Bülow and, in 1872, Rubinstein—had complained on their return of the merciless manner in which they had been driven to work and exploited. Paderewski was not scared by hard work, and as long as the money was good, he was game. The contract obliged him to give eighty concerts in the United States; Steinway undertook to pay all expenses, to guarantee him a fee of £6,000 and to make sure that all the concerts it arranged were of a high standard. Any money that was made over the top of the break-even figure was to go straight to Paderewski, as Steinway was looking for advertisement, not profit.

In October Paderewski went to England, where he gave thirty-eight concerts in London and the provinces, and on 3 November he set off from Liverpool on the steamship *Spray*. Ahead lay uncertainty; behind him he left two disconsolate hearts. "I still cannot resign myself to believe that this cruel moment has come, fatal, irrevocable, without pity or mercy for me," wrote Rachel de Brancovan. "And I feel that as the minutes pass, the reality will impose itself more and more in all its black sadness."[48] Helena Gorska had disapproved of the whole venture from the start, but she tried to put on a brave face, and on the day after leaving Liverpool Paderewski received a cable from her which ran: "Take from the Americans everything you can and do not give them any part of yourself. Here your place will be kept."[49]

It was a daring venture, this American trip, not least because everyone had been trying to dissuade him from it, appealing to his artistic integrity and his duty to become a great composer rather than waste his time being a concert pianist. In May of that year Princess Bibesco had reiterated her argument that he should consecrate his life to composing. "God created you for glory; you cannot make your halo lie! God demands great things from those to whom he has given much!"[50] Only a few days before leaving for America he received an extraordinarily savage letter from young Laurence Alma-Tadema, deploring his continuous tours. "And yet you rush from town to town," she wrote, "drunk on their crude applause, as though this excitement, unworthy of a great artist, had become indispensable to you!"[51]

The girl had in fact hit the point, for behind the financial insecurity, imagined or otherwise, lurked another, which was the result of years of failure and self-doubt. Paderewski needed the money, but he also needed to be continually reassured that he really was a great pianist. Success had not cured his insecurity, but it was nevertheless a potent drug, one to which he gradually became addicted. He was caught in a pursuit of fame and fortune which would lure him on and on, ever further from his fancied aim of settling down to a life of composition.

CHAPTER VI

The New World

The *Spray* sailed into New York on 11 November. Paderewski's first vision of Manhattan was not impressive; he arrived late in the evening, and the only things he saw were "small, dirty, low buildings near the wharf. There were hardly any lights and the impression was rather sordid and depressing."[1] On the pier he was met by Mr. Tretbar of Steinway, who cheerily set about deepening the gloom. "Well," he started, "we hear you have had brilliant successes in London and Paris, but let me tell you Mr. Paderewski, you need not expect anything like that here in America. We have heard them all, all the pianists, all the great ones, and our demands are very exacting. We are not easily pleased here."[2]

Tretbar then took him to his hotel and left him. The place was full of mice and bedbugs, and Paderewski could not bring himself to sleep there. He was so depressed in the morning that he went to the steamship office to find out the dates of sailings for Europe before calling at the Steinway offices, which were then on 14th Street. He complained so vehemently that Tretbar moved him to the Windsor Hotel at Fifth Avenue and 46th Street, which was a great improvement. In fact, he took such a fancy to the place that he always stayed there in future, even when he could afford better.

His despondency returned when he was informed of the programme Steinway had planned for him. This consisted of three orchestral concerts in the first week, with hardly any time between to rehearse the different programmes. "I longed for the earth to open and swallow me up," he wrote, but immediately started practising for the first concert.[8]

This took place at Carnegie Hall (then known as the New Music Hall) on 17 November 1891. The orchestra performed an overture, with Walter Damrosch conducting, and then Paderewski came nervously on to the platform. As the *New York Tribune* pointed out, he had been "dangerously well advertised," and the hall was full. He had put his programme together for maximum effect. He started with Saint-Saëns' Fourth Piano Concerto, a well-known test piece in which he could show off; this was followed up by a group of Chopin solos, in which he excelled; and the performance ended with his own Piano Concerto, which provided an obvious climax to the evening. He felt he had been "well received, but not yet any kind of sensation" as he left the hall and went to a dinner arranged by Steinway, but he greatly underestimated the impression he had made.[4]

"The foreign press had prepared us to expect a great artist, but the extent of that greatness was hardly comprehended," began one of the notices, going on to say that "we almost hesitate at the terms of superlative praise which instinctively and inevitably come to mind."[5] Most of the reviewers felt no such hesitation, and the superlatives rained down, in phrases like "a pianist among pianists," "he stands alone," "an intoxicating triumph" and "the greatest of them all . . . a giant . . . a master."[6] The *Evening Post* could not resist remarking that "his fingers glide over the keyboard as if it were all done by electricity."[7] But the more serious were no less enthusiastic, like the distinguished critic James Huneker, who wrote, in the *Musical Courier:* "Ignace Jan Paderewski played the piano last night at the New Music Hall, and played it in such a wonderful manner as to send a huge audience mad with enthusiasm and recall memories of Rubinstein in his prime, but a Rubinstein technically infallible. . . . In the dual role of a composer and virtuoso, Mr. Paderewski won a triumph that was genuine and nobly deserved . . . mere brutal display and brilliant charlatanry are totally absent." Huneker found Paderewski's playing of the rather dull Saint-Saëns Concerto "totally overwhelming," and thought his own Concerto came close to genius. The whole evening was "a success that was stupendous."[8]

Paderewski had no idea of what was awaiting him in the press the next morning. What he did know was that he had an orchestral rehearsal late the same morning for the concert to take place that night, and as he needed to practise before the rehearsal, he had no option but to stay up all night. He could not practise in his hotel room, so he went to the Steinway warehouse, where he worked for five hours while the night watchman and Goerlitz snored on benches beside him. On the next day he got through rehearsal and concert. "Paderewski was again acknowledged to be the grandest pianist now before the public—the only peer of Rubinstein," in the words of one critic.[9] But Paderewski hardly noticed what anyone said or wrote any more. Between the second and third concerts, which were only one day apart, he practised for seventeen hours. His arms were "dropping off" when he ascended the platform, but somehow he managed to forget the fatigue and the pain, and to play magnificently.

After the three orchestral concerts came six recitals, to take place in the smaller Madison Square Garden Hall. Recitals were not popular or frequent in the United States, and smaller audiences were expected; but after the first two, on 24 and 26 November, the box office was so besieged that the remainder were removed to Carnegie Hall, which was packed for the remaining four, with all 2,700 seats and 1,000 standing places taken. At the end of the second of these the audience, led by women, rushed on to the stage and mobbed Paderewski.

He had hardly any time in which to consider his success, or to answer the frequent letters from Helena begging him to take things easy, as he was immediately whisked off to the next stop on his tour, Boston. Here he was met by his old Warsaw friends Timothy and Joseph Adamowski, who had settled in America and now played in the Boston Symphony Orchestra, which Paderewski thought one of the finest in the world. Its conductor, too, earned his immediate esteem; "I have known many splendid conductors, but the closest to my heart was Arthur Nikisch," he wrote. The concerts were both satisfying and successful, but there was no time to enjoy Boston, for he was off again. In Chicago, too, he found a magnificent orchestra and conductor, Theodore Thomas, "a real musician, a musician by the Grace of God."[10] At the Chicago

Auditorium he played to his largest audience yet—4,000 people.
Prominent amongst these, he noticed with emotion, were hundreds
of local Polish émigrés who had flocked to the concert at the sound
of his name. Poles or no Poles, the audiences everywhere were enormous and responsive; his appearance in Milwaukee was more like
a football game than a concert, with men standing on their seats
and cheering while tears poured down their faces. When he played
in Cleveland, Ohio, the Lakeshore & Southern Michigan Railroad
had to lay on special trains. In Portland, Maine, over a thousand
people pressed through his dressing room after the performance,
insisting on shaking his hand, which was "swollen twice its
size as a result."[11] As one Boston critic put it, "It is something more
than fancy; something more than fashion; something more than
a contagious enthusiasm."[12]

Paderewski, who was thinking of the dollars as he shook the
thousands of hands, suffered a terrible disappointment. He found
out that when booking the tour the sceptical and wary Tretbar had
sold some of his performances for a fixed—and sometimes very
low—price, which meant that even when a hall was packed and
the takings amounted to thousands, Paderewski received only the
couple of hundred dollars agreed to between Tretbar and the hall
manager, who pocketed the rest.

He complained of this and other hardships in his letters to
Helena, but received little of the sort of support he must have
longed for in return. Not that her letters were infrequent—if anything, they were all too frequent. His departure had robbed her of
all serenity and peace of mind, and she was in a desperate mood;
she sent several letters begging him to drop everything and return
to Europe. Possessiveness alternated with anxiety about his health,
but this gave way to self-pity and reproach when he wrote little
and rarely. "Your last letter was dry as pepper," she wrote in
February. "I have been through many bitter moments in these
couple of months, and unfortunately their memory will remain
forever—it is true that at my age every month must rob me of
some shred of my right to live, to be happy. . . ."[13] She was
constantly seeing signs that his love for her was waning, so aware
was she of his youth, beauty and position in contrast to her own.
"Why do you love me less darling Ignasiek?" she would write.

68

"I need your love so terribly now. Why, why do you forget me?"[14] She was in agonies of loneliness and apprehension, and again and again she asked herself, "Is this really happiness to love the way I love?"[15]

Part of the trouble was that Gorski had just discovered what was going on between his wife and Paderewski. He was not, it seems, remotely angry, since he was himself flirting with Hélène Bibesco and Antonina Szumowska, a young girl from Warsaw to whom Paderewski was giving lessons. Nevertheless, he grew spiteful and unpleasant, and, like some delinquent child, he began to run up debts in his wife's name, foreseeing that Paderewski would end up paying them. "The atmosphere at home is impossible," Helena wrote to Paderewski.[16] "His presence is so irritating to me that it is unbearable,"[17] she wrote in the next letter, at the same time suggesting that Paderewski might find Gorski a job in the United States so she could be finally rid of him. The marriage had been breaking up for some time, but Helena was still shocked by the degree their estrangement had reached: "In the face of all my sufferings [Gorski] has behaved with icy indifference, and from the moment he found me weeping over your letter,—the one that arrived on Christmas Eve—we have not spoken to each other. . . . I do not mourn the fact that our relations have become virtually hostile—but it is sad to reflect that a man who has been near me for so many years cannot even bring himself to utter a word of sympathy when he sees my suffering. . . ."[18]

Gorski told her that she was a free agent and could do what she liked; but this only served to heighten her insecurity, as it seemed to throw her into the arms of Paderewski, to whom she wrote: "Don't you worry yourself about it, for *nothing unwonted* will fall on your shoulders. While little Alfred needs me, I shall stay with him—and afterwards I shall disappear, and will not be a burden to anyone, not even to you, my darling one."[19] Her bravado is touching, but she was a burden to Paderewski already. Many of her letters ask him to send money for herself and Alfred, and now that Gorski was being difficult, someone would have to provide for her son. The very fact that she was spilling out her miseries to Paderewski at a time when he was working harder than ever to try to establish himself was a burden on his already strained nerves. He hardly had enough time to sleep, so he could not have enjoyed the added worry of Helena's problems, particularly since he felt himself responsible. He replied in brief notes and telegrams hastily written between concerts, and sent money. He sometimes also found time to write to Rachel de Brancovan, whose letters to him must have been a refreshing change—always sprightly, amorous and a little saucy. Hélène Bibesco's letters, hundreds of which followed him across the Atlantic, fared less well and remained, for the most part, unopened.

The sheer pace of the tour precluded much thought of anything else. When he was not playing he was rehearsing, and when he was not doing one or the other he was either travelling or being given dinner by local musicians or dignitaries. He only just managed to contrive spending Christmas itself with Helena Modrzejewska, who was acting in New York; it was the first time they had met since Zakopane, and he was happy that she could witness how far her advice had taken him. But he had little time to spend with her or his other compatriots in America, the famous singers Jean and Edouard de Reszke, the vivacious soprano Marcella Sembrich-Kochanska, or the pianist Jozef Hofmann, whom he knew from Warsaw. "In the course of one hundred and seventeen days I played in one hundred and seven concerts and attended eighty-six dinner parties," he later told a journalist. "Mon Dieu, I was cross!"[20] He was in such a state of nervous tension throughout that even if he had travelled and given two concerts on the same day, and however late it was, he found it necessary to play bridge or cribbage with his secretary for hours before he was relaxed enough to go to bed.

He soon found that at this rate he was getting sore hands. He thought the Steinway piano "the most marvellous instrument in the world," but the action was hard and "the actual physical strength required to produce a very big tone from a Steinway piano, as it was then, was almost beyond the power of any artist. The strain was terrific." After long arguments with the managers and then with the workmen at the factory, he managed to persuade them to regulate his pianos in such a way as to soften the action. "My piano then, with all its beauty and power, became gradually quite docile, and my intimate relation to the instrument was most enjoyable. It was no longer my enemy; I no longer had to fight with it—we were friends."[21] But this new-found friend was about to deal him a nasty blow.

One bitterly cold night in January, he arrived in Rochester, New York. From the station he went straight to the packed concert hall and mounted the platform. The piano had been to the factory for servicing, and a regulator who knew nothing of Paderewski's private arrangements had restored the hard action with a vengeance. The result was catastrophic, as he describes:

> As usual, I struck two or three opening chords—when suddenly, something broke in my arm! A terrific pain—an agony—followed. I had the feeling that I must run from the platform, that I would never be able to play again. Of course, I mastered the feeling in a second, because I realized that it would be disastrous for me to do such a thing. But in such dreadful moments one sees everything black. I thought it was the end of everything—that my career was over, because something very serious, I knew, had happened to my arm. It became suddenly very stiff and the pain was indescribable. But somehow I held myself together and began the playing of Beethoven's *Appassionata*. How I got through it I shall never be able to tell you.[22]

After the recital he went to see a local doctor, who said he had torn a tendon, strained others and injured his finger very seriously. The doctor said that only complete inaction could restore the finger to health. This meant that he would have to cancel the rest of the tour, thereby breaking his contract and forfeiting most of the cash. As the doctor had said it was not certain he would ever be quite well again, Paderewski felt that this might be his last opportunity for making any money at all, so he decided that, come what may, he must try to finish the tour even if it killed him. He kept on, playing almost every day and sometimes twice a day. Upon arrival in a place, he would collar the local doctor and get him to massage and bandage for all he was worth. "I had become used to the constant and terrifying pain in my arm, and I had also learned to play with four fingers only of my right hand, and to adjust my will and nerves to the ordeal of going through an almost daily public performance, with the knowledge that each concert brought me nearer my release."[23]

On his return to New York at the beginning of March 1892, Paderewski was at last able to rest for a couple of days. He had fulfilled his part of the contract, but he was faced with a harrowing dilemma. There was great public demand for more concerts, and Steinway, apologetic for the mismanagement of some aspects of the tour, offered to arrange further concerts in such a way that Paderewski would pocket the entire takings. He hesitated. "I felt, as did the physicians, that I might never play again. Perhaps it was the end of my career. . . . What was I to do? . . . I made up my mind to go through with it. I do not know how I did it. I used hot water, massage, electricity, and everything to nurse and galvanize into life my dead finger."[24] He gave twenty-six more concerts, and on March 27 made his farewell to New York and America by giving one at the Metropolitan Opera, the proceeds of which—some $4,000—were to go to the fund for building the Washington Arch. It was the first of many gestures made to show his appreciation of a country to which he was grateful primarily for material reasons, and with which he was to fall in love over the years. He had every reason to be grateful. It had been a nightmare, but—and this was the only thought that mattered as he sailed for England—he had $95,000 in his pocket to show for it, an unheard-of fortune for a pianist; it made Rubinstein's legendary earnings look like those of a barroom entertainer.

Paderewski returned to Paris in May 1892 and immediately set about finding a doctor who could help him. Most of them were categorical that there was nothing to be done except rest, and all seemed agreed that the damage he had done by playing on regardless could never be completely repaired.

He needed little prompting to take a rest, and was soon comfortably ensconced at Amphion on Lake Geneva, in Rachel de Brancovan's Villa Bassaraba. She was delighted to have him back with her, particularly as she had assumed that his constancy would not stand up to the temptations of America. When he remonstrated with her for this lack of faith, she answered, in her disarming way: "Be angry with me, darling, chide me; but you were so far away, so far, and you were so feted, so admired, so adored—how could it have been otherwise? It was inevitable. So, darling, do not be angry, do not chide me; forgive me. It was only natural for me to fear."[25] Encouraged by his reproaches, she now grew more passionate and possessive, which provoked occasional "squalls and storms" between them, for, as she lamented: "Alas! I do everything to make myself less and less loved by you, for I do not know how to love with all the calmness you would like to find in me."[26]

Back in Paris at the end of that summer, he was faced with the more acute problem of Helena Gorska, who had also been reassured by his return from America, and now longed never to be away from him again. "I simply cannot come to terms with the thought that you might stop loving me—you are mine, and you must love me," she wrote.[27] He did love her, passionately, as can be gauged from another letter of hers: "I want you so much, you understand; I want you through whole nights—I cry out and seek your embrace— I want your lips—I want ecstasy, I want you, you.—And you are far away, and life slips by; and without you I feel so empty, cold, sad—so sad. Do not be shocked that I thirst for you—you made me like this. You wanted passion, you wanted abandon; now you have them—be proud of your work and love me—love me, for on top of the delights we have been through, I shall give you many moments of happiness yet. You will see—we shall often . . . be so close to heaven. . . ."[28]

Heaven was some way from Paderewski's thoughts, which dwelt constantly on sealing his success. He had realized that America was a potential gold mine, and gold was what he felt he needed at this stage, in order to be able subsequently to give himself up to a carefree life of composing. Moreover, he had latterly learnt a great deal about the workings of the performer's life. He was quick to appreciate that entertainment, even at the sophisticated level of the concert hall, was an industry like any other, and that the best side to be on in any industry was that of the management.

Traditionally, artists have regarded managers and agents as parasites waiting to prey on them, and Paderewski had at first shared this view. But he now saw that these mechanics of the musical world could be the artist's best friends if only he became their partner in business. Henceforth, he worked only on this principle. He was friendly, generous with his terms, never grasping, and ready to give way on small things in order to achieve what he wanted. He co-operated with the agents in planning tours and programmes, and allowed them to build up his image and his value in the most com-mercial way. As a result, they liked doing business with him, and both sides prospered.

However, when Paderewski showed Helena the contract he had just signed for a second tour of America, she was so dismayed at his leaving again that she threw it in the wastepaper basket and made a tremendous scene, making him feel wretched and guilty.[29] Another obstacle was his injured hand, which showed no signs of growing more flexible as summer turned to autumn. He eventually found a masseur who worked away assiduously, and gradually restored strength to the arm and agility to the damaged finger.

The second American tour, which began in November 1892, was far better organized. Steinway had reaped such enormous advertisement value from the first that the firm was only too eager to make up for the blunders that had accompanied it; Paderewski was now treated with tender care. The pianos were regulated to perfection, and in order to avoid the rigours of seedy hotels and bad food of which he had vociferously complained, Steinway thought up a new system for touring. It hired a private railway carriage, in which he had a bedroom, a dining room and a sitting room with a piano. The car also accommodated his secretary, his valet, a tuner, the tour manager, a chef and two porters. On arrival at a given place, the car was unhitched from the train and left on a siding. Paderewski could then spend the afternoon practising, change, go out to give his concert and come back to find the dinner he wanted waiting for him. The concerts were more widely spaced and fewer. Thus he could expect to find the whole tour much less taxing.

But Paderewski's arrangements were never proof against unex-pected hazards, which always seemed to strike at his most vulnerable parts. After playing at the opening of the Steinway showroom in Philadelphia, his hand was shaken by so many eager people that it swelled up, and he could not practise for a few days. "Another re-ception like this, and I shall not be able to play ever any more," he groaned.[30] On another occasion, in New York, he was recognized in the men's room at Delmonico's by a businessman who insisted on calling in his entire dining party. They all shook hands vigorously with *the* Paddyrooski," which caused more inflammation. Worse was to come.

After a dinner party in New York, Paderewski and the de Reszke brothers agreed to entertain the company with some music. Somehow he had managed to scratch his finger, and the action of playing that evening opened up the wound, which became infected. When he returned to his hotel, the finger began to swell and throb with pain. In the morning he rushed to a doctor, telling him something must be done, as he had to play that very afternoon with the Adamowski brothers, who had founded a quartet and for whom the chance of playing with Paderewski was an invaluable boon. The doctor was sceptical. Although he, and particularly his little daughter Ruth, were to become great friends of Paderewski's in the longer term, Dr. Draper could do little for the pianist at the time. He operated at once and gave a local anesthetic, but the concert was an ordeal: "I played with those four fingers. I had to play a Beethoven trio and a Brahms quartet with the Adamowskis. Fortunately, I was playing only a few solos which were very familiar to me, some Schubert and a little Chopin. But even so, the pain was a torture. During the playing all the effects of the anaesthetic gradually disappeared." The press notices were terrible, and Paderewski decided to postpone the next eight recitals. He started playing again too soon: at the first concert the bandaged wound reopened and blood started seeping out on to the keyboard. "The first time, it made a terrific impression on me. It was an ugly sight. I could scarcely go on playing, but I soon got accustomed to it, I must admit, and during the rest of that tour of twenty-two concerts, I played each one with a bandaged finger and the keyboard was always red when I finished."[31] The audiences must have thought he was going a bit far with his special effects.

Helena felt he had gone much too far, and that her worst apprehensions had been vindicated—he really was killing himself for the sake of money. He must stop all this and come home at once. They would go off to "some quiet corner"—Brittany, Algiers, she did not mind. "You must rest," she wrote, "you must write an opera—everyone expects it of you—everyone awaits your work with the greatest anticipation. It is more important than money; it must be created."[32]

She inveighed against "this nightmare of concerts" not only on artistic grounds, as she had to admit that she missed his presence terribly. "It is so difficult, so horribly sad for me without you," she wrote in January 1893, "that sometimes I feel it might be better to end this life altogether."[33] But although she was prone to sudden violent depressions, she was generally much calmer than in the previous years, and although she still nagged at him in her frequent letters, he was easier in his mind about her. For this, and more practical reasons, this second tour had been less of a strain than the first, in spite of his finger injury.

Again Paderewski chose to show his gratitude to America by giving four charity concerts, and again he could afford to be grateful. His sixty-three professional concerts had netted him a fabulous $160,000 (nearly £40,000), which was serious money for anyone, let alone a pianist. Now he would be able to relax and, above all, to compose.

After stopping off in London long enough to visit some of his friends and to perform his Concerto at one of the Philharmonic Concerts under the baton of Max Bruch, he returned to Paris in mid-June 1893. Almost immediately he set off for Normandy, where Helena had taken a house near Yport for the summer. "It's not the Villa Bassaraba," she wrote, still thinking that it was only the luxury and the social *ton* that drew him towards Rachel de Brancovan, but she assured him that it was very cosy.[34] The atmosphere was certainly calculated to make him feel at home. His sister, Antonina, had come from Poland—she had been married off against her will to an older man, but both he and the child she bore him had died, leaving her destitute and alone. Another who came from Poland for a few weeks was Edward Kerntopf, still one of his very few intimate friends. The greatest pleasure for Paderewski was, however, to be able to spend some time with his son, Alfred. He was confined to a wheelchair by his illness, but was otherwise a lively and intelligent boy of thirteen. He got on well with Helena's son Wacio Gorski, four years his senior, and this companionship helped him to dominate his infirmity and grow up a happy child.

Paderewski felt well in these surroundings and soon got down to composing. In the first five weeks he wrote the Polish Fantasia for Piano and Orchestra (op. 19), which he dedicated, a little ungratefully in the circumstances, to Rachel de Brancovan. The Fantasia is one of his most satisfying works, and certainly his best orchestral composition. It is based on the Polish folk idiom but the themes are Paderewski's. He develops these with skill and imagination, and strikes a finer balance between piano and orchestra than in the Concerto, which was intended as more of a show-piece for the pianist. The Fantasia achieved wide popularity, and maintained it, appearing frequently in concert programmes well into the 1930s.

After finishing this, he turned to a subject which had been preoccupying him for some time—an opera. He had longed to write one for years, and in 1889, in Vienna, he had met a man who wanted to write the libretto, Alfred Nossig. Nossig was the son of one of the elders of the Jewish community in Lwow and a prominent Zionist; he was also a sculptor, a journalist and a playwright, enjoying a certain recognition in Berlin, where he wrote, almost exclusively in German. During their first meeting they had discussed the possibility of collaborating on an opera, and a few years later Nossig had sent Paderewski the draft of a libretto, based on a Polish story, which appealed to the composer. He set to work on sketching the first act, but was soon distracted from it.

Either he was getting a little bored by the seclusion and the domesticity at Yport or perhaps he could not resist the siren's call; in July he suddenly left Normandy and went to join Rachel de Brancovan at Aix-les-Bains. Paderewski adored Helena and was devoted to her. He also loved her passionately and physically, which makes it all the more baffling that he should have felt the need to have another regular mistress. It cannot have been mere lubricity that motivated him, as he could, and probably did, satisfy his sexual needs wherever he chose without forming lasting attachments. He was, in fact, in love with both of these women, in very different ways, and this reflected the dualism in his character. Helena's presence meant warmth, comfort, homely security and complete understanding; it was being with one's own. Rachel de Brancovan represented the outside world, full of glitter, excitement, beauty, but also of challenge; by its very brilliance and sophistication, her world was just a little frightening and foreign to the minor nobleman from Podolia who lurked within the cosmopolitan pianist. It was nevertheless alluring and Rachel de Brancovan was seductive and yielding. "I who am fortunate enough to love you as I do, and to be not detested by you," she had written to him recently, "I consider myself, with pride and joy, to be the happiest of women, and I thank you for it again and again, as I send you my most tenderly grateful kisses—I adore you!"[35]

At Aix-les-Bains they spent hours boating on the Lac du Bourget, basking in the romantically intermittent nature of their relationship, and revelling in the beauty of the scenery. "No, I shall never forget them, those adorable hours," she wrote to him. "I shall count them amongst the most beautiful I have spent—*the* most beautiful!"[36]

After a couple of weeks Paderewski went to Italy, probably with the Princess, and in August they were both at Amphion. The Villa Bassaraba had been built by Napoleon's illegitimate son, Count Walewski, and consisted of a principal house surrounded by small chalets scattered throughout the park. Most of the guests lived in these and came to the villa for lunch and dinner; the rest of the time they could do what they wished. One of the great joys of Amphion was the Princess' yacht, on which the company would sail around the lake, often calling in on others who lived on its shores. That little corner of Europe had been, since the end of the eighteenth century, the retreat of the rich, like Adolphe de Rothschild at Pregny near Geneva; the exiled, like Jerome Napoleon at Prangins; and the elegant, like the Haussonvilles, who lived in Mme. de Staël's old house at Coppet.

Paderewski often went sailing with the other guests, but he also spent a great deal of time working. The Princess had put him in a conveniently situated turret room in her house, with a piano of his own; her daughter Anna would hear him practising there as she sauntered around the garden in one of her exalted moods.

When Paderewski had first met her, five years earlier, Anna was only a little girl, albeit a precocious one. "On the small, frail body of a puny child, she bore the superb head of a goddess of antiquity, but the face, a face of ecstatic beauty, made one rather think of the pious brush of a Fra Angelico," is how he described her then.[37] She was now seventeen and, in the words of the Duchesse de Clermont-Tonnerre "as beautiful as a summer moon."[38] She was burgeoning both emotionally and intellectually, and her recent meeting with Marcel Proust, who was to become a close friend, had set her on a literary course. She wrote poetry of rather fey intensity, musically beautiful but thematically insipid, and she loved to declaim this for hours, usually from her bed, around which sat an admiring audience.

In Paderewski, Anna found the companion she yearned for at that moment in her life. She was in love with him in an exalted way, but her love, like everything else about her, was a mass of contradictory urges. She needed humouring, and he, who may have felt something for her, too, spent hours with her. "The prolific agility of the spirit which animated him," she explained, "spiritually enriched every creature his eyes rested upon," and she always felt that "beside Ignace Paderewski we were like people walking suddenly out of the shade into the sunlight, and experiencing the delight of feeling on their shoulders the light but baking pressure of the aerial heat."[39]

Speaking at her funeral over forty years later, he remarked that she suffered from "perhaps excessive sensibility," but he is reported to have said on a less formal occasion that "she was just like a tap one cannot shut off."[40] He was not the only one to feel this way. "When she talked one felt battered by a hail of diamonds," quipped one Parisian, while one of her lovers, Barrès, complained: "If only she'd keep quiet, I might be able to listen to her."[41] Tiresome as she may have been, she nevertheless exercised strong powers of seduction over men.

Who the other guests at Amphion may have been that summer is not known, but there was usually a lively selection of Parisian literary figures and other friends of the Princess. Paderewski enjoyed the rarefied intellectual atmosphere of the gathering as well as the more obvious attractions of being unconstrained with his beloved Rachel. But soon it was time for him to go, he felt—he must get back to Paris and work at his opera. Rachel de Brancovan was upset that he wished to leave her so soon. She accused him of not loving her enough, and on their last day together they had a flaming row. On the next morning, after he had left, she wrote in despair: "I sent you a telegram this morning, but that cannot soothe

the bitterness in my soul. It is so great, so great, that I must come to you, I must tell you how much I suffer far away from you, my darling, how much I love you, how dull, empty, unbearable life seems *without you!* Oh! How sad and miserable I feel. Sad because you are no longer here, miserable because you left me under a very unfortunate impression. Why cannot I learn to control myself more than I do? Why does my passionate love manifest itself at times in ways that you find too violent?"[42]

His return to Paris was a sort of flight, not from her specifically, but from the emotional and intellectual hothouse of her world; and it did not stop at returning to Paris. Instead of settling down in his apartment on the Avenue Victor Hugo, which was too close to the fashionable world and his mistresses, he rented secluded quarters at Passy, where he was visited by nobody but the valet who came to prepare lunch and attend to his needs. His dinners he usually took at a workingmen's bistro frequented by cab and coach drivers. "The food was excellent," he explained. "The company was not aristocratic, of course, but it was certainly not unpleasant to see all these good people enjoying themselves after their work."

In the spring of 1894 he came out of hibernation. He played during the Paris season, and then made another English tour, mainly in order to give his Fantasia an airing. This time he crossed over to Ireland, playing in Dublin, Belfast and Cork. That summer he stayed at Amphion once again, and the following summer he went to Normandy, but otherwise he stayed in Passy for the whole of 1895 and most of the next year, working, mainly on his opera.

"I turned all my forces towards the great object, a tremendous undertaking that obliterated everything else," he wrote. "I shut myself completely away from the world."[43] At first everything went well and speedily. By the end of 1893 he had finished what he thought would be the final version of the first two acts, and had already sketched out the third, but his pace soon slackened as he started reworking parts of it and having doubts. He interspersed his work on the opera with attempts to write a violin concerto and an orchestral suite, only fragments of which remain; but he kept coming back to what he was beginning to see as a great moral as well as musical statement—the opera, which was blotting out all other writing with its monolithic presence in his mind.

The story on which the libretto is based is about a young gypsy, Manru, who falls in love with a Polish peasant girl and, much to the disgust of his own people and hers, marries her and settles just outside her village. With the heavy hand of late Romantic literature, he is portrayed as wasting away gradually, like a plant in foreign soil, and finally, as a result of the connivance of a gypsy girl and also of a hazy fate, rejoining his tribe to the accompaniment of the suicidal death-rattles of both ladies. Under the influence of the Zionist Nossig and the Romantic nationalist Paderewski, the libretto which emerged cast the elements of love and fate into the background, replacing them with a strange concoction of cultural affinity and racial determinism as the mainspring of the drama. The influence of Wagner is obvious, but while Wagner had thought his ideas through at both the dramatic and the spiritual levels, Nossig had not. It was up to Paderewski to make sense of the libretto, and in this he was hampered and confused by two factors: one was that the ethno-cultural determinism of the peasant girl and the gypsy ultimately eluded the successful pianist sitting in Passy; the other was that he found himself emotionally involved in the plot. It cannot escape notice that the rootless gypsy that Paderewski had become was as tortured as Manru by the choice between cultural assimilation with Paris as represented by Princess Rachel, and return to his own people in the shape of Helena Gorska.

This awareness of cultural frontiers had been felt by Chopin in the same circumstances, but Chopin's art dominated and made up for his life and enabled him to rise above its fortunes. Paderewski's art was only one facet of the man, one talent that he had developed, and it in no way dominated either his personality or his attitude, which was prone to all the nagging complexes of the expatriate. As a result, his flirtation with the artistic life of Paris had been brief and jejune. Gounod, to whom he had instantly warmed, had died that year, and the musicians he saw most frequently now were Saint-Saëns, Fauré and d'Indy. His friendship with the first two became close, but at the personal rather than the artistic level. It is significant that Saint-Saëns described Paderewski as "a genius who plays the piano," while Fauré told a friend that Paderewski was "one of the greatest artists, one of the most magnificent characters, and one of the most noble hearts of our times."[44] Both betray regard for the whole man, rather than just the artist.

His contact with them, and with people like Debussy, remained on the whole a social one; he laboriously forged on along his own course, led not so much by inspiration as by force of circumstance. The preoccupation with his own predicament and that of his people was turning gradually from an emotional response, as in Chopin's case, to a political one, and this was becoming one of the main motors of his urge to compose. This in itself isolated him from his French contemporaries in the cultural sense, while his career and his life-style isolated him from them in the physical sense. Between his composing, his tours and his social life, he hardly had time even to go to concerts.

His ploy of earning enough money by exploiting the concert platform so that he could retire and compose had been misguided, for he discovered, as everyone does, that a fortune dictates tastes. In his case, many of them had always been there; he came from the Polish nobility, which, however impoverished, has always had a talent for spending. It almost goes without saying that the moment he made any money at all, he started to indulge various of these tastes, which usually masqueraded as necessities. The perfectionist at the piano was a fastidious dandy when it came to dress, so fortunes were spent on silk shirts, waistcoats, evening coats, patent-leather pumps and *bottines* made to measure in London, fur coats, hats from Lock's, exquisite watches, cuff-links, tie pins and cigarette cases. Every time he set off anywhere, there were more pieces of luggage.

Next came that very Polish trait, the compulsion to give presents, to send flowers, and to distribute largesse to anyone in need, or even to scroungers. Here the resemblance with Chopin is striking —money was just a means, and any consideration of the wisdom of saving it was far outweighed by the joy of being surrounded with beautiful, expensive things, and by the voluptuous pleasure of giving them.

Perhaps the most ruinous of the traits he had inherited from his national, and particularly his social, background was the minor nobleman's virtual lust for "land." For the Pole of that class, land was something to be loved and possessed; a nobleman without land was like a knight without a sword, a grounded albatross. It is therefore hardly surprising that even before the first American tour Paderewski had collected every spare penny he had and bought an estate in Poland. He had set foot there only once before selling it a year later, at a loss, and buying another. This was to be managed in his absence by a cousin of Helena's. The man had no qualification for the job, and since Paderewski's instructions were to turn it into a model farm and not to skimp, oceans of money disappeared as the place was refurbished and stocked with everything from the latest machinery to thoroughbred horses.

Paderewski was supporting his father and sending money to his sister, Antonina; he was keeping Helena Gorska and her son, Wacio; he was paying the most expensive doctors for his son, Alfred; and he was employing a number of servants, including Alfred's valet and his own secretary, Hugo Goerlitz. It soon became apparent that the money he had earned could not last very long at this rate, and little pruning of expenses was possible with so many people dependent on him. There was nothing for it but to look to America once again.

The land of promise did not disappoint him. During his tour, which began in the autumn of 1895 and ended in the spring of 1896, he gave ninety-two concerts which netted him the princely sum of $280,000—well over two million pounds at present-day values. It was an astonishing triumph both materially and artistically, as one American critic explained:

> No clearer illustration of the magical power which lies in music, no more convincing proof of the puissant fascination which a musical artist can exert, no greater demonstration of the capabilities of an instrument of music can be imagined than was afforded by the pianoforte recitals which Mr. Paderewski gave in the United States in the season of 1895–1896. More than three-score times in the course of five months, in the principal cities of this country, did this wonderful man seat himself in the presence of audiences, whose numbers ran into the thousands, and were limited only by the seating capacity of the rooms in which they gathered, and hold them spellbound from two to three hours by the elo-

quence of his playing. Each time the people came in a glad-
some frame of mind, stimulated by the recollection of previous
delights or eager expectation. Each time they sat listening to
the music as if it were an evangel on which hung everlast-
ing things.[45]

This was the polite way of putting it. What really went on during
these tours seems to belong more to the 1960s than the 1890s.

CHAPTER VII

Paddymania

"Drama on the Ocean!" ran the headline. Reading it, an innocent might have leapt to the conclusion that a ship had gone down with all hands. In fact the article under that heading in a New York paper described how, during a rough night, the piano in Paderewski's cabin had broken loose from its moorings and rolled across the cabin, making it rather difficult for the pianist to get out of his bunk until his valet arrived with breakfast.

Paderewski had become a star. His extraordinary popularity in the concert hall had drawn more and more people, and had turned his recitals—normally events appealing only to serious music-lovers—into the most widely attended musical entertainments, transcending boundaries of class as well as nationality. Unprecedented scenes took place at box offices whenever a Paderewski recital was announced. In London, people queued from the early morning with chairs and picnics. In Boston, they arrived at eight a.m. for an evening concert. Again and again, thousands had to be turned away for lack of space. Whether in London or Sioux Falls, South Dakota, the houses were full, the enthusiasm unbounded and the earnings immense.

The press was not slow to take more than a critical interest, particularly in America, where it was keener on "a story" than on mere news. Paderewski certainly made good copy. In the headlines he became "The King of Pianists" and "The Wizard of the Keys," and the editors did not have to look far for their ghastly puns.

85

"There's Music in the Hair!" announced the front-page headline of one New York paper as Paderewski sailed in for his tour. The hair was, of course, one of the first things they seized upon. Soon after his first New York concert, the following little rhyme appeared in one of the newspapers:

> What's the useki,
> Paderewski,
> Of your phalangial skill,
> When your playing
> Goes sasshaying
> With your frontal hirsute frill?
>
> You're not so-so
> Virtuoso
> But a reg'lar, 'way-up player;
> Still your phrasing
> 'S not amazing
> As your perturbating hair.
>
> You can churn
> The sweet nocturne,
> Of th' andante you've the hang;
> But your pounding
> Lacks the sounding
> Timbre of your towzled bang.[1]

"Like Samson, he depends for his effects not upon his fingers but his hair," intimated one reporter. "It is said that Paderewski's hirsute Chrysanthemium is thinning out," awesomely reported another. Some claimed it was a wig; others, that he shaved his head completely when not on tour. Journalists wondered what he washed it in and what he put on it. The *Chicago News* confidentially informed its readers that the distinctive colour of the artist's hair was the result of his habit of eating a whole fresh lemon every day.[2] It was not long before shampoos were marketed with more or less direct assertions that they were based on "the Paderewski formula." And if it worked for shampoo, it could work for anything. A candy-manufacturer brought out sticks in the figure of the pianist, closely followed by a soap-manufacturer. Paderewski wigs were marketed as party jokes, and even a mechanical toy was produced, in the image of a little man with a vast mop of golden hair sitting at a piano. When wound up, the little man would leap about, banging the keyboard madly. The image was in the popular mind, and it could therefore be exploited in any and every way.

Shane Leslie, travelling from London to Paris in 1895, recognized Paderewski, who was in the same carriage, "from the skits which were played at music-halls by comedians with hearth-rugs attached to their heads."[3] A circus performer in England drew crowds by changing his name to Paderewski and putting it about that he was the great pianist's brother. The name was used to sell just about anything. "Paderewski—the man who astonished the world—takes Nuxated Iron Pills. You try!" ran one advertisement in a Chicago paper. "Paderewski—Prince of Pianists; Finckelstein's —Emperor of Dry Goods," announced another.[4]

The next object of fascination for the American press was the financial aspect of the pianist's successes. His earnings were published in the papers—with good reason, for they were indeed news, as no single musician had ever pocketed such sums before. One journalist calculated that, even including encores, Paderewski was earning, on average, over $1,000 for each piece he played.[5] A typical rider to this was speculation as to how much his hands were insured for. Nobody could find out, but fabulous sums were suggested. When, in 1905, his train was derailed near Syracuse, New York, there was a veritable orgy of interest and conjecture in the press across the United States. First came the "human drama," complete with artists' impressions of Paderewski lying in bed being nursed by glamorous women, and diagrams showing which tendons in his neck had been strained. Then came the money. Nobody actually knew how much insurance he received, but the New York Central Railroad Company announced that it had got off cheaply, as Paderewski had accepted only $7,000 in compensation for the concert he had to postpone.[6] The papers then went on to speculate how much his life was worth, and suggested figures based on an estimated income of around one million dollars per year; but even they were outdone, for the American tour of the previous year—

only about half of his yearly appearances—had netted him over one and a half million.

From there it was just one step to the subject of how he looked after his health. It was known that he bathed his hands in warm water before playing, but that was simply not good enough; secret potions and preparations were hinted at darkly. People wanted to know how much he ate, what he drank and how many cigarettes he smoked. The *Popular Phrenologist* of London devoted its January 1903 issue to an inquiry into Paderewski's mind, character and intelligence, not to mention musical ability, based on phrenological deduction. He only had to sneeze or lose his watch to make headlines.

This sort of thing was not entirely unknown in America, and Jenny Lind's tour in 1850 and, to a lesser extent, Anton Rubinstein's in 1872 come to mind. Jenny Lind had met with astonishing ovations from the crowd, and her name, too, had been exploited, to the extent of being used to sell coal-burning stoves. But there was a subtle difference between this and Paderewski's case. Jenny Lind and Rubinstein had enjoyed world-wide reputations long before they came to the United States, and their visits to that country were seen almost in terms of divine condescension: Americans were being allowed to catch a brief glimpse of the most excellent in Europe, and they were determined to show their receptiveness and appreciation. Paderewski, on the other hand, arrived in New York not as the world's greatest pianist but as one among many, and it was partially in America that he established his paramount reputation. The image was therefore not one of divinity descending from heaven, but truly of an earth-born, almost home-grown American idol. "Paddyroosky," or just "Paddy," as he came to be known throughout the United States, inspired affection, not awe. This, combined with the frequency of his visits, made the American press and public take a far more personal interest in the details of his life.

The private railroad car in which he travelled across the United States was the symbol of a princely way of life, and therefore attracted that new and growing fascination with "how the other half lives." Paderewski was one of the first victims—and beneficiaries—of the plot by the media to persuade their readers that some people's lives are magic, and that by reading on they will be vouchsafed a peep into this land of dreams. A full-page article in the *Minneapolis Journal* of 9 December 1913 begins thus:

When the North-Western Limited steamed out early today it carried with it in its observation car and day coach "886" the two cleanest cars that ever left Minneapolis, for yesterday the two were scoured and scrubbed, polished and primped no less than eight separate and distinct times. All yesterday the two had stood in the North-Western yards at Plymouth Avenue and River Street, and between them was tracked the private car of Ignace Jan Paderewski, the pianist, and all day in his car the great master rehearsed over and over again the wonderful compositions that are to make up the program of his recital tonight at the Auditorium, and to hear which Minneapolis must pay.

An admiring audience of car-cleaners heard him yesterday without charge and earned a day's pay besides, for as long as they worked nearby they could hear, all of which explains why the two North-Western coaches, standing on either side of the pianist's private car, had to be cleaned so many times that they would have shone resplendent if there had been a sun anywhere around to help them out.

In vain did A. Deck, the boss car-cleaner, call to his fifty-two hands to work elsewere, insisting that it might be as well if some of the other cars in the yard were at least swept out, but the fifty-two cleaners cold-decked Mr. Deck, the boss, and worked away on car "886" and the observation coach with a vigor that some day may make one of them president of the road. At 2 p.m. Harry L. McClure, the rotund superintendent of the North-Western's commissary department, gave it up, and with his clerks moved from the little frame building at the end of the yards and established headquarters in the observation car, with an open window about two feet from where the master practised calmly on, deaf to the engine whistles and the din of the noisy neighborhood.

If some of the North-Western's dining cars are shy of a few things today, Mr. McClure hopes he won't be blamed.

"I am inclined to think," observed John Olsen, as he used up the third box of metal polish on the brass rails of the observation car," that Jan plays the Beethoven concerto in A minor with much more delicacy of touch than he employs in Liszt's rhapsody in E major. What do you think, O'Reilly?"

"Well," responded the window-washer, who was then on the fourth round of the car's windows, "personally I am more inclined to admire the technique of the lighter passages of the sonata in major opus 106, and he reads Wagner well, don't you think? And Olsen, tis a fine ring-side seat we've got."

That is only the introduction. The article, which is about eight times as long, then gets down to business. It lists the personnel of the private car: the English manager, the American manager, the treasurer and bookkeeper, Paderewski's valet, Marcel, the piano-tuner, the two porters and finally the black cook, James Copper. Copper was always willing to be interviewed; he went on at length about Paderewski's diet, and how it was really his doing that the pianist was as well primed as he was. Copper enjoyed talking to anyone who cared to listen, and stood in awe of nobody. One day after dinner Paderewski told his valet to compliment Copper and tell him that "the fish was excellent, the roast perfect and the dessert sublime." A few moments later the valet returned from the kitchen and announced: "Mr. Copper thanks you, sir, and says the soup was very good, too."[7]

The fact that not one but three of the major Minneapolis daily papers had sent their hacks to hang about dirty railway yards all day long in order to be able to produce long and tedious "stories" tells its tale. Paderewski was news, and if authentic news could not be come by, stories would have to be improvised. Artists' impressions of his "studio" in Paris were published, and, not surprisingly, they did not accord very well with one another, since none of the artists had ever been near his Paris home. His Polish estates were discussed at length, often with the wildest exaggeration, and he was perennially reported to be "secretly" married to a selection of gypsies, Roumanian princesses, and German baronesses.

The sexual element in Paderewski's success was, of course, exploited to the hilt. From the start there had been, as with Liszt and Paganini, serious over-reaction on the part of women to his playing, and it was reported with glee. "At least a dozen ladies had to be carried out in a fainting condition," wrote the amused critic of a recital in Edinburgh in 1894.[8] At a New York concert "a large number of hysterical ladies had gathered to the front and, seeming to hang on the edge of the platform by their chins, became almost hypnotized."[9] More alarming manifestations were on the way. In 1893 a London newspaper reported that "Paddymania has reached such heights that three New York ladies have embroidered musical phrases from the *Minuet* on their stockings."[10] Paderewski used to receive hundreds of requests for photographs—of which he learnt to keep a trunkful always at hand—hundreds of love letters, and even proposals of marriage.

After a concert which they had given together in the Queen's Hall, Paderewski and Henry Wood came out by the stage door in Riding House Street. There was, as usual, a small crowd waiting to catch a glimpse of the pianist, and Henry Wood spotted two girls standing together. "Yes—go on," cried one of them, "be quick!" while the other whipped out a pair of scissors, snipped off one of Paderewski's curls and made off with it.[11] On another occasion two women forced their way into Paderewski's hotel room brandishing scissors and pursued him through the suite with a look of cruel determination which sent him diving into the nearest closet, where he was besieged until help arrived.

The American press reported all these symptoms with relish. "Matinee Girls on Rampage!" screamed one newspaper; "Girldom in Throngs—Our Reporter was Crushed by Femininity in Carnegie!" howled another; while the *New York Herald* explained to those who had missed the point that "The long-haired pianist bears about the same relation to the women of New York as a cookie-jar does to an orphan asylum."[12] The *New York Telegram* began its review of one of the concerts with a sort of subdued lament:

The mere announcement that Paderewski is to give a recital causes among the two sexes that attend piano recitals as much excitement as does the intrusion of a death's-head moth into a hive of bees. There are indeed two sexes that attend piano recitals. Inasmuch as the women are the stronger and the more energetic of these two sexes, the women yesterday had captured all the seats for the Paderewski recital in Carnegie Hall, while their hats, mostly white, had captured all the view.[13]

Another critic was evidently more alarmed by this inequality:

There I was, simply girled in! A huge and dominant gynarchy seethed around me. There were girls in shirtwaists of silk and of flannel; there were girls in loose corsets and in tight corsets. There were large and bouncing girls, and short and stubby ones. There were girls in hats, and girls in bonnets. There were girls who wore wedding rings and girls who didn't. There were girls....[14]

This kind of thing was good for the box office, but as the popular idol loomed larger, the pianist was gradually eclipsed. Many serious music-lovers and critics reacted to all this enthusiasm with a certain disgust which caused them to mistrust their original judgements. They began to feel, as critics will, that if this man was so ludicrously popular with people of little or no musical education, that popularity must be based on something other than good musicianship. At a less sophisticated level, too, the publicity had its ill-effects, if Osbert Sitwell's description of a scene which took place in a British Officers' mess in 1912 is to be believed:

One day, when I was sitting there, I watched a Major reading the newspaper and noticed his face begin suddenly to swell, twitch and turn plum-purple. At last—I had not dared to break the silence and ask if I could be of any help—he threw down the rustling pages, and appeared to be making a struggle to frame words. Seeing this, a brother-officer came immediately to his aid, patting him on the back and saying, "What's the matter, Snorter old boy?"—or Piggy, or Pongo, or whatever may have been his regimental, taboo nickname. I listened carefully and tried to gather the gist of what he was trying to tell us. He had been reading, it appeared, the report of an incident on board a ship going to South Africa, when someone had insulted Paderewski. "I wish to God the feller'd killed him," the tongue-tied Major bellowed, that organ at last freed by emotion from its years of atrophy. "I don't believe he could play a choon if he wanted to! He ought to be shot, that—Padderoosky!"[15]

In the case of other artists, envy combined with disapproval as they sat in their garrets or their empty halls and thought of Paderewski counting his millions. People began to say that it was all a question of long hair and showmanship, that his playing was deficient and that he could not be considered a serious artist, and this opinion gained weight with time.

Paderewski was not a born pianist in the sense that Liszt, Chopin and Rubinstein had been. But he was endowed with certain musical gifts, and by painstakingly developing these he had ultimately achieved technical brilliance. Although there were occasional accusations from critics that he blurred his chords and pounded too hard, his technical excellence went unchallenged in the main.

"In purely mechanical skill," wrote one critic, "it seems impossible to exceed the limits of his amazing achievements."[16] "He seems to shake the notes from his sleeve like a prestidigitateur; technical difficulties do not exist for him; indeed, from his playing, one might fancy that there was no such thing as a difficult piece," wrote the American critic Henry T. Finck.[17] William Mason, a pupil of Liszt, thought that Paderewski was "always master of his resources, and possesses power and complete self-control."[18] Even Bernard Shaw found that Paderewski was always sure of his notes.[19]

"It seems to me that in the matter of touch Paderewski is as near perfection as any pianist I ever heard," wrote William Mason.[20] He thought Paderewski superior to Liszt in variety and richness of tone colour, and in this he was echoed by other critics.[21] This tone was achieved partly through varying the use of finger, hand and arm weight, and partly with the aid of the pedal, for which he developed his own technique. He could, for instance, produce an extraordinary *legato* effect by using the pedal in syncopation with his hands. "He seems to do almost as much playing with his feet as with his hands," wrote the critic W. J. Henderson.[22] "Paderewski is the wizard of the pedal," claimed Finck. "No other pianist, except perhaps Chopin, has understood the art of pedalling as Paderewski understands it. In this respect he is epoch-making; his pedalling is a source of unending delight and study to connoisseurs."[23]

The acquisition of such skill by someone to whom it did not come naturally was achieved by intelligently applied hard work. What form this work took is best gleaned from the accounts of the few people to whom he gave some lessons at this stage in his life. However advanced they might be, he would make them do finger exercises every day, first slowly, with a deep lingering touch, in order to examine the tone produced. The exercises would then be done with the wrists pressed against the edge of the keyboard so that only the fingers could move, and the pupil would have to go through them varying the strength of his touch. The exercise would then be played very fast, after which it was done very slowly once again. The purpose was to make the pupil listen to the tone he was producing. "No doubt you feel the beauty of this composition," Paderewski would say to his pupil Stojowski, "but I hear none of the effects you fancy you are making."[24] It was complete denial of the instinctive, and continual calling into question of acquired skill. And Paderewski practised this system himself. "After playing a composition a great number of times in public recitals he will go back to his house and play it as slowly as if he were a beginner," wrote Antonina Szumowska, another pupil.[25] He would rework every piece and listen to his playing of it, reevaluating his rendering from the point of view of clearness, tone and timing.

It was on this very point of timing that he was severely criticized by many people. It was said by many that his use of *tempo rubato*—poetic licence with regard to rhythm—was exaggerated, even outrageous. Judging by recordings of his playing, his use of the principle whereby tempo can be varied was indeed often too *outré* for modern tastes, which demand a more meticulous observance of the printed instructions. This was not so in the 1890s, when Paderewski's dictum that "a musical composition, printed or written, is, after all, a form, a mould; the performer infuses life into it" was not merely acceptable but accepted.[26] While rehearsing a Brahms Trio in Paris, he decided to replace a *diminuendo* in the score with a *crescendo,* whereupon his two colleagues protested, pointing to the clear instructions Brahms had written. "It is not a question of what is written," he snapped impatiently, "it is a question of musical effect."[27] This would be considered sacrilege nowadays, but then it was noted by a musician as a sign of his greatness.

Paderewski had strong opinions on the subject of strict time, to the extent of writing an essay on it.[28] "Rhythm is the pulse of music," he wrote. "Rhythm marks the beating of its heart, proves its vitality, attests its very existence. Rhythm is order. But this order in music cannot progress with the cosmic regularity of a planet, nor with the automatic uniformity of a clock. It reflects life, organic human life, with all its atttributes, therefore it is subject to moods and emotions, to rapture and depression. . . . There is no absolute rhythm. In the course of the dramatic development of a musical composition, the initial themes change their character, consequently rhythm changes also, and, in conformity with that character, it has to be energetic or languishing, crisp or elastic, steady or capricious." Few people would disagree, but it is a question of degree—and that changes with the prevailing fashion.

In the 1890s most critics found this very aspect of Paderewski's playing the most fascinating. "His playing is the negation of the mechanical in music, the assassination of the metronome," wrote Finck.[29] "His irregularity of movement is so natural, so unconscious, that one might easily suppose he was playing in strict time," he explained, "yet any incarnate metronome trying to keep pace with his hands—right or left—would soon be landed in a madhouse."[30] "Mr. Paderewski's rhythm is flawless," claimed another critic. "He never offends the most judicious listener either in quantity or in dynamics, but, on the contrary, accentuates in such a manner that the phrasing of a composition comes out in the clearest possible light."[31] Wanda Landowska, too, was captivated by "his passionate phrasing, his refined touch, the vehemence of his movements, and the nobility of his *rubato*."[32]

It all boiled down to a question of interpretation as opposed to mechanical skill. Liszt had been surpassed in the purely technical sense by people like Thalberg, but he could give a far greater performance of a piece of music than Thalberg could aspire to. And this because he had a higher understanding of music, because he was an artist and not just a pianist. Much the same was true of Paderewski: "His playing is not mere musical mechanics," explained one critic, "he possesses that temperament which distinguishes the *artist* from the *pianist*."[33] The word "temperament" is misleading, for this insight and understanding were to a slightly lesser degree than with the technical aspects of playing, the result of application and intelligent study. The process, too, was the same. The long hours spent going over a piece again and again were to ensure that every single little technical point had been taken and mastered, but they were also employed by Paderewski to develop a closer understanding of the piece. Phrase by phrase, Paderewski would examine the composer's intention and his meaning. "There is no other known method of finding out the inner meaning of a composition equal to that of playing it over and over to oneself," he claimed. "New beauties present themselves; we get nearer and nearer to the mind of the composer."[34] It was then, and only then, that the pianist could, in Paderewski's words, "put his own personality resolutely, triumphantly into his interpretation of the composer's ideas." [35] Stojowski summed up this process as follows:

> A great artist's performance of a noble work ought to sound like a spontaneous improvisation; the greater the artist, the more completely will this result be attained. In order to arrive at this result, however, the composition must be dissected in minutest detail. Inspiration comes with the first conception of the interpretation of the piece. Afterwards all details are painstakingly worked out, until the ideal blossoms into the perfectly executed performance.[36]

The result of this was that, as Edward Baughan put it,

> Paderewski's playing represents the beautiful contour of a
> living vital organism. . . . It possesses that subtle quality
> expressed in some measure by the German word *Sehnsucht,*
> and in English as intensity of aspiration. This quality Chopin
> had, and Liszt frequently spoke of it. It is the undefinable
> poetic haze with which Paderewski invests and surrounds all
> that he plays which renders him so unique and impressive
> among modern pianists.[37]

Insistence on the *meaning* of a musical work can have disastrous consequences; interpretation can all too easily turn into
parody. However, Paderewski was an intelligent and discriminating
man, and a great believer in self-control, and his long studies of
composition in Warsaw and Berlin made him one of the most
highly educated pianists of his time. His interpretations met with
a rare consensus of approval.

"No matter how rapid or mechanically difficult the passage,"
wrote an American critic,

> the result of Mr. Paderewski's private study as revealed to
> his hearers is manifested in this remarkable insistence upon
> the artistic relations of the thousands of tones in a composi-
> tion, coupled with a mastery of tone-colour which preserves
> at all times the vocal illusion. And behind all this lies a men-
> tal grasp of the organic unity of the musical work, which
> gives us a symmetrical and satisfying interpretation.[38]

Bernard Shaw singled out this musical "intelligence" as Paderewski's most impressive quality, as it permitted him to seize ten
nuances in a composition for every one the average pianist picked
out, and for this reason, Shaw felt that he would have made a fine
conductor. The great conductor Henry Wood, who often worked
with Paderewski, found it a strange experience. "His unity with
the orchestra was amazing," he wrote. "He never seemed to be listening to his own playing, his whole attention as usual being given
to the orchestra."[39] A corollary to this understanding of what he

was doing was, as Shaw points out, a deep and intelligent sympathy with all kinds of music.[40]

Paderewski played Bach, for instance, not as the great Romantics played him, but as a classicist. Every voice was studied and brought out, every part of the work received its full share of attention; nuances were never neglected, nor were they in excess. The emotional and intellectual content of the work were in perfect balance.[41]

It was in this combination of an emotionally live rendering based on a deeply intellectual understanding of the pieces he played that the key to Paderewski's extraordinary popularity can be found. "The secret of Paderewski's permanent success lies in this," wrote Finck, "that he makes us forget that there is such a thing as technique by his supreme mastery of it and by making the musical ideas he interprets so absorbingly interesting to all classes of hearers."[42] "There are many persons who shun piano recitals as intolerable bores," he explains, "but who never miss a Paderewski concert, because, when he plays, Bach and Beethoven are no longer riddles to them but sources of pleasure."[43] These observations explain how Paderewski managed to cast his spell with equal force over the urbane European music critic and the small farmer of the American Midwest. But there was more to it than just a pleasant and accessible rendering of great music.

Paderewski's mastery—significantly, a word he often used in this context—of a composition and his apparent understanding of its sense gave his playing an authority the critics were quick to take up. "He has the most extraordinary ability in impressing the belief upon his hearers that an interpretation is the only correct and logical one, because he has done it that way," wrote a Chicago critic.[44] When Paderewski played a well-worn piece, the audience had the impression that this was the first time they had ever heard it, even that he was improvising it himself. He seemed to play everything the way people played their own compositions, and Bernard Shaw, after hearing him play the Schumann Concerto, felt that, had he not known the contrary, he would have assumed that Paderewski had written it.[45]

There was certainly inspiration here, and it must have accounted for a great share of the delirious enthusiasm of his audiences, but it did not quite account for all of it. Nor did it account for some of the more hysterical manifestations of that enthusiasm, for, as the pianist Abram Chasins pointed out of one concert, "there were few present who were not mesmerized long before Paderewski placed a finger on the keyboard."[46] The dimly lit hall, the finely chiselled head with its mane of golden hair and the flowing white knot of Paderewski's tie can in no way account for this. Nowadays they might seem theatrical, but at the time he must have seemed, if anything, restrained. Rubinstein, with his Beethoven head, thundered and pounded his pianos to splinters, the very image of the Romantic Titan; de Pachmann explained to his audience that the waistcoat he was wearing had belonged to Chopin, and then proceeded to speak asides throughout his performance; but Paderewski would walk on diffidently and play with a minimum of physical motion, and with his eyes nearly closed.

The famous hair is always listed, even in serious works of reference, as one of the factors contributing to his success. The hundreds of poor pianists who thought likewise and grew striking heads of hair in an attempt to reach the limelight provide, through their failure, proof enough of the absurdity of the contention.

Paderewski's hair was not, in fact, very long—certainly not as long as Rubinstein's—and the striking effect it had on his audiences was largely self-induced. They *willed* to see him as the transcendent artist, they willed to see him beautiful, magnificent, almost divine. The audience's desire and the artist's expression fed on each other, producing an atmosphere in the concert hall that was highly charged.

Waves of something other than sound were felt by those who came, and they found themselves carried along in a state of near-hysteria. James Huneker, a staid critic and not a young man, writes: "I assure you that I have been at Paderewski recitals where my judgements were in abeyance, where my individuality was merged in that of the mob, where I sat and wondered if I really *heard;* or was Paderewski only going through the motions, and not actually touching the keys? His is a static as well as a dramatic art. The tone wells up from the instrument, is not struck. . . . Is this the art of a hypnotizer? No one has so mastered the trick, if trick it be."[47]

It is often said that Liszt possessed a mediumistic quality

which allowed him to induce hysteria, particularly in women, as he played, and there are certainly, as with Paderewski, plenty of examples of the effect he produced. Finck attempted an explanation by suggesting that Paderewski concentrated so hard on the music that he gradually hypnotized himself with it, and that because there was anyway a very special rapport between him and his audiences, he would, like some kind of medium, draw them into the music with him. Strange powers are not something, however, that can be constructively discussed.

It is easier to induce a trance with the aid of insistent heartbeat rhythms of African music or with Indian ragas than with classical European music, but all music can be used for this purpose, whether the performer is a medium or not—indeed, whether one believes in mediums or not. On the other hand, it seems odd that a critic like Huneker who went to dozens of concerts a month for year after year should suddenly have his powers of discrimination torn away from him by works he had heard many times before simply because they were being played by Paderewski. To this must be added the fact, also very widely attested, that, on or off the stage, Paderewski exerted a strong magnetic appeal.

This appeal was to some extent based on his beauty—not the physical beauty of features and forms, but an allusive and suggestive beauty. Proust's friend Montesquiou writes of "the beautiful face of a thunderstruck archangel, whose ardent mystery was so well captured by Burne-Jones's pencil; under the hair of a cleverly tousled Masaccio, the tormented visage of a Lucifer whose halo had been turned to mere hair."[48] Elsewhere he calls him "the exquisite standard-lamp,"[49] while an American critic described his appearance as "slender and orchidaceous."[50] Even Queen Victoria was struck by Paderewski's "aureole" of hair, a word used again and again to describe that head.[51] The young Arthur Rubinstein, when visiting Paderewski a few years later, was shown into the drawing room, where he felt intimidated.

> I was really on the verge of running away, when—a miracle happened; the centre door went wide open, and there appeared the Sun, yes, the Sun. It was Paderewski, the still young Paderewski in his middle forties, dressed in a white

suit, white shirt, and white Lavallière tie; a shock of golden
hair, a moustache of the same colour, and a little bush of
hair between his mouth and his chin gave him the look of a
lion. But it was his smile and his charm which made him
appear so incredibly sunny.[52]

The American poet Richard Watson Gilder noted that, like
Swinburne, Paderewski was "all nerves and sinew, but the body
subordinate to the spirit—always."[53] "He is electric as life," noted
an English lady. "Splendidly restrained, he is almost never tem-
perate. There is a subtle violence about Paderewski that is quite irresistible. However civilized you are, it makes your soul rise as a
wave to the West Wind, as the hooded cobra to the pipe of the
charmer."[54] Chasins recalls how, while playing in a room full of
people, he suddenly felt something electric in the atmosphere
and, turning round, saw Paderewski standing in the doorway. "I
shall never forget that leonine authority, that quiet dignity and regal
poise—the way this man's presence illuminated that room crowded
with his most celebrated colleagues, as though a blinding light had
been turned on."[55] Henry Wood, appearing with Paderewski at the
1897 Promenade concerts, was struck "by his quiet, forceful and utterly dignified bearing."[56]

It was not just artists or aesthetes who picked up these emanations, as a down-to-earth reporter noted after an interview:

The outward man is six feet tall. Not a lumbersome, obvious
presence, because his remarkable patrician face holds every
bit of your attention to a complete effacement of everything
else about him. After sitting across the table from him for
some time, one remembers nothing about his clothes, his
bodily presence, his height. My chief recollection of him is a
very low collar, a plain white tie tucked into a bow under
it, and an athletic breadth of shoulders. A faithful report,
according to modern standards, should include a description
of his boots, perhaps, but I didn't see them, so entirely absorbing and complete was the spiritual importance of his
face and head.[57]

Implicit in this "spiritual importance" was Paderewski's tremendous intelligence. Not an arrogant, sparkling brilliance but a deep, human intelligence. "His mind is one of the most extraordinary I have ever come in contact with," wrote Walter Damrosch, who knew him well. Montesquiou spoke of "his informed and refined mind,"[58] For Paderewski did not look at the world through the prism of his art or his career. Anna de Noailles noted with appreciation that, unlike most artists, Paderewski did not see himself as a being from another sphere temporarily condemned to exile on earth.[59] He never sought to cut himself off in any way from his fellow-creatures, and was always aware of them.

This was the root of his goodness, which manifested itself through astonishing generosity. His was not just material generosity, although this was indeed prodigious as well as prodigal: his tips were legendary, he gave presents and money at the drop of a hat, he made sure that his servants always gave food or money to tramps (the private railroad-car was a sort of travelling soup-kitchen for the needy during his American tours) and he certainly gave more money and benefit concerts for various causes than any other artist before or since. But giving money is one thing, caring is another, and Paderewski cared for anyone who asked him for help as well as a good many who did not. He would happily give a dozen encores after a concert, often playing for up to an hour over his normal programme, which was always long anyway—just in order not to disappoint the audience.

People the world over knew of this goodness, and he was frequently petitioned for some favour or some material assistance, which he rarely denied. It is not remotely surprising to find in his papers a letter from a group of Armenian students in Geneva in 1904, begging him to help them collect money for Armenian political prisoners in Turkey, as they knew he would help. They were not disappointed, for he immediately gave a benefit concert for their cause. Often he would not wait until he was asked. One day he read in the paper that a poor workman had been run over by a train outside Baltimore, and that his pregnant wife had, as a result of shock, given birth prematurely but, for lack of money, was about to be thrown out of the hospital she was in. No sooner had he read this than Paderewski went to the hospital, settled the bill, took the woman and her child to a good hospital in New York, where he visited her daily until she was better, and finally made a settlement for her and the child. This awareness of other people, of their needs and problems, was a striking feature of Paderewski's character. A less spectacular but no less eloquent example is provided by Henry Wood. Paderewski asked him, after a concert, whether he could meet Wood's father, having heard that the old man always came to his son's concerts. Wood obliged, and later his father said, with tears in his eyes, "Of all the great artists appearing in Queen's Hall, possibly not one ever gave a thought or wondered whether you ever *had* a father—except Paderewski, the greatest of them all."[60]

This attitude to his fellow-men undoubtedly contributed to the charm and to the impression of warmth and light which he exuded. He was alive to his audiences more than most performers. He always knew which areas of a given audience were responding to his playing, and which were cool or hostile. He was even aware of individuals in the audience, watching for the face of an old man or a little girl who would come to hear him each time he played in a given town, or else playing to particular groups or people whom he had noticed. The first time Pablo Casals went to hear him in the Salle Erard, he was astonished to find Paderewski staring at him throughout the performance. Afterwards, when someone tried to introduce them, Paderewski declared: "I already know this young man; tonight I played for him." He then fixed the disconcerted cellist with what Casals called a fiercely penetrating look and announced: "This youth is *prédestiné.*"[61]

At the same time Paderewski was conscious of the fact that, once an audience had assembled, it became a "colossal collective individual, and primitive to excess. It is never guided by reasoning, but always by intuition, by feeling and instinct."[62] This instinct could sense in Paderewski the extraordinary man he was, and it could also tell, apparently, that he loved his audiences and cared for them. One can quite see how all this helped him to manipulate his audiences and to absorb them in his playing. As one young man said after a recital in Lwow, "It wasn't a concert, it was a religious ceremony."[63] It was, above all, what they wanted.

Some people, however, began to feel that these extraneous elements were the *only* basis of his popularity, with the inference that he was not, ultimately, a very good pianist. Certain critics would sit through his concerts counting the wrong notes and the blurred chords, while pianists like Alfred Riesenauer and Moritz Rosenthal expressed contempt for his technical ability. This view became fashionable with many musicians and critics in the 1920s and 1930s, and has remained so ever since, to the extent that on the sleeve of a recent recording of the Piano Concerto a pundit can declare that anyone playing like Paderewski "would be laughed off the stage" by a modern audience in Carnegie Hall. This astonishing assertion is widely accepted, and the recordings he made are often used in support of it.

Paderewski recorded some fifty rolls for the Welte-Mignon and Duo-Art systems in the first decade of this century, and, beginning in 1911, almost a hundred gramophone discs. These have to be treated with reservation, for they can provide only the haziest impression of what his playing sounded like. "Paderewski, from the first, diffidently consented to record and never completely reconciled himself to the ordeal," writes F. W. Gaisberg, who made all the recordings. "He always doubted whether a machine could capture his art. . . . His art involved such broad and unrestrained dynamics—the faintest *pianissimo* crashing into a great mass of tone. In other words, he painted on a vast canvas, and the gramophone could only reproduce a miniature of his mighty masterwork."[64]

There are various practical reasons for this. In common with many other artists, Paderewski always took time to "warm up," and it was only by the second or third piece in a programme that he had shed his stage-fright and got fully into his stride. The early recordings had to be set up and made one at a time, in a sterile atmosphere. Had it been possible to make "live" recordings at a concert, the great performer would have sounded more relaxed and more in command. It must also be remembered that the first recordings were made when he was fifty years old and having serious nervous problems with his playing, and the majority were made in his sixties and seventies, when he was not only long past his prime but also more free and self-indulgent in his readings. Above all, the quality of the discs makes them more useful for detecting wrong notes and lapses of timing than for appreciating delicacy of touch and richness of tone. As Gaisberg writes: "Of the greatness of Paderewski and Chaliapin neither gramophone nor film can give anything but a faint suggestion."[65]

Even this faint suggestion, however, is quite enough to expose the silliness and arrogance of today's prevalent view. There is indeed no shortage of wrong notes in these recordings, but this was true of most pianists of the day, and it is only comparatively recently that performers have concentrated on eliminating these from their playing. It is also true that Paderewski's timing is both free and irregular, but so was Chopin's and Liszt's. A change of taste in the attitude to the printed score cannot be invoked against *their* greatness. And greatness certainly comes through the hiss and crackle of Paderewski's recordings, which reveal not only the power, the delicacy and the astonishing fingerwork of which he was capable, but also a profound, thoughtful, majestic and sensuous understanding of the music he played.

Whatever one may think of them, the recordings are in a sense irrelevant. Nowadays the majority of concert-goers and gramophone-owners do not play or even read music, so they want an accurate and objective reproduction of the score. In Paderewski's day a similar majority did play and read music, and what they expected of a pianist of his stature was a great interpretation, and a subjective one, of a piece which they or their wives or children could play quite acceptably. This is precisely what they got from his concerts. They were performances, complete experiences, involving and absorbing the audience to a degree probably unique in the annals of classical music. That is why a serious critic like Fuller Maitland judged him as "one who seems to me to unite in himself all the greatest qualities of all the greatest pianists that have ever lived."[66]

His performances were still satisfying to other musicians, as well as critics. As the pianist Arthur Friedheim, who had every reason to resent Paderewski, having had his own career eclipsed at just the wrong moment by the Pole's meteoric rise, affirms: "Quite apart from the great magnetism of his personality, he was the foremost all-round player of his time."[67] Chasins firmly believed that the magnetism, or whatever it was, "goes into the making of music as well as into the making of a career,"[68] while the American composer Edward MacDowell put it more succinctly when he said: "Some call it hair, I call it piano-playing."[69]

There seems little point in speculating whether or not Paderewski would be laughed off the stage nowadays. One can only surmise that if he managed in his own time to bewitch literally millions of people, many of whom had never listened to classical music before, and at the same time satisfy the most discerning critics, he would still have been the most popular pianist in the world if he had been born fifty years later. As Anton Rubinstein conceded shortly before his own death: "He must know his business . . . the crowd does know."[70]

CHAPTER VIII

The Travelling Circus

We have been, let us say, to hear the latest Pole
Transmit the Preludes, through his hair and fingertips.

T. S. Eliot, *Portrait of a Lady*

The idol who does not fall from grace soon becomes an institution, and this is what gradually happened to Paderewski. The process which had begun with the recital in the Salle Erard in 1888 swept him along with its inexorable momentum, subtly distorting his plans and his original ambitions. By 1896 he had reached a pinnacle of success vouchsafed to very few indeed; he was probably more widely known throughout the world than any previous musician had been in his own lifetime, he was genuinely respected and loved, and he was earning millions. The next decade should have been one of leisure and fulfilment; the security he had longed and struggled for since childhood was his, and it looked as though he would now be able to realize his other dreams of composing and of doing something for his country. In fact it was to be a decade of disappointments, of harder work than ever, and it was to witness the death of at least one of those dreams.

He was thirty-five years old and felt a strong urge to settle down and reorganize his life. His affair with Rachel de Brancovan burnt itself out finally in 1896, without recrimination or ill-feeling on either side. In one of her last letters to him she wrote: "I owe you my life, my darling one; I owe it to you *twice over,* for it is thanks to you that I have come to know life and to love it."[1] Their relationship had been happy and uncomplicated, and as a result they remained friends for many years to come.

With his reputation, his millions and his seductive personality,

Paderewski was now in a position to have just about any woman he chose, whether for passing amusement or for marriage. The fact that he loved Helena Gorska had not prevented him from seeking pleasure elsewhere before, so it should not have done so now. Nevertheless, Helena's presence was becoming increasingly central to his life; without either of them willing it, a mutual dependence bound them to each other more firmly with every year that passed.

Gorski had begun to shirk his duties the moment he realized that his wife was Paderewski's mistress; he flirted with other women and made hardly any effort to support his wife and child. Since Paderewski was already contributing to the expenses of the Gorski household on account of his own son, it was natural that he should help whenever money was short, which it increasingly was. Very rapidly a complete transfer of financial as well as conjugal and emotional responsibility for Helena and her son took place, leaving Paderewski in the position of being husband to Helena and father to young Wacio Gorski as well as his own son, Alfred, in all but name.

In the circumstances, he could not think of abandoning her. Nor did he wish to. Throughout the twenty years he had known her, she had been his staunchest friend and support. She had assumed the role of the mother he had never known, and combined it with that of the most perfect of sisters. She had lavished on him everything from advice on his career to her homemade cures and lotions for his hair; she had soothed his nerves, helped him conquer his doubts and assuaged his fear of the stage; she believed in his genius totally and passionately. She looked after his son, she looked after his affairs, and was prepared to take charge of anything that might distract him from his work. It was she who dealt with all the details of life too complicated or too personal to be entrusted to his secretary, particularly those connected with his family affairs and his estates in Poland.

He was grateful to her for all this, deeply grateful. He was also imbued with a sense of absolute loyalty towards her. But these were not the grudging sentiments of a man conscious of his obligations. They were bound up with his love for her—the simple, enduring love that only a mind as emotionally uncomplicated as his could feel. He might occasionally hanker after other women, he might see in them things that Helena could not give him, but he would never leave her; she was his companion, the best companion imaginable, and he was hers.

In 1895 Helena had applied to the Warsaw archepiscopal court for an annulment of her marriage to Gorski. Her move was dictated as much by her wish to be free of the tiresome attentions of the man as by any plan to marry Paderewski. Her letters make it clear that she felt her claim on his affections to be weak; although still a handsome woman, she was no dazzling bride for the idol of European and American womanhood, while her age would preclude her bearing him children. But they were happy together, and soon after she obtained her annulment, in May 1899, they married quietly in Warsaw.

As man and wife they went to spend the summer on Paderewski's estate at Kasna in southern Poland. He had never before stayed more than a couple of weeks at a time, although he had poured a minor fortune into it; he had laid out and planted two hundred acres of parkland, he had built greenhouses, started wine-growing, stocked the river and ponds with fish, imported superior strains of cattle, and he had even bought some sheep from Balmoral—everything had to be of the best.

The Paderewskis did not, however, settle in Poland, for two reasons: it was not conveniently situated as a base for his tours, and Alfred needed an alpine climate and easy access to specialist doctors. Paderewski had already found a place which fitted the bill perfectly on both counts, in Switzerland. During one of his last sojourns at Amphion, Rachel de Brancovan had drawn his attention to a large villa not far from Lausanne which was to let. He had rented it as a holiday home, and two years later he bought it outright.

The Villa Riond-Bosson at Morges, near Lausanne, was a curious place. It had been built in 1823 by the Duchesse d'Otrante, widow of the French statesman Joseph Fouché. But her heir had rebuilt the house completely in 1883, with unfortunate results. It looked like a cross between a chalet and a Venetian palazzo, with something of a Ritz hotel thrown in. Arthur Rubinstein thought it resembled "neither a villa nor a chateau, reminding me rather of a comfortable, large pension de famille at a summer resort."[2] The house was, in fact, hideous, but this was made up for by its setting, in a park of five hundred acres planted as an aboretum stretching down to the shore of Lake Geneva. The most pleasant feature of the house was the large terrace, and the view from it was magnificent: the park fell away in a gentle slope towards the lake, on the other side of which rose majestic mountains topped by the peak of Mont Blanc, always fascinating as the rays of the setting sun played upon its mantle of snow.

The interior of the house was no less curious than the overworked façades. The first thing to strike the visitor as he entered the front door was the stairs. Since the large hall rose to the full height of the house, piercing two upper storeys, the stairs which disappeared on their way up to the first floor were magically in evidence again as they climbed to the second. The large landings peered down into the well of the hall through Italianate colonnades, giving the appearance of an opera set, while the multitude of potted palms and chairs likened it more to a hotel lobby. Both of these effects were to some extent cancelled out by the presence, in the centre of the hall, of a huge billiard table at which Paderewski enjoyed whiling away his evenings.

The drawing room was dominated by two Steinway grand pianos, their keyboards facing each other. They were draped with Chinese embroidered silk hangings and bore a collection of framed photographs, each with its personal dedication to Paderewski—from Queen Victoria, Princess Alexandra, the King of Italy, the Pope, Gounod, Saint-Saëns and a selection of other crowned heads and public figures. On the wall hung a vast portrait of Helena by Siemiradzki and two of Paderewski, by Burne-Jones and Alma-Tadema.

Next door was Alfred's room, situated on the ground floor on account of his wheelchair, which he seldom left. Opposite this two large doors opened into the dining room, very *fin-de-siècle* with its heavy table and sideboards, and its walls covered in red brocade. The principal painting here was a gloomy triptych by Malczewski depicting a group of Polish political prisoners sitting down to their Christmas dinner of bread and tea in Siberia; not, perhaps, the obvious choice for a dining room. Just outside, in the narrow pantry, stood the only telephone in the house. Paderewski's dislike of the instrument was such that it had been put in the least obtrusive place, where using it would entail the greatest possible discomfort.

Also on the ground floor was a large room housing the extensive library he had built up over the years—an impressive record of his taste in literature and his continuing urge to improve his education.

Paderewski's study on the first floor gave the impression of someone trying to live in an antique shop. A huge Louis XVI desk submerged in papers occupied the centre of the room. Around it stood the upright Erard piano on which he did his practising, a sofa, two tall bookcases filled to overflowing, and a large glass cabinet containing a collection of extremely precious Chinese figures and porcelain on which he had spent millions to gratify a passing interest. The walls were studded with pictures, and the tops of the furniture with cabinet photographs, busts and objects. No personal style was evident in the arrangement of the house, and even this sanctum was devoid of real character. The same went for Paderewski's bedroom, which was ascetic and cold; he slept in a tight single bed and preferred to wash with ewer and basin rather than use the adjacent modern bathroom.

Helena's domain showed more personality, if that is the right word. Her room had elements of the head nurse's and the schoolgirl's in it, with its desk bursting with papers and account books on the one hand, and its collection of dolls, photographs, knick-knacks and medicines on the other.

Her sway extended well beyond the confines of this room and into the grounds. While Paderewski indulged his horticultural urge by planting acres of fruit trees and building greenhouse after greenhouse to be filled with every conceivable variety of grape, peach and berry, and marshalled an army of gardeners, exhorting them to produce bigger and better fruit, Helena gave free rein to her own passion—poultry-rearing. Mary de Navarro recalls that "before I met the second Madame Paderewska I asked her husband about what I should speak to her; he answered with a smile: 'Chickens; she is so fond of chickens.' Therefore, when introduced, I told her I had heard of her interest in breeding chickens. Oh yes, she loved them, and added: 'I have made great searches for the purest, finest breed of roosters, and when I have found him, I show him to Paderewski, and he say, "That is a so fine bird—do not kill him:" ' "³

The practical result of this passion was that ever rarer strains were bred and ever greater acreages devoted to sumptuous chicken runs. It grew into a minor industry, bringing Helena prizes—over three hundred between 1899 and 1914. It also brought in a good deal of money, but any potential profits were swallowed up by heavy and consistent over-investment. In 1913 she started a scheme whereby impoverished young ladies from Poland came to Riond-Bosson and took a course in poultry-rearing. There were some half-dozen of them at a time, living in a small house in the park but taking some of their meals at the villa.

Riond-Bosson seemed to attract women. Paderewski's sister, Antonina, was imported from Poland and put in charge of running the house. She had never re-married and she now slipped into the only possible role for someone in her position—that of complete subservience in the shadow of her great brother. Helena played no part in the running of the house; she had her own business to attend to, and she had her own little establishment within the household: her own maid and even a sort of lady-in-waiting, a penurious distant cousin.

Their existence at Riond-Bosson began under a cloud. In June 1900, less than a year after they had moved in properly, Alfred—who had brought and held them together, and who had constituted one of the main reasons for buying the house—died unexpectedly of pneumonia. They had known that he would never leave his wheelchair, but Paderewski refused to despair and kept sending him to new doctors; his sudden death of a completely different complaint while consulting specialists in Paris was unexpected and poignant. In spite of not having seen his son during the first ten years of his life and of having seen him only intermittently during the second, Paderewski had struck up a close relationship with Alfred, who was extremely intelligent and precocious. They corresponded assiduously when they were apart, and spent hours talking or playing chess when they were together. Alfred's short span of life, tortured and forever reminiscent to Paderewski of the death which had brought it into being, was one more link with those days of sorrow whose memory made him shiver. The tragic end to this pathetic life, itself the product of a searing loss, was a phantom that Paderewski refused to contemplate. Alfred's room became the bridge room; Alfred's valet, Marcel, became Paderewski's valet; and Alfred's name was not to be mentioned. Every time Paderewski was in Paris he would visit his son's grave, but, once he was out of the cemetery, the nightmare was banished from his thoughts.

Life at Riond-Bosson fell into a pattern which sometimes verged on the pompous. Paderewski lived in a sort of royal isolation in his rooms; Helena was so insistent that he should never be disturbed that nobody would have dared knock on his door even if the house had caught fire. He would emerge for lunch when he was ready, and since he was oblivious of time when absorbed in his work, the assembled household and guests might have to wait an hour or more on occasion. This infuriated the already tetchy Antonina, who never knew what time meals would actually begin and had only the vaguest idea of the numbers.

Paderewski's hospitality was legendary: there were always people coming to tea or dinner from the surrounding area, from Lausanne and Geneva. Friends and acquaintances from further afield would come and stay for a few days or weeks, while musicians were constantly dropping in for a day or two in the middle of their tours—Nellie Melba, Leopold Stokowski, Enrique Granados and Saint-Saëns were frequent guests.

The style of the hospitality was equally remarkable. Paderewski had developed a taste for good living, and one of his first acts on taking up residence had been to lay down a cellar of exquisite quality. Dinners at Riond-Bosson were grandiose and refined; lobsters swam in vintage champagne in the memory of departing guests. Paderewski loved entertaining, and, apart from the innumerable dinners, picnics and boating parties, he always gave one great party every year on his name-day, the feast of St. Ignatius on 31 July. There would be lunch, followed by boating on the lake or other amusements, and in the evening a huge dinner was followed by some elaborate musical entertainment, dancing and fireworks. The park would be hung with festoons and lanterns, the best wines flowed freely and the food was nonpareil. "These fetes," as one guest pointed out, "were carried out in a truly regal way."[4]

This grandeur, itself the reflection of Paderewski's taste and of Helena's idea of the position he had attained, was to grow on him over the years and affect his behaviour and his attitude. The place was run like the court of a minor Balkan principality, and the rich young nobleman who had bought it slowly grew, in his forties, into the role of minor potentate. In spite of having a strong sense of humour, he began to take himself a little more seriously and, with the aid of Helena's continuous pandering to his ego, began to see himself more and more as some sort of public figure. This is a common feature of performers who have become idols, but in Paderewski's case it was tempered by his intelligence and his innate modesty, and in large measure justified by a conscientious fulfilment of certain self-imposed duties.

To understand this compulsion and the nature of these duties, one needs only to consider the traditional upbringing of the minor Polish gentry from which he sprang. Their ethic was inspired by the ideals of medieval Christendom and deeply marked by the humanistic spirit of the Renaissance. It was hardly affected by the enlightenment of the eighteenth century, but the struggles and the captivity of the nineteenth had both hardened it and protected it from the influence of modern materialism. This produced a doctrine of service to ideals which were often vague but all-embracing—a sort of religious and cultural patriotism not to be confused with ordinary nationalism. The Cossacks who had dragged off Paderewski's own father and the Germans occupying areas of Poland were not merely enemy warriors. They were the agents of states which were trying to change the way of life and the way of thinking of the Poles, and this was primarily why they had to be resisted. It was also the ground on which they *could* be resisted.

From the moment Paderewski attained a certain position, he had begun to use that position and the money it brought him in very specific directions. The principal motive behind his purchase of estates in Poland had been the desire to own land, but the subsequent lavish investment in an attempt to turn them into model farms was dictated by a sense of civic duty. He wanted to refurbish a small plot of his native land, thereby improving conditions locally and setting an example. The same is true of an idea which he had put into effect a couple of years previously. He set up a consortium, in which he was the principal shareholder, to build a grand and very up-to-date hotel in Warsaw—the magnificent Hotel Bristol, a little scruffy now but still in operation. It was an invaluable addition to the city, and one more example of how he tried to use his earnings to benefit his country.

Paderewski contributed to any charity and could be counted on to give benefit concerts for any cause. He often made unbidden gestures to countries he admired: he gave a concert for the Transvaal War Fund in England, and in America he established a competition for young American composers with a $10,000 prize. But his philanthropy was increasingly directed towards his own countrymen, wherever they might be. He set up or gave funds for innumerable projects, such as a Polish paper for Detroit; an exhibition in Paris; a Kosciuszko monument for Chicago; cultural activities in Wilno; Polish students' organizations at American universities; a new college for Cracow University; and various other schemes, most of them designed to help at the social and cultural level. The sums involved were never symbolic, and in his lifetime he gave away the equivalent of millions of present-day pounds for such minor causes.

In view of this commitment to patriotic philanthropy, there could be no question of retiring from the concert stage as he had hoped he might. Since he had assumed the role of universal benefactor, there was nothing for it but to keep earning. Between 1896 and 1914 he toured the world, vindicating his early triumphs and packing houses wherever he went. He covered Europe repeatedly, from Lisbon to Minsk, from Edinburgh to Naples. He made two tours of Russia, half a dozen of the United States, and he meandered across South America, Australia, New Zealand and South Africa. He was the first musician to exploit new transport facilities to such a degree, and by doing so when their destinations were often still highly primitive, he was able to count on an element of the sensational that later performers could no longer expect. The arrival of this man—in perfect evening dress and pumps, pungent with the atmosphere of Paris salons—by the weekly packet in Tasmania was at once so wonderful and unlikely that it was irresistible to European peoples culturally isolated in some new world.

He travelled like a nabob—he with his valet, Helena with her maid, with a secretary, a tuner, the English manager and well over a hundred pieces of luggage. When the party docked in some foreign port, they were joined by the local impresario or agent with his own staff of secretary, bookkeeper and porters. This escort of up to a dozen people enhanced the magic of Paderewski's arrival in a remote place, even if it did little to simplify the travelling arrangements. Paderewski had got these down to a fine art in Europe, where he knew which hotels to stay in and which trains to travel on; in America he had achieved perfection with the private Pullman coach. The prepared timetables read like military operations, with minute instructions as to which train the carriage was to be coupled to at what time, which siding it was to be left on, and when it would have to be shunted up to a platform so Paderewski could emerge to go and give his concert; but he remained detached from all this and could relax in its comfort, keeping his own hours.

Nevertheless, things often went wrong, particularly outside Europe and America, and each tour was an adventure, a constant challenge to his endurance and his reputation. A typical example is the Russian tour of 1899, where sabotage was added to the number of hazards. As was his wont in countries where there were no Steinways available, Paderewski had a couple of Erard pianos shipped out to St. Petersburg. When he went to check the instrument half an hour before his first recital was due to begin, he found that one of the pedals had been neatly sawn through so it would break off at the first pressure. Further examination revealed pins sticking up between the keys in such a way as to cause horrible injury to anyone striking a chord, which was what he always did at the beginning of a recital. This turned out to have been the work of a local piano-manufacturer who was incensed that his instruments were not being used, but there was jealousy elsewhere, too, particularly amongst the staff of the Conservatoire. Here the cult of Rubinstein reigned absolute and manifested itself in hostility towards any other pianist of note, particularly one who had been favourably compared with the great man.

116

Annette Essipov was teaching at the Conservatoire, and she received Paderewski with joy. She introduced him to Cesar Cui and Borodin, who were cordial and flattering, but all the other musicians he met were unfriendly and remained so in spite of his giving two benefit concerts for the students and widows of teachers.

Moscow turned out to be just as alarming, in different ways. The conductor of the Conservatoire orchestra, the famous batonless conductor Vassili Safonov—a former pupil of Leschetitzky—was charming, but had one great flaw, presumably inherited from his father, a Cossack colonel: he drank. Nor was he the only one, and a drunken horn-player managed to ruin a performance of Paderewski's Polish Fantasia by butting in at the wrong moments with off-key bellowings. More unpleasant was the fact that the Polish parts of the programme—Paderewski's works and Chopin's—were hissed and jeered by some members of the audience, and on one occasion the police had to be called to restore order.

With monumental equanimity, Safonov told Paderewski to pay no attention, and took him out to dinner at the Hermitage Restaurant, where they sat and drank until six in the morning. Paderewski found the alcohol and the Russian attitude to it rather depressing. It was carnival time, and there were people revelling all night in his hotel, the *Slavianski Bazar,* so he moved to a quieter one. Here he found a piano in his room, but after touching the keys and producing no sound, he lifted the lid and saw that there was no trace of any works in it. He asked the hotel manager to explain the riddle. "Ah, Mr. Paderewski, that is not a piano," replied the beaming manager, "it is a gold-mine!" He then explained that the favourite pastime of gay young blades in Moscow was to get thoroughly inebriated and then pour champagne into a piano, and each time they did this they had to pay for a new instrument.[5]

The Tsar had expressed the wish to hear Paderewski, but then sent a haughty note explaining that he had not the time, so the recital was given to a multitude of grand dukes instead. Queen Victoria, however, did have the time, when Paderewski was in London the following year, to hear him at Windsor. She looked old and tired, but still listened with pleasure and then spoke at length to Paderewski on musical matters; her mind seemed unimpaired by age, while her bearing and dignity were enhanced by it. Less dignified altogether was the behaviour of the future King Alfonso of Spain. When Paderewski gave a command performance to the royal family during his 1902 tour of Spain, the prince insisted on dancing to the music, much to everyone's embarrassment.

A few days later, when Paderewski played in Barcelona, the audience was so enthusiastic that after the performance a crowd of students surrounded his carriage, unharnessed the horses and dragged him through the town and finally back to his hotel amid scenes reminiscent of Liszt's triumphs in Vienna.

Later in the same year Paderewski toured Germany, avoiding Berlin, and was put out to find the stolid, middle-aged citizens of Magdeburg rushing on to the stage and mobbing him. More so to find himself confronted in Bremen with an audience made up entirely of old people, who showed their appreciation by hurling hats and then umbrellas on to the stage, cheering all the while. "They completely lost their heads," writes Paderewski, describing the scene. "Anything they had, they threw on the platform, and it really became very dangerous. I can assure you it was a shower of missiles. It was a very odd audience."[6]

In 1904 Paderewski set off on his greatest adventure—a tour which was to take him to Australia and New Zealand. This time the usual entourage was swelled by a Parisian doctor, as he wished to take no chances. They sailed from Marseille in May and reached a cold, wet Melbourne thirty-five days later. Paderewski had been ill throughout the crossing and fell into a depression as he sat in his hotel room trying to keep warm. He found the food virtually inedible and sent Helena and his English manager out to the market to buy food, which they then cooked as best they could in their rooms.

In an attempt to cheer up the gloomy pianist, the Australian manager bought him a talking parrot. "That was a very unfortunate idea of his," explains Paderewski, for Helena was so delighted with the creature that she immediately went out and bought thirty more birds, which she brought back to their hotel room and which thenceforth travelled all over Australia and New Zealand with them. The prodigious collection of luggage was now joined by a multitude of cages containing this flock of screeching and multicoloured creatures. "How did I endure it?" mused Paderewski. "I do not know, except that I am an animal of exceptional patience—if I were not so patient, I should have been dead long ago!"[7]

There were, however, brighter aspects to the tour; he was treated everywhere as a great personage. In Melbourne, Lord Northcote received him with cordiality; in Wellington, Mr. Seddon, the Prime Minister of New Zealand, called at his hotel shortly after his arrival, while the Governor-General, Sir William Plunkett, gave dinners for him. When he arrived in Launceston, Tasmania, he found the whole town draped in bunting in his honour. At Rotorua the Maoris dressed him up in their own costume and showed him round the hot springs and geysers.

Houses were packed everywhere, and Paderewski was pleased with the Australian audiences. "The level of musical education was quite respectable, not only in Melbourne, but in Adelaide, where we went afterwards," he wrote. But it was New Zealand, where he played in Auckland, Napier, Christchurch, Dunedin, Invercargill and Wellington, that astonished him in this respect: "It was like playing in London."[8]

From Tasmania he returned to Melbourne, and thence sailed for San Francisco to begin his next tour of the United States. Luckily, Helena was prevailed upon to get rid of most of the parrots there, and only the original one was kept. Paderewski had grown very fond of him, so he was taken back to Riond-Bosson, where he lived for many years. He talked incessantly, using filthy language, and was eventually trained to speak Polish, but his favourite amusement was to perch on Paderewski's foot while he was playing the piano and from time to time exclaim, mimicking a swooning dowager: "Oh, Lord! How beautiful!"

The tours went on. In 1911 Paderewski covered South America, playing in Rio, São Paulo, Buenos Aires and elsewhere. He grew petulant when he discovered that audiences in Argentina were wont to talk in the concert hall, and he soon silenced them. In the following year he went to South Africa, which was "a very unpleasant experience altogether."[9] He found the South Africans rude and aggressively boorish. In Durban, where he played in Holy Week, a crowd of devout Boers gathered outside the hall and chanted psalms so loud he had to interrupt the recital. But culture-conscious South Africans could be worse: in Pietermaritzburg he was literally besieged in his hotel room by a lady who wanted to discuss music and other things.

However strenuous and occasionally unpleasant, this way of life held one great attraction for the provincial Polish gentleman born in poverty—he saw the world and he met people. In the course of his comings and goings he came in contact with the international musical fraternity, and also with the society of the countries he visited and, almost invariably, with the reigning powers, whether it was Porfirio Díaz of Mexico or the Queen of Roumania. Since he was interested in everything and anything, he absorbed what he saw and heard and compounded it by reading a great deal, with the result that soon he was widely and well informed about the state of the world, more so than many a foreign minister. He assimilated all this information avidly, for at the back of his mind lay Poland, and the future status of Poland depended on world developments of one sort or another. In his thoughts he was always building alliances and seeking parallels, as well as models, hoping one day to be able to use them in the service of his country.

He loved Switzerland because it was civilized, comfortable and reliable. He adored Paris, still for him the cultural hub of Europe and the scene of his success and happiness; but he did not see in France the staunch friend of Poland she was made out to be. The two countries which impressed and fascinated him most were Great Britain and the United States.

"I always feel the English quite different from other peoples, markedly different," he wrote—a common reaction amongst Poles, who generally find the English more difficult to understand and assess than other nations.[10] Paderewski, however, was not put out by this difficulty; he learnt the language quickly, he read the literature and the history, and, most important, he got to know the people. Throughout the 1890s and 1900s he dropped in on England at least twice a year, and his acquaintance grew steadily.

He always saw the Alma-Tademas, whose daughter Laurence concealed her love for him under the guise of warm friendship and passionate interest in Poland. Through them and the Lewises he met more and more musicians and artists, while his society friends, notably Jennie Churchill and Lady Barrington, introduced him to the exotic world of Late Victorian aristocratic life, with its seasonal rituals and its seemingly incompatible contrasts of stolidly be-whiskered dukes and the extravagance of their country houses. Paderewski is only once recorded as having broken a hammer in a piano—while staying with the Duke of Portland; and who can blame him for his lapse of control in the gorgeously absurd archi-tectural wedding-cake of Welbeck Abbey, the least of whose eccen-tricities was to be approached through an underground drive.

Paderewski also met many figures in British public life. These contacts were of the greatest interest to him, and later of the greatest usefulness. He met Alfred Harmsworth in 1895, just be-fore he founded the *Daily Mail,* and they became friends. Some twelve years later, in December 1907, Lord Northcliffe, as he had become, came to a recital given by Paderewski in a private house, and it was there that he got wind of the negotiations over the fu-ture of *The Times.* He acted on the intelligence gleaned that night and finally bought *The Times;* this had ever been his dream, and he used to tell Paderewski that it was thanks to him it had come true. His misdirected gratitude was later to prove of the greatest consequence. [11] Equally valuable were Paderewski's contacts with British political figures. He had met Asquith in 1891 and often saw him when passing through London, and over the next few years he met Lord Haldane, A. J. Balfour and Rufus Isaacs, the future Lord Reading.

An artist of renown is always welcome in society, but it is un-usual to find one being actually befriended by people such as these. Yet there was something about Paderewski which transcended the charming and witty pianist—a refined intelligence which these people instantly recognized and trusted. He was worth talking to and worth listening to; he was a mine of sagaciously observed information, and he often talked about his country, of which people in England knew very little. He never bored his listeners with it, being too aware of the joke about the Pole who, when asked to write a book about elephants, produces an authoritative tome en-titled *The Elephant and the Polish Question.*

It was undeniably a privilege for the Polish pianist to have din-ner with and talk to the leading political figures of what was still the greatest world power, and it inspired him with a lasting respect for Britain. The man who impressed him most of all was Balfour. "It is very rare to find a mixture of such great refinement, such wonderful education and culture, and at the same time such real simplicity and kindness of heart. If ever there was a gentleman, it was Balfour," he later wrote. "In an age of wise and splendid men he stood apart."[12] Balfour and people like him came to epitomize Great Britain for Paderewski, which largely explains his remarkable faith in that country as a bastion of civilization and political equity.

The United States struck a very different chord in him. No East European born in his circumstances, particularly one with his idealistic outlook, could fail to be gripped by the appeal of the American dream. His introduction to America had been hardly calculated to kindle enthusiasm; when he first set foot in New York on that dank November night in 1891, the city was not an impressive place. Apart from a few elegant streets and the cathedral, the most impressive thing to Paderewski was the huge reservoir at Fifth Avenue and 42nd Street. "There was not very much imagination about the building," he explains, "but it appealed to one as an old fortress, something from the remote past, something like a medieval castle."[13] He then proceeded to tour the country —in winter, let it be remembered—and saw most of it from railway lines. "Outside of a few cities like Boston, for instance, and beautiful cities like Washington," he goes on, "the whole country was dirty and disorderly. . . . On the railway lines, the landscape, when it was not strikingly beautiful by the Will of God, was absolutely exasperating and disgraceful by the awkwardness of man."[14] Yet he was impressed, particularly when he came to Chicago. There were three really colossal things in the United States, he claimed, "But while Niagara Falls and the Grand Canyon were the result of brutal forces of nature, Chicago appealed to me then as being the result of all the tremendous but intelligent forces of mankind."[15]

His enthusiasm was not confined to the megalithic aspects of America. To his surprise, he found orchestras of a very high standard as well as perceptive audiences. "They came from the small surrounding places, from the little provincial towns, and the majority of them came with their music, with the notes to follow me," he explains.

They listened with a beautiful silence and followed me very reverently with their music. They made a kind of musical congregation, I felt. . . . I remember particularly two concerts in Kansas City during my second tour. . . . Several hundred people arrived from Texas, all armed with their volumes of music. They crowded the hotels; they gathered in clusters at the street corners, and they stood in line in front of the box office—all with their music in hand. . . . During that season, I had in my audience in Los Angeles people who came even from Phoenix, Arizona, and at Salt Lake City a train full of music-lovers, young students from faraway Montana, came to the concert.[16]

He found the Americans just as personable outside the concert hall. He was lionized from the moment he arrived in New York. He already knew several Americans from Europe, like Joseph Pulitzer, who gave parties for him in New York. He liked Pulitzer and his family, and he found Pulitzer's love of music touching, though his taste and knowledge were "somewhat deficient." In later years, when Pulitzer had lost his sight, Paderewski never failed to go and play to him at home, "to lift a little the curtain of his dark days."[17]

Through Pulitzer he came into contact with some of the more colourful figures in New York, such as "the most picturesque and typically American," Chauncey Depew; Joseph Choate, the future ambassador in London; and George Vanderbilt, whom he thought "a delightful fellow." Andrew Carnegie, whom he also met during his first American tour, was friendly and hospitable, and even offered to become Paderewski's banker, a service which the latter refused out of a misguided feeling of pride. Another, who did at one stage act as Paderewski's banker, was J. P. Morgan, that millionaire of millionaires, who loved collecting rare and precious things and could hardly resist adding this bird of paradise to his collection of friends.

Amongst the millionaires it was William Waldorf Astor who captured Paderewski's affection in a lasting manner. "Astor was a prince among hosts," he thought, not least because when he played at Astor's evenings at Carlton House Terrace in London later on, "the guests were always quiet and as attentive as in a concert hall. It was a joy to play there—he *imposed* silence."[18] The only "at home" at which Paderewski played during his first tour of America had been in marked contrast. It took place in the studio of the painter William Merritt Chase, and not only did the guests talk throughout, there were so many of them that he could hardly move his elbows. This was clearly not the problem at the house of James Montgomery Sears in Boston, where the music room was large enough to accommodate not only Paderewski and a reverently silent audience but also the entire Boston Symphony Orchestra to accompany him.

One of the first friends Paderewski made in America was the poet Richard Watson Gilder. "Paderewski is one of the most extraordinary experiences in our lives," Gilder wrote to a friend soon after the first meeting, and he made him as welcome as he could, with the result that the Gilder house on Eighth Street became, in Paderewski's words, "a real home during those first years in America."[19] They kept open house for the literary set, and Paderewski met, amongst others, Bram Stoker, the author of *Dracula*, and Mark Twain, whom he loved as "someone that only America could have produced, in the quality of his mind, his humour, and character."[20]

He saw America as being capable of producing extravagant and questionable behaviour, on account of the extreme rapidity with which new arrivals there could make fabulous sums of money, and he was in no doubt that it was America which was responsible for the affectations of an Andrew Carnegie. The pleasure of staying at his Skibo Castle in Scotland was, for instance, marred by his insistence that the guests should be woken from their slumbers by a piper skirling into their room. "The intention was charming, but the experience was not always agreeable," notes Paderewski, who suffered from a headache all day as a result.[21] He felt that one could expect almost anything from the Americans, but he was not taken in by the superficial eccentricities, for, just as in England, he became acquainted with the public figures, whose serious purpose impressed him.

In his early days in New York, Paderewski met future President William McKinley while playing pool in the lobby of his hotel. It was the first of many encounters with American heads of state, and half a dozen became personal friends of his. He knew Grover Cleveland, and he knew William Howard Taft, for whom he played at the White House. He also played at the White House for Theodore Roosevelt, who "always listened with charming interest and applauded vociferously and always shouted out, 'Bravo! Bravo! Fine! Splendid!' even during the performance." He admired Roosevelt as a "strong, brilliant, and exceptionally well-informed man, knowing a great deal about European conditions."[22] Roosevelt had read all the historical novels of Henryk Sienkiewicz and as a result felt great sympathy for and interest in the Poles; he spent hours finding out more in long conversations with Paderewski, who little imagined that one day he would be saying the same things to an equally interested President in the same rooms at a crucial moment in the history of the world.

A meeting which hardly seemed portentous at the time but was to prove immeasurable in its consequences occurred during Paderewski's second tour of the United States. Two students from Stanford University had decided to entice him to come and give a concert in nearby San Jose. As well as enhancing the cultural life of the place, they hoped to make some money for themselves out of the enterprise, since they were both working their way through the university. Unfortunately, they did not advertise the concert well, and since it fell in Holy Week when many people would not go to entertainments and the students were mostly away on holiday, attendance was poor; they had fixed the price of the seats very low, so the takings were a mere $1,000. They had guaranteed Paderewski $2,000, and they still had to pay the expenses of hiring the hall. In despair, they went to see him and explained that they would do their best to work off their debt to him over the next couple of years. He was amused by their confusion. He told them to settle all the expenses, take twenty percent of the remaining money for themselves and give him the rest; he refused to hear of any money coming out of their pockets. Paderewski promptly forgot the episode, and it was not until many years later that Herbert Hoover came up to him and reminded him that he had been one of the two students. He repaid his debt a thousandfold in 1919 by feeding millions of Paderewski's starving countrymen.

Paderewski and America responded to each other perfectly in many ways; the spirit of enterprise and the idealism of the people were very much after his own heart, and he soon felt quite at home there, while the story of his career, his personality and his attitude were irresistible to most Americans. He quickly became a figure to be pointed out as an example of determination and achievement, and took his place amongst those used to illustrate the possibilities of the American dream.

However financially rewarding and intellectually gratifying this progress round the world may have been, it was carried on at enormous physical and nervous cost to Paderewski. He never let up on work and practising, since he did not rely on his own talent to see him through performances, but on sound methodical preparation. The old feeling of inadequacy did not disappear as his successes piled up—it took on a different guise. It turned into a haunting nightmare that he might lose control of his resources, that he might stumble on account of not having prepared a piece well enough. "That fright, that terrible inside nervousness, practically fear of everything, of the public, of the piano, of the conditions, and of the memory too, was nothing else but a bad conscience," he explained. "In a repertory which contains fifteen, eighteen, and sometimes twenty or more pieces, it is enough to have only a single piece, one little phrase, that you have not mastered, to completely unnerve you and beget the most dreadful fear."[23]

Paderewski lacked completely the sort of self-confidence which characterized, for instance, Arthur Rubinstein's early career, and this mainly because his fingers wanted a certain natural suppleness. The same Arthur Rubinstein, while staying at Riond-Bosson in 1902, listened to Paderewski practising, "repeating certain difficult passages slowly a hundred times. I noticed that his playing was greatly handicapped by some technical defects, specially in the articulation of his fingers."[24] This was why he did not shed his stage-fright with time; the problem grew, if anything with the years, and in order to keep up a degree of control over his fingers, he had to work constantly. As his reputation grew, so did his nerves; he began to resemble a sportsman straining to defend his title, and during his tours everything was geared to be just right, to put him in the most favourable position to maintain it.

In order to keep himself in prime condition, he did physical exercises every morning, and even lifted dumb-bells to give himself strength. On the day of a concert he would get up as late as possible, both in order to be well rested and also to shorten the ordeal of anticipation; and he would eat nothing all day. Before playing, he would bathe his hands in hot water and massage them. His seat was another matter for concern. He had found the normal piano stool uncomfortable and somehow unsympathetic, and this minor irritant had assumed gigantic proportions until one day he found a low chair with a back which suited him. He had a set of them made, and thenceforth there were two at Riond-Bosson, two in Paris, two in London and half a dozen in the United States permanently at his disposal. Lighting was equally important to him, as he explained: "A dimly lighted hall is an absolute necessity for me. I simply cannot stand a brilliant light shining into my eyes when playing."[25] But even with everything just right, each performance was an ordeal for him, and it was not until he had quitted the platform, had his neck and shoulders massaged by his valet, changed his clothes, drunk some champagne and smoked several cigarettes that he could sit down to dinner; and after dinner he needed his game of bridge to relax him for sleep.

Much of this was seen as affectation. "One should understand that in trappings and appearance a Paderewski piano debauch differs from all other musical festivalling," wrote a critic in the *New York Telegraph* in 1909. "The first thing that strikes your eye as you enter a Paderewskorium is the blackness of a black hole. That black hole is the stage. Paderewski does not allow lights on the stage; he would fain utter his profound Orphic sayings from a half-Erebus."[26] The semi-darkness undoubtedly contributed to the atmosphere of intimacy which pervaded the proceedings, and was conducive to emotionalism in the audience. The atmosphere and the emotionalism, however, were created by the audience, not by the pianist, whose showmanship was entirely passive in nature: the hair, the looks and the dim lighting. "During the rendering of his soul-moving passages, he sits almost impassive," explained another critic.

"He does not rock upon his seat, nor throw his halo-surrounded head to the rhythm of the music. Neither do his hands fly from the keyboard after the manner of the third-rate performer." Even his bowing was restrained, and the same critic noted that "no young girl after a course at a school of deportment bows half so gracefully as does Mr. Paderewski."[27] Bernard Shaw, it is true, was less impressed by "that curious little bow of his which is so like the action of a critic who, falling asleep at a concert, nods forward until he overbalances and recovers himself just in time to avoid falling with a crash on his nose."[28]

Occasionally the prima donna did come to the fore, particularly if someone in the audience dropped something or banged a seat. At the last concert of the 1902 American tour Paderewski was nervous the minute he came on stage. "As he glanced over the vast audience he quivered like a frightened canary," according to one of the critics, and the performance was fraught throughout. He stopped in the middle of a piece and started again from the beginning, and plainly lost his way in another. When he was playing his encores at the end, a lady tried to sneak out from the back of the audience, but Paderewski noticed. He stopped playing, glared at her and, in the words of the critic, "bristled with wrath like an infuriated chrysanthemum."[29]

The reason he quivered "like a frightened canary" was that he suffered from stage-fright—so much so that on one occasion Helena had to get piano-shifters and stage-hands literally to push him on to the stage. Once there, he was so desperate to keep control of his memory and his concentration that anyone breaking the spell brought out his ire. There were moments in the 1900s when he was pushing himself so hard that not only were his nerves in a raw condition, but he was also beginning to resent what he saw as a kind of servitude—the necessity of playing when he wanted to do other things.

He had been caught up in a ludicrous financial spiral from which he found it impossible to break out. He made vast sums of money, much more than any popular musician today, but it slipped through his fingers at an alarming rate. Huge sums were spent on keeping Riond-Bosson and the Polish estates going, fortunes were expended on causes and individuals, and Paderewski was, almost inevitably, taken advantage of liberally by various people. The agent of the estate in Poland embezzled and stole by the cartload, while the gardener grew rich by exploiting and finally selling the greenhouses Paderewski had spent so much on.[30] When, in 1903, he sold the last of his Polish estates, it was at a loss. His investments fared no better, and their story makes distressing reading. His large share in the Hotel Bristol, for instance, had repaid itself by 1914, but just as the hotel was going to start making money for him, it was requisitioned by the German military authorities for the duration of the war.

Since he seemed incapable of stemming the outward flow of resources, there was nothing to do but to keep the income at a steady rate. The dream of building up a fortune which would make him independent had turned into a nightmare; his ten fingers were his fortune, and he had to keep playing. He resented this fact not merely for itself but also because it prevented him from doing other things—he still wanted to be a composer.

Manru, the opera he had started in 1893, had been abandoned. He tried to take it up again several times over the next several years, but he never found enough time between tours to make any significant progress. It was not until 1900 that he devoted some time to the project, and then he managed to finish it in a matter of months —"rarely did I do any work with greater interest and pleasure," he admitted.[31]

What gave him equal pleasure was the work connected with the opera's production, for, unlike many a composer, he did not have to wait long for this; he finished it in January 1901 and the première took place in Dresden on 29 May. He worked with the singers and attended the rehearsals, and felt that "nothing could have been better" than the final result. The première was well attended and immensely successful. Paderewski sat between Leschetitzky and Joachim, and praises rained down on him from all sides. A few weeks later the opera opened in Lwow, then in Cracow. Over the next eighteen months there were productions in America, which toured New York, Boston, Philadelphia, Pittsburgh, Baltimore and Chicago; in Bonn, Prague, Zurich, Warsaw and Kiev. A Paris production was scheduled, but never materialized, since the translation of the libretto, entrusted to the poet Catulle Mendès, never did. Plans for a Covent Garden production ended in a concert performance in London.

It is extremely rare for a composer, even a composer of note, to see his work given such wide exposure in such a short space of time, and it speaks volumes about Paderewski's universal fame and popularity. The managers of opera houses did not sit around discussing *Manru*'s merits; they knew it would draw vast audiences wherever it was put on. The halls were indeed full, and most of the criticism was favourable, if a little polite; the opera was treated as an important event in the musical world.

Manru's success was ephemeral, and it was not long before people had to admit that it is simply not a very good opera. The libretto is weak and, as the Warsaw critic Antoni Sygietynski pointed out, "has neither action, nor psychological drama, nor poetry; it is a scenic hotch-potch in which the length of the dialogue is only rivalled by the drabness of the language."[32] As a result, the whole structure of the opera lacks coherence and, inevitably, the music poetic unity. As with most of Paderewski's work, there is here a mixture of influences, and those of Schubert, Verdi, Liszt and Wagner can be detected. Paderewski was the first to admit his indebtedness to Wagner: "Wagner changed the standards of opera, and imitation was absolutely necessary," he explained. "Because of the subject I chose, however, it was possible to introduce much of a lyric nature into the score, and in this perhaps I have followed what is called the Italian method."[33] Whatever the methods he was following, the result is a patchwork rather than a whole piece, and although it contains elements of real beauty, there is no strong individuality or inspiration to weld them together into a satisfying whole.

Paderewski himself was pleased with his work, and many years later he wrote: "Whatever may be the shortcomings of that opera, those of which I know and those of which I am completely ignorant, I am thankful to say that the orchestration, even when I look back at it after so many years, gives me complete satisfaction."[34] The orchestration is indeed rich and colourful, a fact picked out in many of the notices. "One should consider a performance of *Manru*," writes Sygietynski, "not as the performance of a lyrical drama, for there is none, but as a real lesson in orchestration."[35] Paderewski thought there was more to it than that, and felt that by concentrating not on love but on the broader theme of racial and cultural alienation he had introduced a new element into opera. One could argue for that as well as against it, but there seems little point, since the work made no significant impact on other musicians, in spite of its world-wide performance, and whatever innovations Paderewski may have made were therefore of no consequence.

Once the excitement had died down, all the factors which had worked to help *Manru* gain such wide exposure began to work against Paderewski. Richard Strauss, who liked the opera, wanted to revive it in a new production in Berlin in 1903,[36] but these plans came to naught. Worse and certainly less interesting operas have been occasionally revived, but *Manru* never has been produced again, bar a few performances in Poland in 1910.

Paderewski managed to spend most of the year 1903 at Riond-Bosson, and he used his time well. He wrote the Piano Sonata in E flat minor (op. 21), which he described as "one of my most important and best works," with some justification. It is a grandiose and thoughtful work, and one can understand why an American critic hailed it as "one of the most important essays in what may be the pianoforte music of the future."[37] But it has its defects. Passages of beauty and originality alternate with almost clumsy effects and phrases which seem to derive heavily from Chopin, and this impairs the unity of the composition as a whole. It is overwritten and sins by its length, and it is also extremely difficult, which helps to explain why it never achieved great popularity.

After the Sonata he wrote twelve songs to poems by Catulle Mendès, and then completed the Variations and Fugue in E flat minor (op. 23), which he had begun at Strasbourg nearly twenty years before. "This work is my best piano composition, I think," he wrote. "It is extremely difficult and perhaps too long, but it contains quite a few things which were then almost a revelation in their character and novelty."[38] It is impossible not to agree with him. The twenty variations, which follow each other disconnectedly at first and gradually fuse together into a dramatic build-up, are both masterful and stimulating. Each is an original departure, sometimes sentimental, sometimes humorous, into a different style of writing, and the last seems to plunge one into the world of Scott Joplin's rags with its busy yet lilting pace, only to run majestically into an elegant classical fugue. The Variations give eloquent proof not only of Paderewski's craftsmanship but also of his originality of thought, which, contained by the rigorous form of this composition, does not turn into a meandering quest for new effects, as it does in his next work, the Symphony.

The Symphony provides the climax to Paderewski's second phase of composition, and it displays all the traits which prevented him from becoming a great composer. He started sketching it in 1903, but it was not until 1907 that most of it was written, and not until the following year that the finishing touches were put to it. The result is a work of three parts, lasting one and a half hours, which would be trying even if it were great music. The Symphony also has a theme to it—the fate of the Polish nation over the last couple of centuries—which is developed not as a strict programme but rather as a series of images. Since the expression is highly dramatic and the illustration vivid, the end-product is not so much a symphony as a sort of operatic tone-poem. What worked for Smetana in *Ma Vlast* does not, unfortunately, work for Paderewski; the Symphony rambles on through images of suffering and grandeur without seeming to get anywhere. There are some glorious moments and some lyrical ones, but the grand passages are too rhapsodic and fail to build up to anything, while the lyrical themes are not developed as delicately as they might be. There is nice use of the organ in the first movement and a beautiful melody in the second, and one could point to other effective features, but the overall effect is one of monotony. As one critic put it: "There is no moment at which it seizes on the mind and lives afterwards in the memory: its actual substance is flaccid, amorphous, invertebrate."[39]

Ultimately, the Symphony relies for its appeal on the sentimental and dramatic content, but the sentiment behind it, as one critic pointed out, is more of a personal grievance, and the drama is principally made up of great clashes of sound. The orchestra is used masterfully, but it is nevertheless wielded like an army to batter the message home, and one is not so much moved as exhausted after listening to the work.

Stylistically, the Symphony is disconcertingly varied. It contains shades of half a dozen composers, including Tchaikovsky, Mahler, Elgar, Debussy and even something which sounds very like Gershwin. No personal flavour or individuality is apparent in any part of it. Karol Szymanowski, who heard it in Vienna, called it "an unbelievable abomination for which no words are insulting enough."[40] It was nevertheless performed widely, and most critics had something good to say for it, if only that it showed Paderewski could write in large forms competently, while a good many saw elements of genius in it.[41]

As a composer, Paderewski defies easy categorization. Although most of his works are disappointing, he cannot be relegated to the ranks of third-rate composers so numerous in the nineteenth century. Even Bernard Shaw, who consistently criticized Paderewski's works, calling them "immature and secondhand," stated firmly that to compare Paderewski with Rubinstein as composers was like comparing an ancient Greek with a modern Bulgarian.[42] He pointed out that Paderewski had intelligence, ideas and a competence in writing for both piano and orchestra which placed him in a class above the second-rate. There are certainly enough great passages in his work to bear this out, and there can be no doubt that he had all the makings of a great composer—yet his oeuvre as a whole fails to establish him as one.

The principal defects from which his music suffers are verbosity, the incidence of cliché and general aimlessness, which all seem to point to absence of inspiration. Much of the time he is writing for the sake of writing rather than for the sake of communicating. At other times he is labouring a point which nevertheless remains obscure. Yet he had plenty to say, and he did not lack the method of putting it across, since he was technically a very competent composer. The root of the trouble lay in the nature of what he was trying to put across, and in the character of the man himself.

Success and public acclaim never managed to break down the barriers erected by Paderewski's insecurity and even fear of others. The façade of the relaxed, elegant, urbane idol of concert hall and salon was an uneasy one, and behind it lurked a man open to very few. Many have used their art to utter things they dare not otherwise express; but Paderewski's reticence affected even his powers of musical expression, so, while he could put all his feelings into the interpretation and transmission of another composer's outpourings, he either repressed or hedged his own. He decked his youthful lyricism in the conventional garb of salon phraseology, and buried his feelings under heaps of musical verbiage, with the result that the greater part of his work lacks poetry.

There was, however, another, stronger, impulse driving Paderewski to compose—that of the little boy who wanted to help his country. Nationalism was a perfectly legitimate sibling to love, death and all the other offspring of the Romantic movement, but Paderewski's nationalism was not metaphysical, like Chopin's, or pastoral, like that of so many late nineteenth-century composers, but practical. This meant that he used music as a medium for making political points, for which purpose it is simply not suited. In *Manru* he develops an argument instead of implying it by giving an impression of two cultures. In the Symphony he laboriously tells a story, instead of expressing an attitude or a mood of suffering or heroism, as Chopin would have done. The very nature of Paderewski's theme in this work condemns it to monotony and bombast.

His best works are those in which he is making no particular statement, only indulging a mood or the pleasure of developing a theme—as in some of the short pieces from the Strasbourg period, in the Fantasia, the Sonata and the Variations and Fugue. But even here he has to contend with his tendency to over-write, which is responsible for the excessive length of many of the compositions.

Another characteristic which spoils much of the music is his eclecticism, and this was aggravated by his chaotic musical upbringing and the isolation to which he condemned himself by his career as a virtuoso. His education had been sporadic and disconnected as he moved from Warsaw to Berlin, Vienna and Paris, nowhere fitting into, or reacting against, any formal tradition or school, but always a little lost and alienated. This is clearly reflected by his taste in other composers.

He loved Bach above all; he liked and played a great deal of Scarlatti and Handel; he adored the Romantic composers, particularly Schubert and Schumann, with whom he was in great sympathy. He naturally identified with Chopin, by whom he was deeply influenced at every level. But when asked what single score he would save from a universal conflagration, he replied, without a moment's hesitation, that it would be Wagner's *Die Meistersinger,* which he thought "the most prodigious effort of the human brain in the domain of art."[43]

He liked none of the Russian composers, with the exception of Scriabin—but this dislike, although he claimed it was aesthetic, was almost certainly nationalist in origin. Rachmaninoff, who loved to hear his native tongue when abroad, once spent a whole evening in a New York restaurant talking to Paderewski in French. "And two days later," Rachmaninoff expostulated, "I found that he speaks perfect Russian! This Paderewski of yours!"[44] Paderewski was particularly ill-disposed to those who, like Tchaikovsky and Stravinsky, came from Polish families which had become Russified.

Paderewski was deeply suspicious of the French composers, with whom he was thought to have some affinity; he liked Gounod, Saint-Saëns and Fauré, but there it ended. "The modern French are witty, clever, brilliant, but they are not writing music," he declared to an interviewer.[45] He liked Debussy's short piano pieces, but not his orchestral or chamber works, and his remarks on the subject reveal a complete failure or refusal to comprehend the essence of the music.

There is no more order in these views and tastes than there is in the variations of style in his own works. If one were to listen to Paderewski's music without knowing who had written it, one would place some of it in the French school, some in the late German Romantic tradition, and some in the Polish one. He is neither a great Polish composer nor a particularly cosmopolitan one; he simply does not seem to belong anywhere, which may be why he no longer gets the attention he deserves.

Paderewski was aware of his own shortcomings as a composer, and he was convinced that he could do better, in which he was probably right. But what he needed if he was to carry out this conviction was more time spent in one place and freedom from the physical and nervous strain of his way of life as a virtuoso. He appreciated this and it added a new dimension to his resentment of this way of life. He eventually began to develop frightening neuroses regarding the piano itself, the symbol of his servitude.

During a tour of France, Spain and Portugal in 1906, he wrote, "Something was happening to my nerves that made me completely *hate* the piano. . . . I no longer wanted to play. No matter what I played, I did not feel in touch with the instrument. It was a kind of torture."[46]

The doctors he consulted advised him to retire from the stage for a time and to turn his mind to something else. He went back to Riond-Bosson and concentrated entirely on looking after it. He worked hard in the garden, which he enjoyed very much, introduced bees and rabbits, and even acquired a couple of goats to swell the already impressive contingent of St. Bernards, pugs and Pekingese which lolloped behind him as he strolled around the grounds. He revelled in this Trianon-like dabbling in husbandry, and it kept him busy, but apparently not busy enough. On the one hand, he taught himself Spanish (he was already fluent in Polish, Russian, French, German, English and Italian) and started cheerfully reading his way through the works of Blasco-Ibáñez and Ortega y Gasset; on the other, he purchased a small estate not far from Morges and set about managing its farm. In Paderewski's case, management was synonymous with improvement and investment; so, while the activity "brought a certain kind of healing with it," it also used up all his spare cash and inevitably sent him back to the concert platform after a couple of years.

But those two years spent farming and putting the finishing touches to his Symphony had been beneficial, and on his next American tour, at the end of 1908, the critics noticed the change in him. The *Musical Courier* of New York, which had been consistently uncomplimentary about his playing over the last ten years, carried an article entitled *"Paderewski Redivivus."* "Even Paderewski's appearance has undergone a change," it ran:

> The jaded ennui, the indifference and listlessness have disappeared, and in their place have returned the old leonine manner, the magnetic movements and gestures, and the proud assurance of the artist who knows he is supreme master of himself and his craft and feels he is justified in that knowledge. . . . Such a ringing triumph has not fallen to his lot here since his first monumental performance in New York

a decade and a half ago. Nobly did he vindicate himself yesterday, and when the greatest musical lion of his time came to life again there was no one to gainsay the majesty and authority of his presence, and the commanding eloquence and compelling power of his utterance.[47]

Notwithstanding such accolades and the, as ever, frantic demonstrations of the public's esteem and love, Paderewski soon began to suffer from nerves again. His Symphony was being played all over America, and the response, although favourable on the whole, was not as enthusiastic as he might have hoped, a fact which further depressed him. It is almost as though he realized that it was the last work he would ever write, and that it had gone wrong in some fundamental way. Towards the end of the tour, in the spring of 1909, he broke down completely and had to cancel the remaining engagements and return to Europe.

He tried all sorts of medical cures, including hypnotism, and felt well enough by the end of the year to set off on a short tour of the Riviera. He struggled through the Monte Carlo concert, but in Bordighera he started hitting wrong notes. "It was impossible," he explained. "The easiest pieces I had in my repertoire I could not manage. My fingers were just like cotton. I could not produce the tone. The touch was so strange to me. The slightest action was an agony of my whole body."[48] The only thing to do was to stop playing again and to throw himself into something which absorbed him more completely than gardening—and there was something.

CHAPTER IX

The Politician

As soon as the little boy from Kurylowka had become "somebody"
—which he had beyond his wildest expectations—he began to indulge his other childhood dream, of helping his country. The urge
to become a great artist had never succeeded in distracting him from
this ulterior goal. If anything, the dream had overshadowed and
even, it could be argued, submerged his artistic development. The
artistically harmful need for money was in large measure dictated
by his desire to play a semi-political role. His patriotic outlook had
cut him off from other composers and imposed not only nationalistic
but even political functions on his own works, particularly in the
case of *Manru* and the Symphony. Some of the resentment he felt
towards the piano was the result of frustrated ambitions which were
not those of a composer.

Paderewski had helped Poland indirectly in myriad ways. He
had given money to individuals or groups of his countrymen and,
by the example of his success, encouraged them. To the world at
large he had played the part of cultural ambassador, taking every
opportunity to acquaint foreigners with the plight and aspirations of
his nation. In Poland he used every concert or banquet to make a
statement which, however veiled, told his compatriots to take heart
and look to the future. And he now embarked on his most ambitious
project to date, which was to be a gesture to his country and a
clarion call to Poles throughout the world.

When only a boy Paderewski had been much stirred by accounts of the Polish victory against the Teutonic Knights at Grunwald—which the Germans call the Battle of Tannenberg—in 1410. The pride he felt in this event, comparable to that felt by an English schoolboy when he reads of Agincourt or Waterloo, had remained with him, accentuated by the bleak reality of the present. The approaching quincentenary of the battle had fixed itself in his mind, and he had determined to commemorate it in some way. In 1908 he met in Paris a young Polish sculptor, Antoni Wiwulski, and commissioned him to make a project for a monument. The project met with his approval, and he decided to go ahead with the plan. For the site he chose Cracow, in Austrian-ruled Poland, which had been the capital at the time of Grunwald.

The monument was ready by January 1910 and the unveiling ceremony was set for July. The event was anticipated with excitement throughout Poland, and when the day came, hundreds of thousands gathered in the old city. There were the political leaders, the aristocracy, but there were also peasants from the depths of Lithuania and the Ukraine, as well as Poles from America. The day began with a mass followed by a procession; then came the unveiling, after which Paderewski made a speech to some 150,000 people gathered round the monument. It was a brilliant piece of oratory, perfectly judged; it could cause offence or irritation to no country, yet it stated Poland's right to existence and affirmed the union of purpose of Poles throughout the world. "The work which we see before us did not spring from hatred," he said.

> It was conceived by profound love of our motherland, not only for her past greatness and present misfortune, but also for her brilliant future. . . . We ardently hope that every Pole and every Lithuanian, from every one of the former provinces of Poland, and from beyond the ocean, will look on this monument as the sign of a common past, a token of common glory, and the herald of better times. . . .[1]

The speech was greeted deliriously and Paderewski was the hero of the hour. The unveiling was followed by lunch and a number of concerts, meetings and other festivities. The event had turned into a sort of jamboree bringing together patriotic Poles of all kinds, and

Paderewski was at the centre of it. His speech had made a strong impression on politicians and peasants alike with its tone of promise. Wladyslaw Reymont, the novelist and Nobel Prize winner, admitted that he had wept.[2] Laurence Alma-Tadema, who had over the years extended her love for Paderewski to include all he held dear, and had therefore followed him to Cracow, was so deeply moved that a few days later she wrote to him the following confession she had wrung from herself:

> I understood on that day that the indestructible love which I have born you, often against my own will, for almost twenty years was not to be a sterile thing; I understood that God brought me back to you every time I attempted to be unfaithful to you by running away from the suffering I was ultimately to conquer, for he demanded of me a devotion of which I was not yet worthy. Do not be afraid, my friend, of the word I have dared to utter; you know just as well as I do that I have always loved you, and love when it is old, tried and purified like mine, becomes a sanctification—which should bring no blush to him who gives it or him who receives it.
>
> The day of Grunwald, I gave myself—not to you, but to your country. I can see very clearly that my whole life has been a preparation for the future; I see that I am destined to the service of Poland. . . . I feel at the moment the same gravity as a woman who knows she has conceived a child; I do not know what it will be, this child, but I know it will be beautiful, because it is yours. . . .[3]

She remained true to the feelings uttered that day; she devoted the rest of her life to helping Paderewski and his country. She died a spinster, a few weeks before him; but for many years she had been the best of mothers to a Polish orphan she had adopted.

The significance of 1910 was not limited to commemorating the Battle of Grunwald. It was also the centenary of Chopin's birth, and after spending what remained of the summer at Riond-Bosson, Paderewski was back in Poland, in Lwow this time, for the celebrations.

Jan Paderewski with his sister and baby son

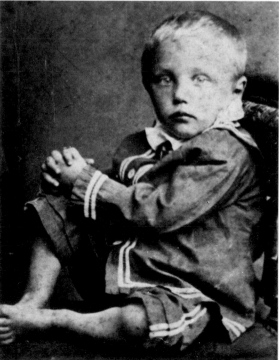

Ignacy Paderewski as a child

Ignacy with his sister, Antonina

At the piano, aged ten

The environs of Zhitomir, a watercolour by Napoleon Orda

Ignacy Paderewski
in his late teens

Antonina Korsak, Paderewski's first wife

Helena Gorska

Annette Essipov

Helena Modrzejewska,
a portrait by T. Ajdukiewicz

Paderews[
at the time of h
Paris deb

Theodore Leschetitzky

By Violet, Lady Granby

By Edward Burne-Jones

Paderewski in 1891,
painted by Lawrence Alma-Tadema

Great Audience Carried Over Gamut of Human Emotion by Art of Player.

By Max Beerbohm

PADEREWSKI NOT A MUSICAL FREAK

Interviewer Finds That He Possesses Much Distinction Apart from His Hair.

An Impression of Paderewski.

Chef Takes Credit for Much of Pianist's Success—Secretary Is G. Sharp—Private Car Has Flat Wheel.

Helena Gorska with her son Wacio
and Alfred Paderewski

Princesse Rachel de Brancovan

Camille Saint-Saëns

Paderewski in the 1890s

The Villa Riond-Bosson, near Morges

On the way to Australia, 1904

Paderewski and Helena with the staff of their private railcar
during the 1900 American tour

Paderewski speaking in Chicago, 1916

Helena in 1916

Paderewski and Woodrow Wilson
at the White House, 1917

Paderewski, Herbert Hoover and Pilsudski with Polish officers, Warsaw 1919.
Behind Hoover is Stanislaw Wojciechowski, Minister of the Interior

Pilsudski and Paderewski
on their way to open the Sejm,
10 February 1919

Jozef Pilsudski

A session of the Paris Peace Conference by William Orpen. Seated,
left to right are House, Lansing, Wilson, Clemenceau, Lloyd George,
and, far right, Balfour. Paderewski is standing just behind Balfour

Paderewski and Gabriele d'Annunzio,
by Max Beerbohm

Paderewski arriving at
10 Downing Street, 1925

With Queen Elizabeth of the Belgians

With Jozef Turczynski,
working on the Complete Works of Chopin

aderewski with Helena at Riond-Bosson
the last years of her life

With Ernest Schelling
at Riond-Bosson

ith General Haller and
incenty Witos at Riond-Bosson

Paderewski at the piano in the drawing-room of Riond-Bosson,
in the late 1930s

With General Sikorski at Palm Beach, Easter 1941

There was a revival of the Lwow production of *Manru* in his honour, and a performance of his Symphony. There were concerts, recitals and meetings. Paderewski was named president of the Convention of Polish Musicians, and made speeches to students. The climax was a symposium on Chopin chaired by the venerable Count Stanislaw Tarnowski, rector of Cracow University, at which Paderewski delivered a florid and emotional speech on Chopin. He argued against the concept of cosmopolitanism and claimed that all art was national in character—even insisting that Chopin's *tempo rubato* was the expression of the changeability of the Polish temperament. The boundary between music and nationalism was blurred as he ended with the words:

> However great a man may be, his greatness is neither outside nor above the greatness of the nation. He is a part of it; a stem, a flower; the greater and finer and stronger he is, the nearer he is to its heart. Chopin doubtless did not know how great he was. But we know that he was as great as our greatness, as strong as our strength, as fine as our culture. He is ours and we are his, since in him is revealed the soul we all have. Let us therefore brace our hearts to endure, to hold out; let us offer ourselves for action, for great and just deeds; let us lift up our souls towards faith—for a nation does not perish when it possesses a great immortal soul.[4]

Again Paderewski met with delirious enthusiasm. Quite apart from the texts, these speeches were delivered with a sense of timing and musicality; they were almost played to the audience.

"In Poland poets are politicians, and the politicians are all poets," runs Bismarck's famous adage. In totalitarian regimes almost any independent action is by definition a political statement. This is why Dostoevsky looked on Turgenev as some sort of traitor, while writers in England simply disliked each other's style. Since Poles could take no part in politics as such, and since it was virtually impossible for them to rise to eminence in any field except the arts, artists—particularly poets—had been the only people to attain a position of moral authority within the community, becoming its natural spiritual leaders. But even in the arts the way was strewn with obstacles, and the censors were ever vigilant. Not surprisingly, it was the musicians who could afford, within the limits of their art, to be the most openly nationalistic, and the music of Chopin, for instance, was regarded as a statement of nationalism every time it was played. Simply by being known throughout the country, and by catering to the aspirations of Poles on at least one level, people like Paderewski were national, and therefore political, figures. Even the press in America began to refer to him as "the uncrowned King of Poland." By funding monuments and making speeches the tenor of which could not escape a single Pole, Paderewski was showing that he was prepared to act, as far as it was possible to do so; and the time was ripe for new leaders to emerge.

The repeated attempts at recovering independence—the rising of 1794; the fight alongside Napoleon; the risings of 1830, of 1846, 1848 and 1863—had all ended in defeat, persecution and, most important, the steady attrition of the nation's most vital forces over several generations. After the last of these risings, in which Paderewski's own father had taken part, a period of intense depression had set in, spawning a new strategy of "positivism," with survival and consolidation as its watchwords. A defensive cultural battle was carried on to keep the nation together, to educate it and rebuild its strength, which was being eroded by the policies of the three partitioning powers.

However, a new generation had grown up which had no memory of the revolts and their consequences, and which therefore tended to reject the "positivist" methods in favour of a more belligerent attitude. This was encouraged by the fact that changes and upheavals within the Russian Empire seemed bound sooner or later to bring about a change in the status of those parts of Poland lying within it, while the growing tension to be felt in East Central Europe as a result of the rival ambitions of the three partitioning powers suggested a conflict between them which would place the Polish question on the cards once again, if only as a pawn in the game. In order to exploit such a situation, it was necessary to take sides.

Paderewski had historical vision—which contrasted oddly with his lack of foresight in small things—and since the beginning of the century he had been predicting a major war between Germany and Russia. He had always felt that the Germans were and would remain intractably hostile to the Poles on racial grounds, so he saw no point in banking on their goodwill. The Habsburg Empire seemed irrelevant to the issue, since its power was visibly on the wane and its interests lay elsewhere. As he supposed the Western Powers would be on Russia's side, he was more inclined to side with those Polish politicians who were building on the Russian alliance. A group of Polish deputies to the Russian parliament, the Duma, believed in gradually carving out a degree of autonomy for those parts of Poland held by Russia, to which could be joined any conquered parts in the event of a war with Germany. Their leader was Roman Dmowski, a very clever and able man. Paderewski had met Dmowski some years before, and again at the Grunwald festivities. He found him sensible and cultivated, although he did not go into his policies in any detail, and he therefore contributed more than once to Dmowski's election fund.

The degree to which Paderewski's activities had enhanced his position as a national figure can be gauged by the fact that Dmowski began to regard him as a potential rival and asked him to declare his intentions. "I state definitely that I do not intend to play any political role," Paderewski wrote to him, "and for several reasons; 1) I am not ready for it and have not the time to prepare myself, as this would take a couple of years' hard work, and there are too many dilettante politicians as it is; 2) I do not have the wish, the education or the temperament for it. Power does not allure me."[5] He wanted to make his contribution, but not to join in the details of political life, of which he knew nothing—he had, after all, lived outside Poland for the best part of thirty years.

Whether he liked it or not, he was soon involved, and in one of the more sordid aspects of the Polish political scene. One of Dmowski's *bêtes noires* was the Jewish minority in Poland: he saw them as a divisive element, as they were more pro-German than pro-Russian—particularly since the Russians had started their anti-Semitic pogroms. Furthermore, they had an important share of the vote, accounting for over a third of the population in Warsaw, which Dmowski represented; and they also commanded influence on account of their position as the backbone of the merchant class. He did not attempt to reach any arrangement with them and, as a result, lost his seat at one of the Duma elections. Dmowski was understandably incensed, because Warsaw was now represented by a Jew who could have no interest whatsoever in Polish autonomy. He therefore launched a campaign aimed at decreasing Jewish influence in Poland. Amongst other things, he advocated a boycott of Jewish trade and shops by Poles, and started a paper which waged a blatant economic and political, though not racial, war against the Jewish community.

One day in 1912, when Paderewski was relaxing in London after his South African tour, roundly cursing the inhabitants of that country, Dmowski turned up brandishing copies of the paper. Paderewski was horrified when he saw what Dmowski had been up to—more so when he discovered that, having used some of the money Paderewski had contributed to his election fund in order to finance the paper, Dmowski had used his name as one of the founders.

Paderewski had no political views on the Jewish question in Poland, and as for Jews themselves, he felt warmly toward them. It is significant that at a moment when the whole of French society had been divided by the issue, all his friends, including Rachel de Brancovan and her set, had been rabid *Dreyfusards*. Luckily, Paderewski learnt from his Jewish friends in Poland that nobody had taken his involvement seriously over there.[6] But this did not stop rumours spreading to America.

When he arrived there for his next tour in 1913, he came under fire from various Jewish political groups, which circulated handbills, tried to get people to boycott his concerts, and even sent threatening letters through the post. As a result, the police department assigned two detectives to him, which only made him uneasy. Paderewski was a man who thrived on adulation and longed to be loved by everyone; he therefore felt miserable. He was suffering from neuritis in his right arm, so he broke off the tour after the Seattle concert and set off with Helena to Paso Robles in California for a mud cure.

There he was finally tracked down by an official from Washington, with an affidavit for him to sign. It had been drawn up by some of his influential friends in New York who, particularly the Jewish ones, were embarrassed and worried by the affair. Paderewski signed the document, which disclaimed any involvement in supposed anti-Semitic campaigns, and it was published in all the major papers. The matter was closed, but Paderewski never forgot it, and he never forgave Dmowski for having caused it. On the other hand, he still saw him as "the most exceptional of all modern Polish politicians," and therefore continued to collaborate with him.[7]

Early in 1914 Paderewski left California, where he had bought a ranch near Paso Robles, so delighted was he with the place, the climate and the mud baths. On his way home he stopped in London, where he gave a concert and visited all his friends. He was "longing for a much needed rest," and was delighted to return to Riond-Bosson, but by the beginning of summer the mounting tension of international relations was reflected in the thoughts of Poles everywhere, not least in Paderewski's. With the assassination of Archduke Francis Ferdinand at Sarajevo on 28 June war seemed inevitable, and the various Polish political groups began to act on that assumption. Towards the end of July Dmowski came to Riond-Bosson to co-ordinate plans in which there was a unique part for Paderewski to play.

"The hour of doom was approaching slowly, but oh so surely, and still life went on in the old accustomed way," writes Paderewski. "Friends came and went; we laughed and talked and made music, and a particularly beautiful summer lay lovingly upon all the land."[8] On 31 July there were the usual celebrations on the occasion of his name-day. The company was large, including a heavy sprinkling of musicians: the singer Marcella Sembrich-Kochanska and her husband; the Ernest Schellings; Felix Weingartner; Timothy Adamowski; Zygmunt Stojowski; Jozef Hofmann; Rudolph Ganz; and Gustave Doret. Szymanowski was to have come, but never made it. There were local artists like Jean and René Morax, and others from abroad, like the sculptor Wiwulski from Paris and Laurence Alma-Tadema from London. In the evening they all dressed up in Chinese costumes provided for the occasion by the wife of the American Ambassador in Bern; there was a sumptuous dinner, followed by fireworks and various musical entertainments. But as Marcella Sembrich sang and Ernest Schelling played the piano on the terrace lit by Chinese lanterns, as the guests strolled or lounged with their champagne glasses in the balmy fragrance of the garden below, there was an uneasy and unspoken feeling that something was coming to an end. A telegram from St. Petersburg had called Dmowski away during lunch. The Swiss guests had brought mysterious little suitcases with them, and from time to time the butler would call one or another of them to the telephone; ten minutes later they would re-appear to take their leave no longer in Chinese costume but in their grey uniforms. The American Ambassador was called back to his post shortly before midnight. A few minutes later Paderewski's valet came to whisper in his ear the latest news—that Germany had set an ultimatum demanding Russia's demobilization.

Gradually the remaining guests dispersed. As their cars turned out of the gate, they caught their last glimpse of the warm, smiling face and the mane which always seemed to glow. "This is the end of my artistic life for a time," thought Paderewski as he wearily as-cended the great staircase to his room.[9] The next day was spent in a state of limbo, watching the trappings of the feast being taken down, but in the evening news came through that Germany had declared war on Russia. Poland's two arch-enemies had finally come to blows. It was a conflict full of ominous possibilities for Poland, for, although she was bound to suffer cruelly, they might destroy each other. While he was fully conscious of the horror of the situation, Paderew-ski saw the promise it held out—and he was prepared to act on it.

CHAPTER X

The Great War

During dinner at Downing Street a couple of years before the Great War, Lord Morley turned to Paderewski and addressed him on the subject of Poland. Paderewski expressed, amongst other things, the hope that his country might regain its independence one day as a result of some major European conflict, but Asquith, who was listening, replied, shaking his head: "There is no hope for your country, sir, none!" "Ah, Mr. Asquith," answered Paderewski with a smile, "there are certain things under the sun which even a Prime Minister of England cannot foresee and foretell!"[1]

The climate at the beginning of the century was certainly very inauspicious to Paderewski's hopes. There was a widespread feeling among statesmen that the security and prosperity of the world were threatened by forces which could best be contained by strong government and rigid preservation of the status quo. Change of any sort was viewed as being the opportunity and excuse for the emergence of all sorts of dangerous political tendencies. However much they might have sympathized with its plight, people tended to feel that it was better that a place like Poland should remain partitioned than that it should create an upheaval which might shake up the world.

The outbreak of war in 1914 was an upheaval of staggering dimensions, and out of this, most Poles felt, something could be gained. Since Paderewski and his colleagues believed that Russia, France and Great Britain would ultimately win the war, they wanted the Poles to take a pro-Allied stand and thereby make the point that they deserved some form of autonomy or independence after the Allied victory. It had therefore been decided that while Dmowski and his party would work through their club in the Russian parliament, the Duma, others in Poland would create a network consisting of prominent figures representing the widest possible spectrum of society. Meanwhile Paderewski and others in the West were to mobilize Poles and friends of Poland in Allied countries and try to create a climate favourable to the Polish cause. Since no overtly political bodies could be set up, charitable committees were established to collect and distribute supplies to the needy population in war-torn Poland.

On 22 January 1915 the Swiss government authorized the formation of the "General Commission for Polish Relief" at Vevey, under the patronage of Paderewski and the Polish novelist Henryk Sienkiewicz. Paderewski then went to Paris, where he called on Poincaré and various ministers, seeking permission to start a similar committee in France. They all told him that he could do so only under the patronage of the Russian Ambassador, since Poland was, as far as Great Britain and France were concerned, an internal problem of Russia. Paderewski was unwilling to let the committee become a Russian body; those in Poland who were siding with the Central Powers would then be able to denounce it for being collaborationist. He sought the advice of the British Ambassador in Paris, Sir Francis Bertie, who was helpful and suggested that Paderewski invite the French ex-President Loubet and the Russian Ambassador, Izvolsky, to be joint honorary members of the committee along with himself. Since it was clear from the start that Bertie and Loubet were purely symbolic members, Izvolsky would have to be as well. The ploy worked, and Paderewski succeeded in putting together an impressive committee, including the minister Delcassé, the academician Gabriel Hanotaux, the princesses de Polignac and de Brancovan, and a smattering of Polish grandees. He also asked Edmond de Rothschild, in consideration of the Jewish minority in Poland.

By the middle of March he was in London with the same purpose. This time he took the bull by the horns and went straight to see the Russian Ambassador, Count Benckendorff. "To my great surprise I found in him the most charming personality," he noted, and the whole matter was settled at once.[2] A Polish Victims' Relief

Fund was established, and its membership was a tribute to the wide acquaintance and popularity of Paderewski. The honorary chairman was Asquith, and the committee included Lord Rosebery, A. J. Balfour, the Marquess of Crewe, the Duke and Duchess of Norfolk, the Duke and Duchess of Somerset, Lord Ripon, the Duchess of Bedford, Lloyd George, Bonar Law, Winston Churchill, Austen Chamberlain, Lord Northcliffe, Sir Edward Grey, Thomas Hardy, Edmund Gosse, Lady Randolph Churchill and Mrs. Leopold de Rothschild. A great disappointment came from Paderewski's countryman Joseph Conrad, who cabled: "With all deference to your illustrious personality, must decline membership committee where I understand Russian names are to appear."[3] But on the same day he received one from Kipling, who announced that he would "feel honoured" to join.[4] A few days later Nellie Melba, who was in Australia, cabled: "I shall give concert in Sydney for your committee. Hope it will help some." It certainly did; some time later she sent the sum of £15,000 to the Fund.[5] Charles Stuart-Wortley induced Elgar to join, and Emil Mlynarski, who was planning a charity concert for it with Thomas Beecham, persuaded him to write something —Elgar had raised a great deal of money for the Belgian relief committee with his *Carillon*. The *Polonia* he wrote in the space of a week, using a theme of his own, two Polish folk melodies suggested by Mlynarski, a theme from Chopin and the opening phrase of Paderewski's Fantasia, was a messy piece and never achieved the same popularity as *Carillon*.

While in London Paderewski sounded out all the politicians he knew and tried to explain the Polish problem to them in the best light. Towards the end of March he dined at No. 11 Downing Street with Lloyd George, who "admired him greatly," as Frances Stevenson noted in her diary,[6] and took the opportunity to ask him what hope he thought there might be for Poland. Lloyd George was sceptical; he said that all Poland could possibly hope for after the war was greater autonomy within the Russian Empire.

Having set up these two committees in countries which, as allies of one of the partitioning powers, could not allow any activity not strictly related to relief work, Paderewski wasted no time in going to meet the real challenge—America. Just as twenty-four years earlier he had set off in the hope of making money and at last establishing his financial independence, he now set off with the greatest political hopes.

Paderewski believed in America. He knew the country thoroughly—more thoroughly than most Americans, since he had travelled far and wide over every single one of the states and had come into contact with all strata of American society. He knew the people and he had seen what the country was capable of in terms of both resources and industry. As he watched Europe sliding helplessly into the conflict which would destroy so much of it, he became convinced that it was America, with her vast and fresh reserves of power and her idealism, who would come into the war and settle the issue.

In Europe, Poland could find no allies. Of the five principal belligerent nations, three were her enemies, and the other two, Great Britain and France, were bound by alliance to one of these enemies. But America could be made into an ally, and that ally could find itself in the strongest position of all at the end of the war.

Paderewski and Helena sailed from Liverpool on board the S.S. *Adriatic* on 7 April 1915, with what amounted to little more than a wild dream in their heads, but the next time they were to see the shores of Europe, three and a half years later, that dream would have come true and their hopes have been thoroughly vindicated. This was not at all apparent when they reached New York. There were already Belgian and Serbian relief committees at work raising money; there was a good deal of pro-German feeling and agitation, and the Americans were less keen than the British or the French on being honorary members of committees. But, as one American politician pointed out, Paderewski's name was better known and more widely respected throughout the United States than that of many a politician.[7]

Paderewski set himself three tasks. The first was to raise money for relief work, as in England and France; the second was to put the case for Poland whenever and wherever possible; and the third was to form the scattered Polish community in America into a strong lobby.

He set up a Relief Committee with ex-President William Howard Taft as chairman, including people like Cardinal Gibbons of Baltimore, Cardinal Farley of New York, Joseph Choate, Cyrus

Curtis of the *Saturday Evening Post* and Melville E. Stone of the *Associated Press*. He collected money from his vast circle of friends and managed to induce the Rockefeller Foundation to give generously. He then turned to the Poles and made appeals for large donations. But the Poles were poor while the Americans had no idea of the Polish question, so money was slow to come in.

Paderewski hated collecting. "There are people for whom it is easier to give a thousand than to ask for hundreds. I am one of those people," he had once written to a recalcitrant donor.[8] To cap it all, he found that he was running out of money himself. He was going to need a great deal simply to keep himself and Helena going. Some idea of the sums involved can be had from the fact that in the four years of the war he spent over $30,000 merely on telegrams in the pursuit of his aims.[9]

The obvious thing to do was to start playing again; but this time he decided that he would talk as well as play. He would give a concert and accompany it by a short address on the Polish question and an appeal for funds. To his own and everyone else's astonishment, he turned out to be a brilliant speaker in English. "Ladies and gentlemen," began one of his earliest speeches, "I have to speak about a country which is not yours in a language that is not mine."[10] He certainly learnt to use it masterfully. "I have heard nearly all the great speakers of our time, excepting Gladstone," wrote one American, "and I have heard none who seemed to have the power of Paderewski and the sincerity that made me think of what the great Greeks and Romans must have been."[11] Upton Sinclair was deeply impressed when he heard him, while the British Ambassador in Washington, Lord Reading, said that the speeches were amongst the finest pieces of oratory he had ever heard.[12] It was noticed that, just as with his playing, he exerted a strangely magnetic charm over his audience, which was carried along by what he was saying, its enthusiasm melting its power of discrimination. He even managed on one occasion to reduce a roomful of journalists to tears. The texts do not point to any great profundity, being rather clichéd and pedestrian, which suggests that it was the quality of rhythm, voice and, above all, personality which made the speeches so effective. And effective they were. In Chicago, for instance, where he played and spoke to a packed hall, he collected $43,000 for the committee.[13]

Between his arrival in April 1915 and the end of the war in November 1918, he gave some 340 speeches and almost as many concerts. Money began to pour in and, what is more, Poland and her predicament became increasingly familiar to Americans.

Paderewski's most difficult task during these years was to unite politically the four million or so Poles in America. Various problems were involved. One was that the American Poles tended to come from humble origins and their level of national consciousness and education was correspondingly low. Over the years Paderewski had indirectly done much to improve this. The very fact that there was a star known and loved throughout America who took every opportunity of underlining the fact that he was Polish had given them something to be proud of. His encouragement, from his first visit in 1891, of all Polish societies, of all attempts at national identification —whether through building monuments or by founding clubs—had also done a great deal, and he knew most of the local leaders of such clubs and communities, as well as most of the priests of the Polish parishes. But any attempts at fostering greater national consciousness were complicated by the fact that the Poles in America were severely split by political factionalism and had taken different sides in the European conflict. Those who had come from Russian Poland, the socialists and the Jews, were all fervently anti-Russian, while those who had been forced to emigrate from Posnania by Bismarck's policies loathed Germany above all. This division reflected the situation in Poland itself.

Long before the war the other great man of Polish politics, Jozef Pilsudski, had voiced hatred for the Tsarist system in particular and carried on a running battle of terrorism and subversion against it from the comparative haven of the Austrian part of Poland. At the outbreak of war Pilsudski's supporters were given arms by the Austrians and they marched into battle. They soon grew into a regular Legion of some 20,000 men, with its own insignia and officers. Although they were fighting on the side of the Central Powers, they took every opportunity to stress their aloofness from the German cause; they had entered into an alliance with the Devil in order to fight what they believed to be Poland's greatest enemy —Russia.

On 16 August 1914 Russia had issued a proclamation calling on all Poles to fight on her side, for which they were led to expect some form of autonomy after the war. Its chances of producing the desired effect, however, were ruined by the Russians themselves. Having gone on at length about the necessity for Slav solidarity in the face of the Germanic menace, they reorganized the military government in Poland in such a way that the top ten officials had names such as von Essen, Korff, von Fechtner, several of whom could speak no Polish and therefore addressed everyone in German. The moment the Russian Army took Lwow from the Austrians, they closed down the Polish University there. This kind of behaviour was not helpful to those who were trying to convince Poles in America and in Poland to throw in their lot with Russia. As Paderewski explained to Jusserand, the French Ambassador in Washington, "Russia promised a great deal, but has given nothing."[14] The Western Allies, particularly the British, were also dragging their feet and making difficulties about letting food supplies for Poland pass through the blockade of Germany. In the spring of 1916 Paderewski wrote to Asquith that "It took all the traditional Polish devotion to France, all the unshaken hope and faith in England's supreme equity to bear this most humiliating and undeserved treatment."[15] The allies Paderewski had chosen seemed to care little for Poland. The root of the trouble was, in his own words, that "notwithstanding the fact that during the present war over two million Polish-speaking soldiers have been forced into fraticidal combat, the belligerent powers, the Central ones as well as the Allies, insist on calling Poland a little nation. This would be an insult were it not absurd."[16] While the climate of public opinion—particularly in Britain, where *The Times* had actively espoused the Polish cause—was growing more favourable, the British and French governments remained sceptical and unsympathetic.

The only hope for a breakthrough lay with America, and towards the end of 1915 Paderewski had taken the first step in this direction. Seeing in the papers a photograph of Colonel Edward Mandell House, President Woodrow Wilson's closest adviser, he was struck by a premonition similar to that he had felt when he saw Casals, and he said to himself: "This is the man who must help me, and I shall do anything to meet him."[17] He went about asking his American friends if they knew House, and finally Robert W. Wooley, the Director of the U.S. Mint, offered to take Paderewski to see him. The first meeting was set for 12 November 1915 at House's flat in New York and was to last half an hour. Pacing up and down as he spoke, Paderewski stated his case, explaining why Poland should have her independence restored, how this would help to prevent the kind of war that was going on in Europe, and how only America was in a position to bring this about. He went on for well over an hour, while the other listened with growing interest and admiration. House then asked him what he wanted in the immediate future, and Paderewski demanded American financial aid for the starving population of Poland. "You have convinced me," said House at last. "I promise you to help Poland if I can. And I think I can."[18] Over the next couple of weeks he brought the matter to the attention of Woodrow Wilson more than once, both by letter and in conversation, with the result that the President declared New Year's Day 1916 a day of collecting for Poland by the American Red Cross.

In March 1916 Paderewski was invited to dinner at the White House to meet the President. The two men took an immediate liking to each other; while Wilson seemed to embody everything that Paderewski valued most in America, Paderewski's charm and the righteousness of his cause affected Wilson deeply. It was a providential moment for them to meet, for the President's ideas on the conflict in Europe and its solution were just then beginning to take shape. Paderewski would be able to feed and influence some of these, and at the same time he was the one person who would be able to muster massive support for them in certain areas.

Paderewski now felt the time had come to tackle the second of his aims—to spread propaganda for the Polish cause—and on 12 April 1916 he set up a subcommittee for political affairs. Through this he delivered notes and memos on the subject to anyone who would listen, and the speeches at his concerts became more concerned with Poland's independence than with Poland's lack of food. This showed remarkable determination and faith in his own convictions, for while he was taking it for granted that America would join the Allies, this was not at all clear at the beginning of 1916, and German diplomacy, aided by a strong body of pro-German opinion and the Irish influence in America, was keeping any such conclusion as unlikely as possible. The Polish community was by no means convinced of it, and large sections of it were so gripped with Russophobia that they were not favourably disposed to the idea of becoming Russia's allies.

The Central Powers were running seriously short of manpower and, in their quest for new reserves, decided to dangle a carrot in front of the Poles. On 5 November 1916 the Proclamation of the Two Emperors promised that Germany and Austria would reconstitute a Polish state after the war out of all the areas conquered from Russia if the Poles would join the Central Powers. This proclamation went further than the Russian one of 1914, offering, as it did, something tangible, and many of the Chicago Poles felt it showed who Poland's friends really were.

Paderewski was not taken in. Neither the Germans nor the Austrians were in fact going to give up any of their own Polish territories, so it was a very strange Poland they were proposing. The future constitution was deliberately ill-defined, and it was fairly evident that the state would be no more than a puppet. Nevertheless the proclamation represented a serious threat to Paderewski's plans. It was bound to exacerbate the divisions within the Polish community and to cast doubt on the wisdom of his policy of siding with the Allies. Unless he acted quickly, he would lose control over the American Poles—and this literally on the eve of America's Presidential election. Not being an American citizen, he had refrained from open canvassing, but he had used what influence he had to support Wilson's campaign; and the Polish vote, although no more than some five percent of the electorate, could be decisive if it was relatively united.

He responded to the crisis with energy and authority. On the one hand, he got in touch with House and begged for an interview with Wilson, and, on the other, he penned a public declaration on behalf of the Polish community of the United States in answer to the Proclamation of the Two Emperors. "We protest against the creation out of the remainder of our brothers of an army which will help those who, having stripped Poland of her robes, now offer her rags in return for the last drops of her blood," it ran. "We protest, for we do not wish Polish hands to sully themselves by bearing arms against nations which never did us harm, for which our forefathers nourished respect and friendship."[19]

The next day, 6 November—Paderewski's fifty-sixth birthday—

was a momentous one; he was granted an interview with President Wilson. "I shall never forget Mr. Paderewski's face as he stood pleading the cause of his country," Mrs. Wilson wrote in her memoir. "It was so fine, so tragic, so earnest."[20] It was also effective, for at the end of the interview the President said to him: "My dear Paderewski, I can tell you that Poland will be resurrected and will exist again."[21]

Wilson did not know whether he would be able to back up those words when he uttered them. It was election day, and the results were by no means a foregone conclusion. If he won, Woodrow Wilson would eventually take America into the war against Germany and therefore exert a very strong influence on the subsequent peace negotiations. He had already decided that these should rise above mere questions of annexation of territory and reparations between the belligerents, and take the shape of a new "system" based on the principle that every nation, however small, had the right to determine its own fate and govern itself. Paderewski knew of the President's ideas, with all that they implied for Poland, and that was why he supported him. But the President's ideas were not widely known, and his re-election campaign treated the unpopular issue of war with circumspection. Paderewski therefore badly needed a statement of intent from Wilson with which he could whip his straying Poles back into line. Wilson needed Paderewski not only because of the Polish vote and the far from insignificant influence he could exert outside the Polish community, but also because the Pole and his following gave substance to the as yet somewhat hazy ideas on a new configuration of Eastern Europe burgeoning in his head. That was why he made his statement on the future of Poland.

Armed with this statement, Paderewski was able to face those Poles who felt that he had overstepped his authority and acted rashly by issuing a declaration in their name rejecting the Proclamation of the Two Emperors. Triumphantly, he produced out of his hat something which meant far more than the proclamation—the word of the President of the United States. They were impressed, for they realized that he had been right all along and that he had influence in high places. By his action he had managed to unite the

Polish community and to defend his position as its spokesman, and in effect became the undisputed leader of the Poles in America.

His masterful handling of the crisis also impressed a good many Americans, particularly members of the administration, who had at first wondered whether the pianist was not going to make a fool of himself on the political stage, for which he seemed so little suited. In fact his musical career and its vicissitudes had prepared him well for the role he had slipped into—that of moral leader and advocate of a community. His energy, capacity for work and single-minded determination had been tried and tempered by the struggle to become a virtuoso, and this had made him into a celebrity in America. His highly developed ability to charm and persuade individuals as well as huge gatherings was invaluable to a politician of any kind, while his well-earned reputation for generosity, sensitivity and, above all, honesty added weight to his arguments and appeals.

Nobody appreciated Paderewski more than Colonel House, a fine, intelligent man—"the noblest man I have ever had the honour to know," in Paderewski's words[22]—who played a key role during the last months of 1916 in working out the practical aspects of President Wilson's ideas on America's aims in going to war. Paderewski's premonition about House had indeed taken him to the right man.

On 8 January 1917 House turned up to see Paderewski at the Gotham Hotel—since the Windsor had burnt down at the turn of the century, he always stayed at the Gotham, conveniently close to Carnegie Hall. House wanted a detailed memorandum on the Polish question to show the President. He was to leave for Washington early on the morning of 11 January and he must have it by then. Paderewski said this was quite impossible, since he had a concert on the next day for which he must practise. House stressed the importance of the request, so after coming off the stage on the night of 9 January Paderewski got down to work. Thirty-six hours later the memorandum was ready, just in time for him to rush to the station and hand it to House fifteen minutes before his train left for Washington. A week later House was back and came to see Paderewski. "The President was very pleased with your memorandum," he said. "Now get ready. The first shot will be fired very soon, and it will take your breath away."[23]

A few days later, on 22 January, in his address to the Senate on the Essential Terms of Peace in Europe, Wilson stated that "No peace can last, or ought to last, which does not recognize and accept the principle that governments derive all their just powers from the consent of the governed. . . . I take it for granted," he went on, "that statesmen everywhere are agreed that there should be a united, independent and autonomous Poland."

Paderewski was beside himself with joy. People had called him a dreamer and shaken their heads when he had expressed hopes that Poland might live again. Yet here was the most powerful of them all, the man who held the balance and could win the war for either side, stating clearly that it would be so. Paderewski did not realize that a number of different factors were conspiring to make this inevitable, even without Wilson's intervention. As far as he was concerned, "the resurrection of Poland came from the United States and through the United States."[24]

At the same time he realized that this was only the beginning, and that in the struggle which lay ahead the main stumbling-blocks would be lack of unity among Poles and the absence of institutions which could act on the President's words. In Paris, Dmowski and others had constituted a National Committee, of which Paderewski had been named a member, but its influence was limited by the fact that most of Poland was by now under German occupation. In Poland itself Pilsudski had been jailed for refusing to toe the German line and his Legion had been disbanded or interned.

Yet support for the principle of Poland's right to exist grew in the Allied camp during the year 1917. Not long after Wilson's declaration the February revolution in Russia removed the principal impediment; for on 29 March the provisional government of Kerensky declared Poland's right to independence. On 6 April the United States declared war on Germany, with Polish independence as one of its aims.

On 21 June the American Secretary of State, Robert Lansing, wrote to Wilson suggesting that a provisional Polish government be set up and recognized by the United States. On 18 October the Allies formally recognized the National Committee, though without defining its status. The October Revolution which brought the Bolsheviks to power in Russia completely changed the situation.

Since the Bolsheviks themselves repealed all treaties made by successive Tsarist administrations in the matter of, amongst other things, Poland, they in effect cancelled out the partitions and recognized Poland's 1772 frontiers.

The Allied positions were made clearer by a second round of declarations. On 12 December 1917 the Italian Prime Minister, Orlando, stated that a strong Poland was an essential basis for peace; on 27 December the French Foreign Minister, Pichon, said much the same thing; on 5 January 1918 Lloyd George followed suit; on 8 January Wilson announced his Fourteen Points, of which a strong Poland with access to the sea was one. Finally, on 3 June 1918, Lloyd George, Orlando and Premier Clemenceau of France made joint binding promises on the Polish question in the Versailles Declaration.

But the war was not yet over, and the Allies could ill afford to tie their hands too definitely on any point, so, while stating the case for Poland in principle, they kept the final settlement deliberately vague. England felt that the Habsburg Empire should be saved if possible. France had invested heavily in Russia, and until she was convinced that the Bolshevik regime was there to stay, she would not support any Polish claims prejudicial to Russia. This was understandable, but it made it extremely difficult for the National Committee and for Paderewski to exert authority over a scattered and occupied nation without certain guarantees about the territorial makeup of the future state. German propaganda continued its attempts to win over or at least divide Polish opinion, and Paderewski was often the target of unpleasant attentions. A typical example is a series of postcards circulated in America at the time. One shows a Chaplinesque Paderewski sitting outside a French embassy with a begging-bowl. On another he plays "God Save the Tsar" as he does a Cossack dance on the keyboard while a couple of thugs with porcine features wearing British and French uniforms encourage him with their whips.

A great disappointment for Paderewski was the American position on the question of a Polish army. In the spring of 1917 France had agreed to the formation on its territory of an Allied Polish army recruited from prisoners taken in the Austrian and German armies, Polish refugees and Poles with French nationality. Paderewski urged the Poles of America to offer Wilson an army of 100,000 volunteers if he allowed them to fight under their own colours. Newton D. Baker, the Secretary for War, who had started by thinking Paderewski mad and ended up one of his most fervent admirers, was keen on the idea, but General Pershing, the American Commander-in-Chief, was against it; it raised all sorts of legal and constitutional issues and could become an alarming precedent for other minorities in America to follow. As one of the military pointed out, "War in general is an opportunity for consolidating a race, and the movement in question, so much as America is concerned, tends towards division."[25] The project was therefore turned down in the summer of 1917, in spite of British support.[26]

Paderewski finally obtained permission, in October 1917, to recruit in America for the Polish army in France, but he could take only Poles who were not United States citizens and who had not applied for citizenship. The results were predictably disappointing: only 22,700 volunteers came forward. They came from all over the United States, but the strongest contingents were from the Midwest and the industrial Northeast: from Chicago, Buffalo, Cleveland, Detroit, Green Bay, Milwaukee, New York, Philadelphia and Toledo.

The volunteers were trained in camps in the United States and Canada and then sent off to France. With their blue uniforms, their Polish four-cornered caps and the white eagle on their colours, they represented an emotive landmark for Paderewski in his continuing struggle. As he watched them leave for the front, he echoed Poincaré's words to their colleagues in France, that "all the future of a nation is wrapped up in the folds of your flags."[27]

Helena, who had been helping Paderewski in everything and on her own initiative running a small industry making Polish dolls and selling them for the benefit of the Relief Committee, now busied herself with organizing a corps of nurses to go with the troops. As there was some difficulty in affiliating it with the Red Cross, her corps was called the White Cross. It soon grew into a sizeable organization, looking after all the needs of the Polish soldiers in America and in the field in France.

Both of them worked ceaselessly in order to surmount the multitude of obstacles and difficulties which loomed at every turn, and Paderewski himself was still giving as many as three concerts a week, each of which demanded hours of practising beforehand. It was not until the autumn of 1917 that he realized that he could not keep on at this rate and gave up playing altogether. His exhaustion was such that frequent minor setbacks in the progress of the Polish cause would turn it into depression and even illness. On these occasions he and Helena would go to their ranch at Paso Robles for a complete rest, but this could never be protracted, since he had to keep his influence strong where it mattered.

He had managed to consolidate his position as leader of the Polish community during the first months of 1917, and in July of that year he was given a document signed by several hundred associations and other bodies representing in all some four million American Poles. It was an affidavit authorizing Paderewski to speak and to make decisions on their behalf on all matters relating to the Polish cause.

To unite and control millions of uneducated and politically divided people spread over a vast area, using only an idea and an appeal, was, as Secretary of State Robert Lansing pointed out, a great achievement, "a triumph of personality."[28] Lansing, who had been sceptical of Paderewski's ability and therefore wary of his plans, now admitted that he was a remarkable politician. This was also true of Colonel House, who had come to trust Paderewski's judgement as well as his sincerity. "I repeatedly pressed upon the President Paderewski's views, which I had made my own," wrote House. "That was the only real influence that counted."[29]

Unfortunately, it was not quite as simple as that. Wilson had set up a body of experts called the Inquiry, which was to examine all the various possibilities for Eastern and Central Europe, taking into account ethnographic, historical and economic factors, in order to help him formulate his schemes for the area. Colonel House had been appointed head of this body and often consulted Paderewski. "We pored over maps—his and mine—of Central Europe," wrote House, "and together we traced what we thought would be a homogeneous Poland."[30] But the other experts had minds of their own, and their job was to work out as many different schemes as possible.

The combination of their efficiency and Wilson's idealism soon began to make itself felt. Paderewski had based his case throughout on the thesis that Poland, one of the half-dozen great states of Europe, had been artificially removed from the map, and that only by re-establishing it could the balance of power in Central Europe be brought back into equilibrium. This argument was valid only if a truly large and strong Poland were re-established.

The ideas burgeoning in the mind of President Wilson were slightly, but essentially, different in emphasis from Paderewski's and House's. Wilson was not interested in restoring Poland to its great-power status; he had gone beyond that, or above that, to his principle of self-determination, and therefore decided to redraw, if possible, the whole map of Central Europe, breaking the area down into its ethnic groupings. It was an impractical scheme, and ultimately a dangerous one; it aimed to create nation-states where there had been empires or federations of mixed nationality.

When Poland had been dismembered at the end of the eighteenth century, it had been a sprawling conglomerate comprising several nationalities, the most notable, apart from the Poles, being the Lithuanians and the Ruthenians. On top of this there had been very sizeable minorities of Jews, Germans and Czechs, not to mention smaller ethnic groups like Armenians or Letts. The constitution of the state had been flexible enough to absorb any amount of racial or religious differences and, as a result, power had been shared far more widely in the old Poland than in any other European state at the time. This was why, incidentally, the Jews had been not merely tolerated but encouraged to come and settle. The Poles had of course remained the dominant group, and they were spread all over the huge area, while many of the other groups had concentrated themselves at the centre. If Poland was to be re-created in its historical boundaries, it would embrace many nationalities; if it was to be re-created in ethnographic ones, there would be a comparatively small country containing millions of aliens surrounded by a number of other states containing millions of Poles.

To Paderewski the obvious solution, and the only one which would include his own far-flung native province, was the historical one, amended to accommodate certain new developments. He wanted to see Poland, Lithuania, Polesia, Volhynia and Galicia make up the five United States of Poland, in which minority problems would not arise since no single group could afford to treat the others as aliens. In a small, constricted national state, on the other hand, the much smaller minorities would suffer endless disadvantages, while a great many Poles would be enduring the same in surrounding countries. Such a solution was bound, Paderewski felt, to produce a truncated state with a national self-defence complex that would lead to disaster.

Pilsudski and most of the socialists thought along much the same lines. Dmowski and his party, the National Democrats, thought otherwise: that the only future for Poland was as a strong, self-contained nation-state. He also saw Germany as the greatest permanent threat to Poland, and since some of the minorities, most notably the Jewish and the Ukrainian, were receptive to German influence, they represented, as far as he was concerned, a dangerous element. The more dangerous of the two, he had decided long before, were the Jews, who made up the greater part of the city proletariat and were therefore also open to socialist influence. "My anti-Semitism isn't religious; it is political," he explained. "And it is not political outside of Poland. It is entirely a matter of Polish politics."[31] But anti-Semitism it was, and when the National Committee with Dmowski at its head was recognized by the Allies, many American Jews grew seriously alarmed.

Quite apart from foreseeing the damage this would do to the cause, Paderewski was incensed by the way in which, having taken over most of the National Committee with his party, Dmowski was proceeding to make its views official Polish policy. In August 1917 Paderewski had cabled Dmowski that the membership of the Committee was too solidly National Democrat, insisting that it should broaden its base by including representatives of the socialist groups and of the more important minorities, particularly the Jews. He followed this up with other telegrams and letters, and, in November, by an ultimatum. "By refusing to coopt members from the progressive left, and by persisting in its policy of extreme factionalism, the Committee will render my cooperation impossible," he threatened.[32]

Paderewski organized a conference, on 14 April 1918, with the most prominent Jewish leaders in New York, including Louis Marshall, Julius Rosenwald and Jacob Schiff. He had little difficulty in convincing them of his opinion that, once Poland was free, relations between the two races would resume their former harmony, and that the greatest favour the American Jews could do their brethren in Poland was to be seen to help the Polish cause rather than hinder it. They trusted Paderewski and knew that his Relief Committees had been distributing food indiscriminately to a population of which over ten percent were Jews, and running thirty-seven kosher soup-kitchens in Warsaw alone for the last three years.[33] But while they recognized Paderewski's honesty of purpose, they were still worried by Dmowski. When Dmowski came to the United States in August 1918, Paderewski urged him to make a special public declaration to reassure the Jews on his future intentions, and arranged several meetings between him and Louis Marshall, Rabbi Wise of the Civic League and others. But while Dmowski made pious utterances on the subject of toleration and minority rights, he did not manage to sound convincing, and many of the Jews felt an enemy in him.

Paderewski, too, was beginning to sense Dmowski's enmity or, rather, his rivalry. Dmowski made a point of treating him as the mere representative of the National Committee, and once or twice snubbed him gently. It was foolish of him, since in America he himself was virtually unknown outside Polish circles, and in those he was known principally as the leader of a party—a party not everyone supported. Dmowski's presence in America was a nuisance to Paderewski, as it threatened not only to revive the factional animosities amongst the Poles which he had worked hard to assuage, but also to impede his good relations with the representatives of other national interests.

From the moment President Wilson had made it known that he intended to redraw the boundaries of Eastern and Central Europe, Washington had begun to attract a great many Lithuanian, Czech, Ukrainian and other gentlemen clutching briefcases bulging with documents and statistics proving that some area nobody in America had ever heard of should belong to an independent Ukraine or Lithuania. The most vociferous of these patriots were making claims to areas in which Poland had an interest, and they pandered to Wilson's ideas on the rights of small nations to self-determination. This was particularly true of the Czech Tomas Masaryk, an intelligent man who so impressed Wilson as the embodiment of the claims of small nations that he managed to make the visionary President swallow his idea of a large Czecho-Slovak state, which was by no means a logical application of the principles being invoked.

Paderewski employed all his tact and diplomacy in dealing with Masaryk and the others, in particular trying to prevent all discussion of claims and counterclaims of disputed territory. He realized that if Poland were seen to be in conflict with not only the Jews but also all the small surrounding peoples, she would soon become branded as a bully amongst the waifs of Eastern Europe. At one conference of East European nationalities in New York, where he knew that Masaryk was to make various claims which Poland would have to dispute, Paderewski made a speech not about Poland but about the representatives of all the other nationalists, ending up with a paean to Masaryk and the Czechs. Masaryk, who was to speak next, was obliged to return the compliment, and, laying aside his prepared speech, he made one praising Paderewski and his country. Paderewski believed that the inevitable disputes should be enacted at a later stage, between actual countries rather than by expatriate enthusiasts in America. By this policy he managed not only to maintain good relations with the representatives of other interests, but also to prevent the American public being treated to the spectacle of a lot of foreigners haggling over territories they did not possess. Dmowski was less tactful in these matters and less intent on courting opinion. Nor was he quite deferential enough with President Wilson when Paderewski took him to the White House, where Masaryk had made a far better impression.

However, while the Polish cause was beginning to suffer a partial eclipse in America in the sense that it was no longer the only maiden-in-distress available for Wilson's quixotry, it had begun to carry much greater weight in Europe. There were many reasons for this, but perhaps the most important was that the Bolsheviks had gained control in Russia and made peace with Germany at Brest-Litovsk. Russia could therefore no longer be considered as a potential eastern ally against Germany in the future. Some other country would have to take over that traditional role, and the obvious choice was Poland. Thus the idea of an independent Poland, which had received its first official support in the United States, was now more warmly espoused by France and Great Britain. That is why, when the Armistice was signed on 11 November 1918, Paderewski felt he could do no more useful work in America and decided to sail for Europe.

Quite what he intended to do once he got there is difficult to tell. Poland's independence was an established fact, and the way was now clear for the politicians to take over. Paderewski's ambition had been simply to help his country recover independence; he had no wish to get involved in full-time politics, although he was ready to help if help were needed. He viewed himself as a special case, as someone who could perhaps manage certain things better than conventional politicians, who were perforce partisan in their approach. A hint of how he regarded his role can be gleaned from words he had spoken in tribute to the writer Henryk Sienkiewicz shortly after the latter's death a few years previously. "He was no king, yet for many years his own people and foreigners regarded him as the first amongst Poles," said Paderewski. "He was no leader, yet the nation followed him. . . . He was no statesman, yet Polish politicians bowed to his intelligence, to his reason, to his judgement."[34] It would be unfair to suggest that he was trying to sum up his own position in this way; his words are merely useful as an illustration of how the artist-statesman perceived his vocation.

At the same time Paderewski was fully conscious of the effectiveness of his wartime work in America. His first aim had been to raise money, and he had raised it. Between his arrival in New York and the closing of the Relief Committee's books, nearly nine million dollars had been collected.[35] His second aim had been to bring home to the average American the justice and rationality of the Polish cause. In this, too, he had been successful; he had managed to convince people who previously had little or no idea of where Poland lay that they must fight for, amongst other things, that country's independence. More difficult to assess is his influence on the policymakers themselves, and therefore on the course of events.

Woodrow Wilson had, on his own, gradually formed the conviction that he must take America to war against Germany. Since he would be fighting not for a piece of land but for a set of principles, he had from the beginning given much thought to the wider context of those principles and of the war itself. If the United

States must come out of isolation and involve herself in a European conflict, she must do so in such a way as to banish all such conflicts from the future by eventually enforcing a peace settlement which eradicated or scotched their causes. One of the major causes seemed to be the rival claims of large empires to rule territories and peoples to which neither had the slightest right. The solution which presented itself to his mind was that of dismembering the empires in question and granting autonomy to their national components. This could be compounded by an association or league of all the nations, which could guarantee the integrity of those states too small to defend themselves, as well as regulating various other aspects of international relations.

The President knew that there were a great many enslaved nationalities in East Central Europe, but whether many of them were avid for, let alone capable of, independent existence was uncertain. And then, late in 1915, Colonel House brought to his notice Paderewski and his aspirations. The pianist provided Wilson with the first tangible evidence that there was fertile soil in Eastern Europe for his germinating plans. Paderewski was respected and his judgement trusted by many, including Wilson's closest advisers, such as House and Lansing, so the President was inclined from the start to take him seriously and to seek his opinion on matters concerning Eastern Europe, matters on which he could otherwise consult only historians. Paderewski therefore played a dual role of lending foundation to Wilson's ideas on the one hand, and of influencing their final form on the other.

He helped the President in other ways, too, and here his contribution is significant. Wilson's plans to take America into the war against Germany were frustrated by the isolationist mood of Congress and the country at large, and fiercely opposed by the German and Irish communities. German submarine warfare and the plots involving Mexico had, of course, the most dramatic effect on American public opinion and provided the waves of indignation on which Wilson could surge forward, but a great deal of preparation had been necessary beforehand, and Paderewski's work in this field had been highly effective. It is significant that Senator Henry Cabot Lodge, who fought with Wilson on every conceivable issue, agreed with him wholeheartedly on the need to restore Poland—and that was Paderewski's doing.[36] More important was his contribution at the popular level. By uniting the Polish community and transforming it into an articulate lobby, and by convincing countless numbers of Americans of the justice of the course Wilson was going to take, he mustered support for the President. More important still was his effect on the climate of public opinion in general. One cannot begin to compute the effect produced by the most popular entertainer in the country, a man loved and respected by millions, passionately advocating a given policy at every opportunity over a period of three years, but it must have been immense.

CHAPTER XI

Premier of Poland

Paderewski sailed from New York on 23 November 1918 accompanied by Helena and two Polish officers. Unbeknown to him, the British Foreign Office was already making arrangements for his arrival at Liverpool; events in Poland had taken a turn that made him indispensable to the Allies.

The Poles had always believed that they could regain their independence only with the support of one or another of the Great Powers, and all their energy had therefore been channeled into seeking that of either Germany or the Allies. But at the end of the war something totally unexpected happened. The Russian Empire had dissolved into revolution and chaos in 1917, and the whole of Poland found itself under German and Austrian occupation. Then, at the end of 1918, the Habsburg Empire collapsed, followed rapidly by the German. All three partitioning powers had ceased to exist as coherent states within the space of a year, and Poland could re-establish her independence alone.

On 8 November Pilsudski had been released from jail and sent to Warsaw by the Germans. On 11 November, the day of the Armistice, the population disarmed the German troops in the city, and Pilsudski took control. On 14 November he assumed the title of Head of State and called to office a government with a socialist preponderance, and two days later he sent telegrams to the Allied governments announcing the re-establishment of the Polish Republic.

The Allies, who had gradually and grudgingly consented to grant Poland independence, were not pleased by this new development. They had their own government for Poland ready and waiting in Paris in the shape of the National Committee, a group of serious and more or less conservative men whom they trusted. In Poland, Pilsudski, whom they knew little and trusted less, had assumed a dictatorial role and called on a group of unknowns to form a government, without so much as a by-your-leave. It was an irritating affront to the Allies, but it was also, they felt, a dangerous predicament. They understood neither Pilsudski's intentions nor the situation in Poland; they feared that he was some kind of German puppet and that under his rule the country would slide into Bolshevism. They therefore felt that the only hope of saving Poland for Western influence lay in negotiating a compromise between him and the National Committee—and there seemed to be only one man for that.

Paderewski reached London at the beginning of December and immediately got in touch with various people, including Lloyd George and the Foreign Secretary, Balfour, who was keen to see him and received him in a friendly manner. Paderewski asked him how the situation stood with respect to Poland. "In a way it is very good for you," answered Balfour, "but at the same time extremely delicate." He went on to assure Paderewski that Poland had the sympathy of all the Allies and would be well treated at the Peace Conference provided it had a reliable and respectable government. "There is only one thing to do," he concluded. "You must go there . . . go there and *unite* all the parties."[1]

Paderewski went home to think about what he should do. He knew very well that Dmowski and his Committee would not give him much of a brief, and that Pilsudski would not be disposed to take him too seriously as things stood, because he had no political muscle. But he was a born diplomatist and soon thought of something that would do the trick. The following day he again called on Balfour and declared himself ready to undertake the mission, but only if the British sent him to Poland in a British warship via Danzig. He knew that this would be the most efficacious way of demonstrating to both Dmowski and Pilsudski that he had British support. At the same time it was a golden opportunity of immediately stressing the Polish claim to Danzig and other parts of Poland still in German hands. "That is impossible," announced Balfour, who had instantly recognized the implications. He tried to persuade Paderewski to settle for another route, but the latter was adamant. As he showed him out, Balfour repeated, with slightly less conviction: "It is extremely difficult, almost impossible." Paderewski knew he had won. He was more delighted than surprised two days later when a note from the Foreign Office informed him that a Royal Navy cruiser would be waiting for him at Harwich on 19 December.[2]

Paderewski went to Paris, where he conferred with Dmowski and Colonel House, but was back in London on 17 December. He called briefly on Balfour, who left him with the words: "We trust you,"[3] and went to Harwich. His heart swelled when he saw the cruiser awaiting him, and thought it a good omen when he saw its name: H.M.S. *Concord*.

On 19 December the *Concord* weighed anchor and two days later sailed into Copenhagen. There it picked up Colonel Wade and Commander Rawlins, who were to establish a British military mission to Poland, and a group of medical officers. It also took aboard a young Pole, Sylwin Strakacz, who was trying to get home. "I immediately took a fancy to him," wrote Paderewski, who asked him to become his secretary.[4] Strakacz was approved by Helena and remained Paderewski's secretary to the end of his life.

The *Concord* was delayed in Copenhagen for a couple of days by bad weather, and the subsequent journey through the freezing Baltic strewn with mines was laborious and uncomfortable. In spite of having a bad cold, Paderewski spent Christmas Eve in the wardroom entertaining the officers on an old piano with a pedal missing.

H.M.S. *Concord* sailed into Danzig on 25 December. The city was cold and silent, ominously draped in the red flags of the German revolutionary council. On the quayside Paderewski was met by a small group of Poles led by the politician Wojciech Korfanty, and together they boarded the train for Poznan. They had not gone far when it was stopped. German officers came aboard and declared that Paderewski could not go to Poznan, which was still a German city. Wade and Rawlins insisted that the journey had been

ordered by highest Allied authority and threatened the officers with
dire consequences. The train was eventually allowed to proceed, and
steamed into Poznan late that night. The station, covered in Polish,
French and British flags, was bursting with crowds of Poles, who
escorted Paderewski to his hotel in a torchlight procession.

Paderewski's cold turned into bronchitis and he retired to bed
for the next two days. A continuous stream of local dignitaries,
delegations of peasants, soldiers and local landowners, came to see
him. On 27 December a huge procession of school-children marched
past the hotel, waving the flags of the Allied nations. Tension
mounted as the German inhabitants of the city watched the Polish
celebrations, and there were acts of provocation on both sides. At the
height of the demonstration, shots were fired at the rooms that
Paderewski and Wade occupied at the front of the hotel. Paderewski
was moved into another room, while various Poles began to dis-
arm German soldiers and police, and returned the fire; the fighting
rapidly spread through the city.

The German Foreign Ministry had been quick to protest to the
Allies. They were incensed by what they saw as British connivance
in a Polish plot—the province of Poznan was part of Germany and
nothing had yet been decided about its future status, which could
only be settled by the Peace Conference. By staying in Poznan during the fighting, Wade and Rawlins gave the impression that they
sanctioned the Polish action. There was great embarrassment in
London, and Lord Robert Cecil wrote of "the extreme folly of having allowed our mission to accompany Mr. Paderewski in his fili-
bustering expedition." Balfour, on the other hand, was unruffled. As
he explained in a note to the Director of Military Intelligence, who
was in contact with the Germans, "As regards M. Paderewski, Mr.
Balfour has no observations to offer, since H.M.G. can scarcely be
held responsible for his attitude." Everything points to the fact that
Balfour was secretly quite happy with the developments.[5] Paderewski had in effect managed to liberate a whole province for Poland
by his provocative arrival, and his political standing was greatly enhanced by the fact.

He left Poznan in the early hours of 1 January 1919, but did not
reach Warsaw until the next day. His train was stopped at every
small country station by cheering crowds, and he made thirty-odd

speeches during this triumphal progress. At Warsaw vast crowds filled the snow-covered streets. People unharnessed the horses from his carriage and pulled it themselves all the way to the Hotel Bristol. He came out on to the balcony with the Mayor of Warsaw, the President of the City Council and other officials. After they had delivered greeting addresses to him, he made a speech to the crowd assembled below. "I have not come to seek fame, honours or high office; only to serve," he stated, "but not to serve a party. I respect all parties, but I shall not belong to any one. At this moment there should be only one party—the party of Poland!"[6]

This was an important point for him to make; it was a declaration to Pilsudski that he had not come as a rival, and to the various factions that he would not be dragged into their quarrels. This was necessary since some right-wing groups wanted him to demand the Presidency for himself. They felt that only by using his popularity with the masses could they succeed in wresting power from Pilsudski and the left before it was too late. One group of right-wingers was planning a *coup d'état* and came to ask Paderewski for his support. He refused to have anything to do with it.

After seeing some of the more prominent figures in Warsaw, Paderewski drove to the Belvedere Palace on the afternoon of 4 January to have his first interview with Pilsudski. The Head of State was a baffling character. Like Paderewski, he was a minor nobleman by birth. His early life, spent in the ranks of the Polish Socialist Party, reads like a novel, punctuated with terrorist activities and a spell in Siberia. It was an apprenticeship which taught him to be secretive and ruthless. He was prepared to make an alliance with the Devil himself to further the cause of Polish independence, and he cared little for the opinion of others. He was a born fighter and a natural leader of men.

Pilsudski looked the part. He was rough-hewn, solid and gritty, and he always wore a soldier's grey tunic without insignia or decorations. His exceedingly pale face with its drooping moustache and piercing eyes was effective to the point of being theatrical. "None of the usual amenities of civilized intercourse, but all the apparatus of sombre genius" is how one British diplomat described him.[7]

It was a meeting of two extremes when Paderewski walked into Pilsudski's study in the Belvedere Palace. After a few moments during which they sized each other up, Paderewski explained that, both for the sake of internal stability and, particularly, for the sake of securing Allied sympathy at the Peace Conference, a representative coalition government must be formed immediately. There was no objection to Pilsudski remaining Head of State, but the government in power was unacceptable. Paderewski was nervous, as he knew that the right-wingers were planning their coup for that very night. He hoped that if an immediate compromise could be reached and a coalition government announced, it would be stifled. Pilsudski also knew about the projected coup, it appears, and since he, too, wished to get rid of the present government—without, however, provoking the anger of the socialists—he was prepared to let it go ahead. He therefore refused to reach an agreement with Paderewski and enjoyed watching him turn pale as the implications of this refusal sank in.[8]

Paderewski had prudently decided to leave for Cracow immediately after the interview, as he did not wish to be associated in anyone's mind with the conspirators. They struck that night while he was in the train, but the whole affair was a fiasco, and by the early hours they had all been arrested. Pilsudski was delighted; the affair cast discredit on the right as a whole while showing that the government in office was weak and unpopular; his own position was strengthened and he now had an excuse for getting rid of the government and reaching an agreement with Paderewski. He wished and needed to do so for various reasons, not least because Herbert Hoover's American Food Mission, which had reached Poland on 4 January, made it quite clear that its relief was conditional on Paderewski being in office.[9]

In Cracow, Paderewski had been greeted with enthusiasm; a mass rally had been organized, and he spoke to crowds from the foot of the Grunwald monument. On the following night, however, just as he and Helena were retiring to bed in their hotel, there was a knock at the door and a special courier from Pilsudski was announced. The courier was Pilsudski's chief-of-staff, General Szeptycki, an aristocrat of conservative bent who was universally trusted and respected. The General entreated him, at Pilsudski's request, to return to Warsaw forthwith—a special train was waiting. Paderewski needed no time to make up his mind; he dressed in a hurry and went to the station with the General and a flustered Helena.

On his arrival in Warsaw he was driven to the Belvedere, and Pilsudski asked him to form a government. He agreed and immediately set about the task. On 9 January he asked the Socialist Party to join his coalition, but it refused, as did various other groups. Nevertheless, on 17 January he was able to announce his cabinet, which, he explained, was supposed to be a coalition government of specialists. "Willing to undertake this difficult task," he said, "I stand before the people asking for the support and help of all factions."[10] Paderewski's sincerity and his reputation eased the political tensions considerably, and at the same time the generally held view that he had influence with the Allies seemed to guarantee not only a just settlement in Paris but also the rapid supply of food, clothing and credits.

The situation in Poland was catastrophic. As Hoover, whose relief mission had arrived in Warsaw on 4 January, explains:

Here were about 28,000,000 people who had for four years been ravished by four separate invasions during this one war, where battles and retreating armies had destroyed and destroyed again. In parts there had been seven invasions and seven destructive retreats. Many hundreds of thousands had died of starvation. The homes of millions had been destroyed and the people in those areas were living in hovels. Their agricultural implements had been depleted, their animals had been taken by armies, their crops had been only partly planted and even then only partly harvested. Industry in the cities was dead from lack of raw materials. The people were unemployed and millions were destitute. They had been flooded with roubles and kronen, all of which were now valueless. The railroads were barely functioning. The cities were almost without food; typhus and diseases raged over whole provinces. Rats, lice, famine, pestilence—yet they were determined to build a nation.[11]

Vernon Kellogg and Colonel William Grove of the American Food Mission worked out that one third of the twenty-eight million inhabitants were unable to survive without immediate help. Apart from vast quantities of food, they immediately shipped in nearly three million tons of clothing, but this made only a slight impact. Over the next six months the American Food Mission poured in over $100,000 worth of food and clothing and medical supplies just to arrest the death toll from hunger, cold and disease.[12]

The destruction was on a vast scale: eleven million acres of agricultural land were totally devastated, six million acres of forest had been felled, two million head of cattle, a million horses and one and a half million sheep had been taken by the Germans. Some ten thousand motors and pieces of machinery had been removed, along with most of the rolling-stock, and 7,500 bridges and 940 railway stations had been blown up in an operation the German Army quaintly termed the "de-industrialization" of Poland.[13] There were hardly any cars left in the whole country, and the roads were pitted and rutted quagmires. There were four functioning financial systems: the Russian, German and Austrian currencies had been joined by the Polish mark.

The military situation was parlous. Pilsudski, who was Commander-in-Chief as well as Head of State, had at his disposal the remains of his disbanded Legions and several Polish units from the Austrian army as well as a small force of Poles raised by the Germans. Plenty of volunteers and demobilized Poles from the German forces were coming forward, but there was little equipment and less organization. These forces were stretched to breaking-point from the start. They had to hold Posnania against the Germans, who threatened to invade it; they had to fight for the city of Lwow and the province of Galicia against Ukrainian units from the Austrian army; in January the Czechs invaded the virtually ungarrisoned province of Teschen; and as the German front in the east disintegrated, Russian Bolshevik troops began to move into eastern Poland.

In the circumstances, the chances that the elections called for 26 January would take place with any degree of order seemed remote. To everyone's surprise, they went off smoothly: well over sixty percent of the electorate voted, and Dmowski's National Democrats emerged as the strongest of the twenty parties, with the peasant groups of the centre coming next.

On 9 February Paderewski and Pilsudski entered Warsaw Cathedral together for a celebratory mass, and on the following day

Paderewski opened the first sovereign Polish parliament, the Sejm, since the end of the eighteenth century. His opening speech reduced most of those present to tears; it was indeed a moving scene. By virtue of seniority, the first session was presided over by the eighty-five-year-old Prince Ferdinand Radziwill, whose distinguished figure contrasted strongly with the peasant delegates, some of them in colourful folk costumes, others proudly sporting everyday working clothes. A motley assortment of morning coats, Jewish kaftans and noblemen's traditional costumes proclaimed to the foreign observers both the remarkable unity of purpose of the nation and the differences which would threaten it.

A few days later the Sejm unanimously passed votes of confidence in Pilsudski and Paderewski. America had officially recognized the new Polish government on 30 January. France, Great Britain and Italy followed suit on 23, 25 and 27 February respectively. Paderewski had successfully carried through Balfour's plan and put the Polish house in order from the diplomatic point of view, and he could now turn to the task of reconstructing the country internally.

Reconstruction is perhaps the wrong word to use, as in effect everything had to be created from scratch: a constitution, governing institutions, an agricultural and industrial policy, a legal system—the whole apparatus of state, in fact. It was not like reforming an existing system; the country had to be run while the apparatus for running it was being put together. Everything had to be improvised, but this was not easy, as the three parts of Poland had developed different ways of doing things in a hundred years of belonging to different countries. Those who had been Tsarist functionaries found the former Habsburg civil servants maddening, while former Prussian employees found both impossible to work with.

Paderewski rose to the occasion brilliantly. His energy and physical endurance could cope with the hectic nature of his day-to-day existence; his extraordinary memory for facts, figures and faces stood him in good stead when quick decisions were required; his personal charm and magnetism smoothed many ruffled feathers, while his presence and authority imposed itself over stormy meetings.

The apartment at the Hotel Bristol was a hive of activity. Helena was organizing her White Cross in Poland, collecting money for orphans and housing the homeless, but she still found time to keep a watchful eye on her husband, ever vigilant over the state of his health and his nerves. Paderewski worked feverishly, whenever he found the time or the opportunity. He would stay up into the early hours of every morning, as that was when he worked best. This was something he had in common with Pilsudski, who had grown used to working at night during his conspiratorial years. They also smoked innumerable cigarettes and eased their nerves with cards—Pilsudski with endless games of patience, Paderewski with his bridge.

The brooding, taciturn conspirator had more in common with the bird-of-paradise Paderewski than was immediately apparent. They resented each other in equal measure on the same grounds: each felt that he had devoted his life to the cause, and each believed that his contribution had been decisive. Each underestimated the other's intelligence, so neither was particularly afraid of the other. Thus, in spite of the occasional stormy interview—usually at four o'clock in the morning or thereabouts—they got on quite well.

They certainly shared many of the same views. Like Paderewski, Pilsudski wanted a strong Poland and envisaged a federal state, although their conceptions differed in detail. Pilsudski was no more a party man than Paderewski. This he amply demonstrated on the day following his assumption of power, when his erstwhile socialist colleagues came to congratulate him and addressed him as "Comrade." "Gentlemen," he cut them short, "we both took a ride on the same red tram, but while I got off at the stop marked *Polish Independence,* you wish to travel on to the station *Socialism.* Bon voyage—but be so kind as to call me *Sir!*"[14]

Pilsudski needed Paderewski for two reasons. First, he needed good relations with the Allies, who were naturally suspicious of him. With Paderewski as Premier, Poland would get the credits she needed and right-wing opinion would be placated. Second—and this was perhaps the most gratifying aspect of the arrangement—Paderewski had managed, by accident, to eliminate Dmowski from power. Dmowski was the leader of the largest single party in Poland, but he was not as popular as Paderewski, either

abroad or at home. Most of the right had decided to back Paderewski rather than Dmowski in order to get someone of their
own views, as they thought, into power where Dmowski might
have failed. They also thought that his term in office would pave
the way for Dmowski. Exactly the reverse happened: Dmowski
was pushed aside, while Paderewski, not being partisan, did not
use his Premiership to strengthen the influence of the right. Up to
a point, therefore, Paderewski played into Pilsudski's hands. Certainly nobody could have served him as well in the forthcoming
negotiations in Paris.

Paderewski had reserved the post of Foreign Minister for himself, and he had also announced that he would be Poland's principal
delegate to the Peace Conference, with Dmowski in second place.
Therefore, having set up his government of "specialists" in Warsaw
and supervised the opening of the Sejm, Paderewski turned all his
attention to Paris, where he thought his country would be given
definition.

CHAPTER XII

The Peacemaker

The Peace Conference which opened at Paris in January 1919 had two principal aims. The first was to sign a peace with the Central Powers settling the territorial cessions and the reparations they would have to make to the victorious Allies. The second was to redraw the boundaries in Central and Eastern Europe.

Its ability to carry out the second of these was severely impaired by the fact that, although victorious and ostensibly all-powerful, Great Britain, France, the United States and Italy were in no mood for further fighting, and consequently were unable to impose by force the decisions they might make. Another anomaly was that one of the Great Powers, and the one most severely affected by any changes in Eastern Europe, Russia, was in the throes of civil war and therefore not represented at the negotiations.

This meant that the representatives of the Western Great Powers were obliged to make decisions of the most extraordinary import concerning an area largely outside their spheres of interest, of which they knew very little—decisions which they were both unwilling and unable to uphold by force. To complicate matters, each of the Great Powers had different aims and visions. When their conflicting nature came to the surface, original concepts had to be shelved in favour of expediency.

The concept of an independent Poland strong and rich enough to provide an effective buffer against both Russian and German expansion—the concept which had been ceaselessly put forward by Paderewski and adopted by all the Allies—was possibly the greatest casualty. In spite of a certain amount of self-help, the country which was cobbled together as a result was in no position either economically or strategically to defend itself, let alone act as a curb on Germany or Russia.

Poland's position as a party to the Paris Conference was somewhat ambiguous. The country had in fact re-established its own independence, taking advantage of the void created by the collapse of Germany, Russia and Austria. From the very first day of "peace" it was engaged in heavy fighting in order to liberate its own territories and to maintain that independence. The Allies, having been gradually brought round to the idea of granting the country independence, saw that independence as their gift and their gift alone. As a result, they presumed a responsibility for the shape of the future state and the right to impose decisions and judgements on it from on high.

This discrepancy between reality as seen from Paris and reality as seen from Warsaw sums up the weakness of Paderewski's own position in Polish politics. Having spent the whole war in the West, and having learnt to see through its eyes, he saw Polish independence as the work of the Allies. The Poles, on the other hand, having fought in various armies and borne the brunt of the destruction entailed by the war, and having then disarmed the Germans and seized power, believed that they owed their independence principally to their own dogged efforts. However much they may have liked Wilson and Clemenceau, they well knew that, as Joseph Conrad so neatly put it, "if the Alliances had been differently combined, the Western Powers would have delivered Poland to the learned German pig with as little compunction as they were ready to give it up to the Russian mangy dog."[1] They felt that their nation had a right to exist based on their determination that it should do so, rather than on the Olympian decisions of prime ministers of countries which had never lifted a finger to help them when this was inconvenient.

Reality lay somewhere in between. Had Russia still been their ally, the Western Powers would certainly not have pressed for Polish independence at the Conference; when Russia did invade Poland in the following year, they did nothing to defend the country. On the other hand, had the Allies not clothed, fed and armed them, the Poles would have frozen, starved and been slaughtered.

For peoples like the Lithuanians and the Czechs, who had not enjoyed any kind of independent statehood for several hundred years and who at the turn of the century could not have aspired to it in their wildest dreams, the Paris Conference was a trying and none too dignified forum from which they did, however, take home something they could obtain nowhere else—recognition as independent states. For Poland, which, in spite of being wiped off the map a century before, had maintained an extraordinary element of corporate identity and fought four times to establish this, and which had originally raised the whole question of independence for the nations of Eastern Europe, the Conference turned out to be one long series of humiliations, in which Paderewski shared as Premier, as delegate to the Conference, and as private individual.

The Conference opened on 18 January. It was an extraordinary assemblage of people. Delegations arrived from every corner of the world, each with a bevy of legal, financial and military experts ready with maps and statistics to shoot down the arguments of rival experts. They filled the hotels, which turned into veritable Babels of heated discussion, with groups of gesticulating Estonians or indignant Bolivians going over their plans in the lobby, the bar and the lift. "The Ritz has become intolerable," Proust complained in a letter to Walter Berry, "in spite of the presence of Paderewski—without Chopin's Polonaises, alas."[2]

The British delegation took over not only every spare room in the embassy, but also the hotels Astoria and Majestic. They were headed by their far from majestic Prime Minister, Lloyd George—the "pink little man" who dominated the proceedings with virtuosity. He was assisted by his Foreign Secretary, A. J. Balfour, "the most cultivated, the most graceful, the most courteous of all inflexible men," and Lord Robert Cecil, "a Christian who believes and wants to live his creed, with the smile of a Chinese dragon expressing an obstinacy closed to argument," as Clemenceau described them.[3] The delegation included the taciturn Bonar Law, the elegant and remote Lord Milner, the arch-Mandarin Sir Maurice Hankey and a host of others.

The Americans settled into the Hotel de Crillon on the Place de la Concorde, conveniently close to their embassy. Woodrow Wilson himself took a house some way off in what became the Place des Etats-Unis, from the remoteness of which he dreamed of a world restructured on ideal lines. The visionary was distinctly recognizable in every drawn feature of that noble, lean, almost ascetic face, which alone remained unamused by the more comic side of the proceedings. With him he had brought his Secretary of State, Robert Lansing, an efficient man who exuded competence from every pore, and his right-hand man, Colonel House, that "overcivilized being escaped from the savagery of Texas who sees everything, understands everything, and, following only his own idea, knows how to make himself heard and respected by all," as Clemenceau saw him. He was indeed widely considered to be the most important man in the American delegation, and his power over Wilson was overestimated.

The Italians were represented by their suave Sicilian Prime Minister, Vittorio Orlando, and his Foreign Minister, Baron Sidney Sonnino; Japan by a host of Nippon barons and viscounts; the other nations by a collection of curious but impressive personages, including Bratianu of Roumania, Venizelos of Greece, Benes of Czechoslovakia, Hymans of Belgium and, resplendent in his robes, King Faisal of Arabia, who all jostled for space in hotels like the Ritz and the Meurice.

The figurehead of the Conference and its chairman was the small but commanding *père la victoire,* Georges Clemenceau, referred to by all as "the Tiger." He would preside over the sittings, flanked by the representatives of the other nations making up the "Big Four"—Great Britain, the United States and Italy. They convened in a large room at the Quai d'Orsay hung with seventeenth-century tapestries. There they listened to special commissions or the representatives of the smaller states who came and stated their case or defended their arguments against claims made by another side. It was an equitable procedure, but it had one great flaw which undermined the high moral note struck by the Allies when they professed their intention of seeing justice done to all: the final decision on each and every question lay with the Big Four, and they were themselves not divinely appointed judges but interested parties.

Wilson was fired by the creed that every nation had a natural right to self-determination, but he was inevitably confused by the question of what constituted a nation. Further, he believed that, once put into effect, his project of a League of Nations would become such an effective moral power that it did not much matter to whom an area was provisionally apportioned, since its inhabitants would be protected by the League.

The French wanted Alsace-Lorraine and heavy reparations for the damage they had suffered. They also wanted to create a new ally on the other side of Germany. However, they wanted so much themselves from Germany territorially and financially that they had to allow less to go to Poland.

The British knew less than the others about Eastern Europe and did not regard it as their sphere of interest. On the other hand, they were determined that France should not get too much of her own way, and that Germany should not be cannibalized. They were more interested in matters involving colonies and shipping routes. Above all, they were keen to get the Conference over with as soon as possible.

The Italians wanted reparations and pieces of the Habsburg Empire and were inescapably caught up in matters far beyond their sphere of interest. The business of the Conference encompassed the entire world, embracing problems in Palestine and Syria, the fate of German colonies in Africa and even the waterways of Manchuria, in a web of intricate negotiations involving the most widely conflicting interests.

The basic principle allegedly governing decisions on Eastern Europe was the ethnic one: if an area was inhabited by a majority of Czechs, it went to Czechoslovakia; if the majority were Poles, it went to Poland. There were, however, three other criteria on which disputes could be settled. One was the historic: if a province was sixty percent Polish and only forty percent Czech, it might be given to Czechoslovakia on the basis that it had for centuries been an integral part of the kingdom of Bohemia. The second was the economic: if a province was seventy-five percent Polish but contained mineral resources essential to the functioning of the German economy, it might be awarded to Germany. Lagging sadly behind all these was the strategic factor: countries were supposed to have defensible borders and, in Poland's case, access to the sea.

This opened the door to orgies of argument on every issue, to which there was, generally speaking, no absolutely just solution. A sound knowledge of the area might have helped the Big Four at least to reach a practical one, but as they gazed at the piles of reports landing on their desks, describing the whole history of Silesia, its coal output, industry and commerce, with maps showing the racial origins, religion and language of the population, they often had only the haziest idea of where the area lay.

The complexity of these problems was surpassed only by their sheer volume, and it soon became clear that if the peacemakers were to weigh up each one with the requisite care, they would get completely bogged down. As far as the Big Four were concerned, the only sensible answer was to listen to a number of arguments and then reach a decision amongst themselves. The result was, as Balfour had predicted, "a rough and tumble affair" whose outcome was more often the consequence of horse-trading amongst the Big Four than of balanced judgement. Wilson did not want the Italians to get Fiume, but Lloyd George did because he needed their co-operation elsewhere; Lloyd George did not want the Poles to have Danzig, but Wilson did because he had promised it to Paderewski; eventually a compromise would be reached on the lines of: "You can have your way on Fiume if you agree to my solution on Danzig."

Lansing describes how Clemenceau would present the decision arrived at by this method to one of the plenary sessions of the Conference, allow five minutes of discussion, then get up and, glaring fiercely around the room, ask if anyone had more to say. Just as some Roumanian delegate was clearing his throat and summoning up the courage to point out that the decision was unjust, Clemenceau would exclaim, *"Adopté!"* in a tone which brooked no argument.

As a result, a country might find itself losing a historic province on ethnic grounds, an ethnically homogeneous area on historical grounds and one which was its own ethnically and historically on economic grounds. "The important point to realize about the Paris

Peace Conference," writes Harold Nicolson, one of the most sardonic members of the British delegation, "is its amazing inconsequence, the complete absence of any consecutive method of negotiation or even imposition."[4]

A good example of this was the negotiation and final settlement of the Polish-German border. Shortly after the opening of the Conference, on 29 January, Dmowski, the second delegate, was asked to give the full Polish proposals. A specialist Commission on Polish Affairs then produced its report, based on ethnic arguments. The boundaries it proposed were very similar to those suggested by Dmowski, except for a small area of East Prussia around Elbing which they felt should remain with Germany. Such a settlement would have given Poland a reasonable seaboard, with Danzig well connected by a widening hinterland to the main body of the country.

With the arrival of Lloyd George on the scene, things began to turn sour for the Poles. On 4 March the Polish-German frontier was discussed in the Council of Four, and Lloyd George unexpectedly declared serious misgivings about whether Danzig, Upper Silesia and the south-western part of East Prussia should be allowed to go to Poland. Wilson and Clemenceau protested that the frontier had already been decided upon in principle, but by a series of specious arguments and some bargaining Lloyd George finally made Wilson agree with him.

As a result, Paderewski was met by a very worried Dmowski when he arrived at the Gare du Nord on 2 April. They went to the Hotel de Wagram, where Dmowski was staying, and there Paderewski was given a run-down of events so far. He listened with growing horror as he heard the overwrought Dmowski explain that the Polish position was being undermined by something in the nature of a conspiracy.

On the morrow of his arrival Paderewski went to see Etienne Pichon, the French Foreign Minister, at the Quai d'Orsay and told him he would like to meet Clemenceau. Pichon made a telephone call, and a few moments later the old Tiger himself appeared in the doorway. He came up to Paderewski and with a twinkle in his eye asked: "Are you a cousin of the famous pianist Paderewski?" When Paderewski replied, "It is I, Monsieur le Président," Clemenceau exclaimed with mock surprise, "And you the famous artist have become Prime Minister? What a come-down!"[5]

Paderewski proceeded to explain to the French Premier the political situation in Poland and how it might be affected by the final settlement of the peace with Germany. Clemenceau, who had great hopes for Poland as a French sphere of interest and influence, was sympathetic, and as he left the Quai d'Orsay, Paderewski felt that at least he could count on French support.

He then called on President Wilson at the Place des Etats-Unis, where he had a less comforting interview. Wilson's ideas on the peace settlement had been crystallizing resolutely and he was now far less open to influence than before. He was coming to see the future League of Nations as being more important than the terms of the peace treaty itself, and this held one ominous consequence for Poland. Wilson had decided that since most of the population of Danzig, the seaport Poland so badly needed, was German, the city should be given neither to Poland nor to Germany, but instead be constituted a Free City under the guardianship of the League of Nations—a terrifying prospect to all but the most sanguine idealists.

In vain did Paderewski remind Wilson of Frederick the Great's dictum that whoever held Danzig was more master of Poland than he who held Warsaw. On 9 April he was convoked to a meeting of the Council of Four and informed that the original decision of giving Danzig to Poland had been indefinitely deferred. He was also told that the fate of Upper Silesia and East Prussia was to be decided by local plebiscite. This boded ill for Poland, as there was little doubt a plebiscite held in areas under German occupation would be subject to interference.

The following day Paderewski went to lunch with Lloyd George. Also present were Bonar Law and James Headlam-Morley, the British member of the Commission for Polish Affairs. Paderewski and Lloyd George had met before and liked each other, but now that they came together to talk of serious matters, Paderewski made a much deeper impression on Lloyd George, who noted in his diary that day: "There are very few people who have ever impressed me as much as he did. I could have listened to him for hours. More often one is disappointed when one meets great men who have been greatly praised, but this time the fulfilment was much greater than the expectation. He is a really remarkable man. He told us some of the history of the Poles and left one with the impression that they had been a greatly underestimated nation."[6] Headlam-Morley, who also kept a diary, noted that Paderewski had "made a great impression on both the Prime Minister and Bonar Law."[7]

Paderewski made a wonderful impression on everyone and behaved with elegance and tact, but while everybody praised this kind of behaviour, so rare amongst the representatives of the smaller powers in particular, it did not advance his cause at all. The Peace Conference was a forum in which mutual respect and forbearance counted for far less than hard bargaining. Paderewski had come to realize that Dmowski's haunting images of conspiracies were not entirely illusory. There were in fact a great number of different interests at stake in Eastern and Central Europe, and an inordinate proportion of them were in conflict with the idea of a great Poland.

Nobody particularly minded the emergence of an independent Latvia or Estonia; these were states that could be—and were—crushed by Russia or Germany whenever convenient. Given the dismemberment of the Habsburg Empire, the existence of a Czecho-Slovak or Hungarian state was not in itself a threat or even a nuisance to more than one other country. But the resurrection of a strong Poland was a different matter altogether, for several reasons. Poland had been a Great Power once and there was every possibility that, given the chance, she would grow into one again. Like the Habsburg Empire, Poland had always been large and diverse enough to absorb any number of neighbouring peoples, and had been in essence, as well as in title, a Commonwealth.

Russians, White or Red, could not view the rebirth of such a state without concern. There was no reason why it should not, in time, pull back into its orbit all of Catherine the Great's conquests in the west. Germans, whether reactionary or socialist, realized that a strong Poland would thwart all their plans in the east. The Czechs, Lithuanians and Ruthenians could fulfill their aspirations only at some cost to Poland, while a significant minority of the Jews of the area were either for international Bolshevism or for strong German rule, foreseeing in the nationalism of small nations a threat to their future position.

If one considers that England was keen to soften the blow for Germany, that France was keeping the door open for Russia while there was still a chance that the Whites might win, that the United States was open to German and Jewish influence, and that the Czechs and Lithuanians by posing as "little nations" could count on a great deal of sympathy in the West, it is easy to imagine the murderous crossfire the Polish delegation was sometimes caught in.

Some of the sniping, moreover, came from unexpected quarters. The British delegation and Foreign Office, knowing little about Eastern Europe, relied heavily on experts of one sort or another, and the two advising them on Polish affairs would certainly have added grist to the mill of Dmowski's conspiracy theory, had he been able to see their comments. One was E. H. Carr, whose knowledge of conditions in Poland was highly selective, and who advised that the nations of Eastern Europe should not be taken too seriously since their affairs "belong principally to the sphere of farce."[8] The other was Lewis Namier, who knew a great deal about Poland, being a Galician Jew by birth, but did not attempt to disguise his dislike for Paderewski and his government, whom he described as a "collection of nonentities." He, too, liked to make out that the Poles were incapable of running anything, let alone a country, and although this bias earned him strong rebukes from his superiors, it nevertheless helped to cast doubt on the viability of the Polish state.[9] A curious aspect of this is that all reports sent in by Colonel Wade and Commander Rawlins, by Sir Esme Howard of the Inter-Allied Mission, and by Sir Horace Rumbold, the British Minister in Warsaw, were commented on by either Carr or Namier, and that almost invariably the comments suggested, and sometimes stated, that the British representatives on the spot had been in some way misled into being too favourable to the Poles.

The opinion of such experts was lent further authority by the lamentable ignorance of all matters East European that was prevalent in British official circles, and fed the general lack of faith in Polish competence—a feeling fostered by the Germans throughout the nineteenth century and accepted as gospel by, for instance, John Maynard Keynes.

To break through such prejudice was not easy, and Dmowski was not the man to do it. Although Lloyd George thought him "extremely able," he was not particularly liked or trusted.[10] The arrival of Paderewski was therefore timely; he was both liked and trusted by everyone, and he was a great diplomatist. He also had loyal friends in important places, and it is typical that while other delegations were paying newspapers to carry articles favourable to their cause, Paderewski wrote to an old friend and a few days later received a telegram which ran: "My newspapers will be glad to assist you in any way possible—Northcliffe."[11] To be able to count on the support of the *Daily Mail* and *The Times* was invaluable.

Resourceful and diplomatic as he might be, there was in fact very little Paderewski could achieve in radical terms. In order to change the minds of the Big Four, the one thing required was pressure of one sort or another, and this was the one thing that he could not exert. Poland was utterly dependent on the Allies for arms and food, and although she was necessary to them as a bastion against Bolshevism, she could have proved that necessity only by allowing herself to be overrun. To defy the Allies on decisions they might make with regard to her frontiers meant to cut off her own supplies. As one observer pointed out with regard to Paderewski's position, "Lucid intelligence and unflagging will were of no avail against the threat of famine."[12]

Paderewski played the only card he held. On his way to snatch a few days at Riond-Bosson over Easter, he told Lord Acton that he was very much depressed by the Allied, and particularly the British, stand over Danzig, and that unless he could change it he would find it very difficult to stay in power. Acton cabled this information immediately to Balfour, who shortly received another cable, this time from the acting British Commissioner in Warsaw, warning him that "a great many persons believe that the remaining in office of Mr. Paderewski depends to a large extent on whether Danzig will be given to the Poles."[13] Paderewski was using the only threat he could—that unless he brought back the goods from Paris, his government would fall. This was something the Allies did not want to see at all. They believed that if Paderewski went, Poland would either drift towards Bolshevism or else become some kind of military dictatorship under Pilsudski, who they feared would make friends with Germany.

This argument carried great weight as far as France and the United States were concerned, but its force broke against the wall of Lloyd George's indifference. The British Prime Minister's attitude was extraordinary. He had no real interest in what happened in Eastern Europe, since this had already been tacitly accepted by the British as lying within the French sphere of interest; yet he would make quite unwarranted sallies into this sphere, partly in order to protect German interests, partly to frustrate French plans. While Wilson and Clemenceau had formulated general schemes to which they stuck, he tended to act on the spur of the moment, taking each problem in isolation from the others. At times he seemed more concerned with imposing his own will than with the soundness of the final settlement.

Although they were on occasion mistaken for each other in the street—mainly because both sported white manes and moustaches—no two men could have been more different than Lloyd George and Paderewski. The Polish Premier, consistent in his beliefs, burdened with a morality which made him acutely aware of an opponent's point of view, and above all a great believer in the power of truth and justice to convince, could hardly believe the impermeability to argument and the apparent lack of scruple of his British counterpart.

On 10 May, for instance, Paderewski made a speech at the Conference in which he challenged the logic of the recent decisions on the Polish-German frontier. He demanded what conceivable justification Lloyd George felt in calling for a plebiscite in Upper Silesia when even the German census revealed the vast majority of the population to be Polish. If Germany needed coal, Poland needed a seaport, and yet this was being withheld from her on account of a German majority in Danzig. Why, Paderewski asked, were the Allies so unwilling to leave the 200,000 Germans of Danzig under Polish rule when they were prepared to leave three million Germans under Czech rule in the Sudetenland and three million Poles under German rule in various border areas? Lloyd George did not answer the question, and instead moved that the final decision be deferred to a later date.

The answer to this question, as Paderewski well knew, was that neither logic nor principle counted for much in the face of expediency, and that, for all the moral attitudes struck, the aim of the Conference was not to see justice done in some abstract sense, but to rearrange Europe in a way congenial to the Allies. Nowhere was this more apparent than in the intricacies of a minor but irritating problem which had arisen between Poland and Czechoslovakia.

It concerned a not very large area of the Habsburg Empire called the duchy of Teschen, in which Poles outnumbered Czechs by two to one. After the Armistice the local population had drawn a demarcation line through the duchy separating the areas inhabited by the two nationalities, and Warsaw accepted this as a fair division of the area. The Czechs, however, did not, having secretly obtained French approval for their plan of taking over the whole duchy. As one English historian has pointed out, Teschen had very few Czechs but a great deal of coal. Prague argued that, without this, Czechoslovakia could not be a viable economic unit. The Czech army invaded the Polish part of the duchy in January 1919, and before the Poles could send reinforcements, Allied representatives arrived on the scene and arranged a ceasefire, with the Czechs in possession.

It was suggested that Poland and Czechoslovakia reach an agreement between themselves, without involving the Allies, which was not possible—as Paderewski was to discover—for they were already involved. Paderewski stopped twice in Prague on his journeys between Paris and Warsaw, but his lengthy conversations with President Masaryk produced no positive results. Paderewski was willing to compromise on details, but insisted that part of the duchy must revert to Poland, while Masaryk was adamant that the whole province must belong to Czechoslovakia.[14]

When he reached Paris after the second of these talks, Paderewski had an interview on 2 May with Clemenceau, who found him, as he told an aide after the meeting, "particularly alive to all the great political problems of the moment."[15] One that he was awakened to during the interview was that Clemenceau wanted to give Teschen to Czechoslovakia and to compensate Poland for it by giving her Upper Silesia, but there seemed to be complications attached to this.

It did not take Paderewski long to realize the nature of these complications. When he spoke to Balfour a few days later, he discovered that the British delegation was, surprisingly, backing the

Polish claim to Teschen—in spite of the fact that Namier had informed them that the duchy was in imminent danger of going Bolshevik without the presence of the Czech army.[16] The reason for this, as soon became clear, was that Lloyd George wanted to give Upper Silesia and its coal to Germany, and therefore Poland would need to be compensated with Teschen. There seemed little point in Paderewski holding any more meetings with Masaryk.

While Clemenceau and Lloyd George tussled with such eminently practical problems, Woodrow Wilson was preparing a more high-minded surprise for Paderewski and his colleagues, in the shape of special clauses to be inserted into the treaty governing the status of national and religious minorities in the new countries.

The concept of these Minority Treaties, as they came to be known, originated with various Jewish organizations in the United States. Concerned at the rise of anti-Semitism in Eastern Europe in the last decades, and particularly by its worst manifestations, the Russian pogroms, they had argued that the Peace Conference should impose, where possible, binding conditions on the new nations to respect and protect their Jewish minorities. A considerable body of opinion in the West felt that such legislation would be timely, since there had been persistent rumours in the press of pogroms taking place after the Armistice in Poland, Roumania and elsewhere. The Polish government had denied this, but since the rumours and allegations persisted, Paderewski invited Jewish organizations to come to Poland and carry out an official inquiry.

The American Jewish mission, under Henry Morgenthau, spent two months travelling around the country collecting evidence, closely followed by a British one headed by Sir Stuart Samuel. The reports they produced agreed broadly with an independent one written by the American Minister in Warsaw, in concluding that none of the events described in the press could be construed as being in themselves anti-Semitic actions. The reports pointed out that the problem was not racial or religious but socio-economic and sometimes political, and suggested urgent deployment of funds in order to help Polish Jewry out of its crippling poverty, and education to lead it out of its almost medieval condition of obscurantism.[17]

Neither of these reports had, however, been published when, at a plenary session of the Conference on 31 May, Wilson's draft clauses

193

were put to the delegates of the countries in question. They referred
to all minorities, in certain cases singling out the Jews for special
attention, and they guaranteed social and religious equality as well
as a wide range of educational, cultural and social service to be provided by the state The whole tenor of these original drafts is
summed up in one clause, which specified that the teaching language in Jewish schools paid for by the Polish state must be Yid-
dish, while Polish could be taught as a second language. As Paderewski pointed out, the state was on the one hand being ordered
to regard the Jews and Germans as ordinary Polish citizens, and at
the same time to make every effort to turn them into aliens unable
to speak the national language properly.

The delegates of most European states refused even to consider
these clauses. Paderewski got up and spoke, reiterating some of the
arguments he had placed before Lloyd Geoerge in a long memorandum a few days before. He asserted to thoses present that over the
centuries Poland had a record of racial and religious toleration which
far outshone that of any other country represented, including Great
Britain and the United States. For centuries Poland had given
shelter to Jews expelled from every other country in Europe, and
had, as a result, greater experience in dealing with a large Jewish
minority than Western liberals who had once sat next to a Rothschild at dinner. Poland was, he declared, fully aware of her re-
sponsibilities in this field, and one of the first acts of the newly
constituted Sejm had been to appoint a special commission to study
ways of helping the Jewish minority adjust to the new situation.
Finally, he was most insistent that by taking the problem out of
the hands of the respective governments and by making it an issue
of international debate in the League of Nations, the Conference
would be sinning against the sovereignty of the countries in question, preventing the German and Jewish minorities from ever becoming normal citizens of their new countries, and automatically
turning each and every state in Eastern Europe into a miniature
Balkans begging for foreign intervention on some pretext of protect-
ing a downtrodden minority.

It was a fine speech, and it was fitting that it should be the
pragmatic idealist Paderewski who showed up the nebulous nature
of Woodrow Wilson's Samaritan instincts. Just to drive his point

home, Paderewski concluded that for his part he would be happy to sign the treaties as they stood on the sole condition that every single country represented did so as well. It was a neat way of asking why there should be one law for the Polish Jew and another for the American black or the Indian of the British Empire; for, naturally, the Allies had not the slightest intention of emancipating their own minorities to the same degree. As Harold Nicolson mused in his corner, "The Anglo-Saxon is gifted with a limitless capacity for excluding his own practical requirements from the application of the idealistic theories which he seeks to impose upon others."[18]

Paderewski's arguments convinced Lloyd George and also Clemenceau, who needed little convincing—the French, with their highly assimilated Jewry, were entirely out of sympathy with the spirit of the treaties. Most of the participants were for dropping the whole project of the treaties altogether, but Woodrow Wilson stuck to his guns. This led some to suspect that, in the words of Headlam-Morley, he was guided "much more by the vote of the New York Jews than by the real advantages to be won for the Jews in Poland,"[19] which was to misunderstand the American President completely; in such cases he was guided not by political cunning but by breathtaking political innocence. As he explained to the Conference, America would send her armies to defend countries like Poland and Roumania when they were attacked, but she would not be able to do so if she felt that the regimes of those countries were not founded on absolute justice.[20]

Wilson could not know that America would never join the League of Nations, that she would retire into isolation and that she would not lift a finger to defend Poland or any other East European country when it came to war. But, had he been less naïve, he would have realized that America would not, any more than other countries, impose standards of virtue on governments she found it expedient to support militarily. This was not, however, how Wilson's mind worked, and although Paderewski and his colleagues had managed to ridicule the original drafts of the Minority Treaties, he could not be induced to give them up.

As far as Wilson was concerned, a principle was at stake. Paderewski saw that there was nothing to be gained by meeting obstinacy with obstinacy, particularly since he was at the mercy of

American aid, and he therefore agreed to sign a watered-down version of the treaties. He was followed by Greece and Czechoslovakia, and then the other states of Central Europe. In their ultimate form, the treaties did not amount to much more than an irritant and an insult, but their very existence was eloquent proof of the poor bargaining position of the client nations and, at the same time, of the inconsequence of the proceedings. Germany, for instance, was not asked to sign them, which meant that Germans in Poland were to enjoy rights and advantages that Poles in Germany would not.

A nice example of this inconsequence is provided by the decision on reparations. Notwithstanding the fact that Poland had suffered greater destruction at the hands of Germany than any other country with the possible exception of Belgium it was decided that she did not qualify for reparations from Germany because part of Poland had been on the German side. On the other hand, it was also thought to be true that Poland had been part of Russia, and therefore qualified to pay a proportion of Russia's war debt to France and Great Britain—a case of "Heads I win, tails you lose."

Paderewski could not hope to defy the Allies on matters directly affecting them. When they wanted something, they took it, and while it was possible to play them off against one another up to a point, little could be achieved by it. It was different on questions in which they had no direct interest, and here Paderewski and Dmowski were more successful. The Lithuanians had early on staked a claim to the city of Wilno and the surrounding countryside on historical and ethnic grounds. Poland was determined to have the city for herself, since it had a large Polish majority and had been tightly bound up with Polish history in the last five hundred years. The area was soon invaded by the Russian Bolsheviks, and Pilsudski decided to capture it. He coordinated the move with Paderewski, who provided a covering smoke-screen and explanations in Paris and eventually managed to get the Allies to accept the *fait accompli*.

A similar situation arose with regard to eastern Galicia. This western part of the Ukraine had been Polish since the fourteenth century, but about sixty percent of the population were Ruthenians. These were mostly spread over the countryside, while the Poles and the Jews were concentrated in the towns. As a result, it was impossible to divide the province, particularly since even the available figures were unreliable and, as one historian put it, the ethnographic boundaries ran down the middle of conjugal beds. The Ruthenians wanted to join an independent Ukraine which emerged in 1918, only to founder several months later, and therefore tried to take over the whole province after the Armistice. The local Poles defended their areas, and particularly the city of Lwow, to relieve which Warsaw sent all available troops.

The Allies, and particularly the British, who were under the impression that the Ruthenians were the same as Russians, demanded a ceasefire and insisted that the Poles evacuate the whole province. They reinforced their demands by holding back the Polish army in France, which was supposed to be shipped to Poland, and when they did eventually let it go, they stipulated that it must not be used in Galicia. Paderewski was in complete agreement with Pilsudski that in this case Poland must pursue what she felt to be the right policy regardless of the Allies. Paderewski therefore fenced in Paris in order to cover the continued advance of the Polish army, including the contingents which had arrived from France under General Haller. He would send urgent messages to the Polish commanders in the field to stop fighting and withdraw to certain lines every time the Allies demanded it, but the messages would fail to get through, the lines would be misunderstood and local commanders carried on regardless. When taxed with his failure to stop the Polish relief columns, Paderewski would use various excuses, including the one that he had little authority over the military, and that if he tried to impose his will, he might provoke a confrontation which would topple his government. By the summer of 1919 the Poles had the whole area under their control, and the French and the Americans were disposed to let them keep it, particularly as the rest of the Ukraine had by now fallen to the Bolsheviks. The British did not like the idea at all, and, faced by the Polish refusal to evacuate, suggested that Poland be given a twenty-five-year mandate over the area, after which time the League of Nations could decide its future. Paderewski questioned this and managed to put off any decision on the subject for several months. By stalling skillfully he eventually managed to get the

British to drop this proposal, and the entire province was left to Poland unconditionally.

Although he could not point to many such victories, Paderewski was a good negotiator, and, as Wilson himself wrote, "no country could wish for a better advocate."[21] Jules Cambon, the French diplomat and head of the Committee on Polish Affairs, stated categorically that "nobody could have done better in Paris than Paderewski."[22] This is probably true; while he could not hope to exert any real pressure, he could, and did soften whatever blows were coming by having his way on questions of detail, as well as cover Pilsudski's moves on the eastern frontier.

Paderewski's manner in presenting his case or defending his standpoint were universally admired, and in Lloyd George's words, "he developed oratorical powers of a high order,"[23] while Harold Nicolson found his speech always "tactful and sonorous" and convincing.[24] It was his moderation and evident honesty which made people listen and take note, as Robert Lansing, the American Secretary of State, explains:

> Ignace Paderewski was a greater statesman than he was a musician, he was an able and tactful leader of his countrymen and a sagacious diplomat. Nearly everything that he said and nearly everything that he did seemed to be the right thing. He made few mistakes and he never seemed to be in doubt as to the course which he should take. He was wonderfully resourceful and apparently had an instinctive sense of the possible and the practicable. He held his imagination in leash as he did his emotions. He was not carried away with extravagant hopes or unrealizable dreams. His views were essentially sane and logical.[25]

Unfortunately, these qualities were of little avail at meetings of the Council of Four like that held in Wilson's house on 5 June, to which Paderewski had been called. When he came in he was told that it had been decided the future status of Upper Silesia would be settled by plebiscite, and was asked whether he had anything to say. He restated his case, once again asking where was the logic of holding a plebiscite; but he was cut short by Lloyd

George, who had made up his mind and did not want to hear any more about it. On such occasions he was wont to improvise arguments which do not always bear examination, and, on this one he reproached Paderewski with being "ungrateful." He then explained, to everyone's astonishment, that a million and a half Frenchmen, a million Britons, half a million Italians and hundreds of thousands of Americans had laid down their lives in the cause of Poland's independence. He also delivered himself of a tirade against Paderewski on the subject of Galicia, in which he accused Poland and the other small nations of being more imperialistic than the Great Powers. This pained him personally, he continued, because he himself was, in his own words, "a man who had fought all his life for little nations."[26]

Paderewski must have been itching to ask Lloyd George what his government was doing in Ireland at that very moment, but a pupil does not talk of motes and beams to his master unless he wishes to be expelled. Paderewski found these encounters, in which his carefully constructed arguments were dashed by the ebullient humbug of the British Prime Minister, intensely painful and nervously exhausting, and he was grateful that the moment of signing the treaty with Germany was drawing near. Dmowski was inclined to agree that only this would, as he put it, "call a halt to the victorious progress of the British Premier and his conquests on behalf of Germany."[27]

On 28 June 1919 Paderewski and Dmowski drove to Versailles. There were troops and flags along the whole way; the long avenue leading up to the palace was lined on either side with French cavalry in shining breast-plates and plumed helmets, and behind them was a crowd twenty deep straining to spot the personalities as they drove past. Paderewski's head was instantly recognized and there were cheers for him and for Poland as they passed.

When they arrived at the palace, they mounted the staircase and were shown to their seats in the great Hall of Mirrors. At a large table in the centre sat Georges Clemenceau, flanked by Lloyd George and Woodrow Wilson; Vittorio Orlando and Baron Makino of Japan also sat at the table, while the delegates of other countries were ranged along the side of the room. In the window embrasure opposite the table, official artists were busily making sketches for monumental paintings which would be consigned with time to some undistinguished corner in a ministry or a museum.

When all the delegates were in place, the doors opened and the two representatives of defeated Germany were ushered in. Originally it was intended that nobody was to rise for them, but, true to his gentlemanly nature, Balfour had objected and insisted that everyone show them due respect. They signed the great document on behalf of their country, after which the representatives of the Great Powers signed, followed by a long stream of other delegates. As the guns boomed in the park outside, Paderewski and Dmowski came up to the table and appended their signatures and seals to the Treaty.

It was a great moment for the little boy who had dreamt of helping his country, but it was not a happy one. The Conference was by no means over, and this first act augured ill for the remaining negotiations. The whole peacemaking process had, in spite of much wisdom and the best intentions, gone seriously wrong. The highest ideals had been invoked, but they had been cast aside as unsuitable; their place was taken not by disinterested pragmatism but by mere bargaining. The Conference had aroused hopes which it could in no way fulfil, and the result was, in Lansing's words, "in one sense a farce, but in another it was a tragedy."[28] The last word on the Versailles Treaty must, however, go to the anonymous French wit who sententiously declared that it contained "all the elements of a just and durable war."

CHAPTER XIII

Fall from Grace

"The signing of these historic documents did not come easily to us," said Paderewski to the Foreign Affairs Commission of the Sejm on 24 July.[1] He now faced the unenviable task of having to persuade the Sejm to ratify the Treaty, which would not be easy, since he could point to no real victories. The fate of Danzig and Upper Silesia was uncertain, Teschen was in deadlock, while the Minority Treaties and the clauses on reparations looked to the man in the street like insults to his country. As the American Minister in Warsaw summed it up, Poland was given "only that part of the country that had been devastated by years of war and was incapable of supporting its own population."[2] Not the least of Paderewski's achievements was that he managed to get the Treaty ratified, by a majority of over seven to one, on 31 July. This triumph could not, however, obscure the fact that his administration faced a serious crisis.

Paderewski had fulfilled a definite need during the first six months of 1919. As a trusted non-party figure, he had helped to defuse tension, and the state had been able to begin to function in an atmosphere free of party strife. Only with Paderewski as Premier could this ceasefire have lasted as long as it did. The left had accepted him because it thought he had magical powers of influencing the Allies; the right had seen in him a saviour because he could keep the left quiet in this way. The unfavourable terms secured in Paris had, inevitably, destroyed a great deal of his credibility, and now the left began to look at him more critically, while the right began to feel that he had let it down. Both still trusted him, but they began to criticize his government on more tangible grounds, and both saw that his usefulness had to some extent run out.

His government had achieved various objectives. It had helped to master the chaos reigning at the beginning of the year and to bring in food and supplies in sufficient quantity to safeguard the population. It had organized and presided over the elections, put in progress the work of framing a constitution and set up the basic machinery of state. By the summer of 1919 there was, for all to see, a European democracy rising out of the no-man's-land of mud and barbed wire that had been Poland.

It was at this point that Paderewski's government lost both its impetus and its sense of direction. Neither the Premier nor his cabinet, which was in truth neither a coalition nor a government of experts in the strict sense, had any policy other than the policy of rebuilding Poland. Once this had been achieved in essence, they were faced with pressing problems which they had not the equipment to solve.

Agrarian reform was essential, and the strong peasant parties were vociferous in their demands for it. This was a question involving political issues of fundamental import as well as economic ones, and since Paderewski had no strong feelings on the subject, he designated a commission to enquire into the problem, without himself making any significant statement.

Finances were another maze in which he blundered helplessly, as might be expected from his personal financial record. At first he had wanted to bring in American experts to sort out the fiscal chaos and to work out economic policy for the country as a whole, but this came to nothing, and after a couple of months he appointed Leon Bilinski Minister of Finances. Bilinski was eminently qualified, since he had for many years been Finance Minister of the Habsburg Empire—whose economic problems were second to none in their intricacy and diversity.

Bilinski could hardly believe the chaos he found at the Treasury. No attempt had been made to solve the currency problem, while government spending was so unregulated that it was impossible to assess and therefore budget. The reason for this was that in the fever of improvisation every ministry purchased essentials as it needed them, without consulting the Treasury. Paderewski himself had set the example: from the beginning there had been critical shortages of everything, and he had followed the line that certain things—clothing, agricultural equipment, railway engines and so on—must be acquired immediately, simply to get the country moving. This was fair enough, but he acted on his own initiative, making deals either personally, when he was in Paris or London on Conference business, or through agents who were not always government employees. It was also not apparent that he had always bought on the most favourable terms.

When Bilinski taxed him with this, Paderewski insisted that all the deals had been of the utmost urgency, which was why he had not consulted with the Treasury. Petulantly, he stated that he would be glad to make up the difference out of his own pocket if Bilinski could prove that any purchase could have been made cheaper. The Minister tried to explain that this was not the point, and that he had no wish to call into question Paderewski's probity, merely that certain procedures must be observed if the finances were to be tidied up. But the two men did not like each other, and while the Minister quibbled over details, the Premier accused him of trying to introduce "Austrian systems."

Paderewski was not cut out for the day-to-day business of political life. As one of his colleagues noted, "he had kept a childlike trust in the goodness and goodwill of people, which is no help to a politician."[3] He could not understand the lust for power in others or the compulsion to be partisan which is such a frequent feature of party politics. He was occupying the post of Premier not because he wanted power or status but because he was convinced that it was his duty, as he was the man Poland needed just then. This had certainly been true, but it was growing less so as the summer wore on. What the country needed now was a lucid politician with a clear policy and enough cunning to carry it through.

He was also temperamentally unsuited to cope with his position. For the past thirty years he had been the most important person in his own world; he was the one who forced himself to tour and play in order to support the small entourage which had grown around him. That entourage had inevitably accorded itself to his hours, his potential for work and his need for rest, and this had affected his attitudes and habits, which he was incapable of shedding in his new position. So, while he worked extremely hard, he was not attuned to the timetables of others, and he was often late, sometimes hours late, for conferences or meetings called by himself. If pressing matters came up, he would make time for them at the expense of others, and as a result some were put off endlessly or never dealt with at all.[4]

This gave the impression of chaos, and even negligence on his part. The political situation in Poland was delicate, and Paderewski was not as tactful as he might have been. His tendency to bring in foreigners—the project to import American financial experts, and the successful one of getting British policemen to train the new Polish force—were taken as insults in certain quarters. The implication that the Poles could not do these things for themselves was not flattering.

Paderewski also showed lack of sensitivity in his choice of abode. He had originally taken up residence in the Bristol, but soon moved to the Royal Castle. This was a logical step, since the Castle had always been the seat of government as well as the royal residence, but at this particular moment it laid him open to charges of giving himself airs and, inevitably, to jokes of one sort or another. Bilinski noted with ill-concealed venom that "the anterooms pullulated with sentries, servants, aides-de-camp and secretaries as though it were the residence of a monarch."[5]

His image was not improved by the behaviour of Helena. She had always been obsessed with ministering to his needs, both physical and psychological, and now, in spite of being busy with her own causes, she managed to surround him with her care as with a fence. She encouraged his irregularity, insisting he take a nap when he needed one rather than go to a meeting at which he was required. While he was taking his nap she would intercept messages and cables, often opening them to see how urgent they were. It was not long before she began to censor them if she wished to spare him irritation; if she did not think them important, she would put them in her pocket and, as often as not, forget all about them, with the result that papers which were hunted for all over a ministry were finally tracked down in Helena's laundry.

When she felt a meeting had gone on long enough, she seldom hesitated before coming in to break it up. One politician remembers a cabinet meeting during which she came into the room without knocking, sat down on the arm of Paderewski's chair, started stroking his forehead and said: "Give my poor husband a break now . . . you all tire the poor thing out so much; and do you propose to go on for long, gentlemen?"[6]

Apart from being irritating and making everyone's life difficult, this sort of thing tended to make Paderewski look ridiculous, particularly as Helena insisted on calling him by endearing nicknames and diminutives. Those who saw the Premier of Poland descending the staircase of the Ritz on his way to sign the Treaty of Versailles might well laugh when his wife screeched, "Iniuniu, my little animal —have you taken your scarf? It's cold today!"[7] Her behaviour was marked by total absence of self-consciousness, as was the way she dressed. Harold Nicolson saw her with Paderewski one night at the Opéra and thought she looked "like Hell in orchids."[8] She was usually swathed in clothes that might have been fashionable some twenty years before, had they been made to fit her. With her shapeless hats and drooping shawls, the look of the exhausted prima donna on her face and a yapping Pekingese clasped to her sagging bosom, she was the obvious butt for jokes and caricatures of the most vicious kind.

The reason the satire was vicious was that many people believed her to be actively meddling in the affairs of state. "It was really Madame Paderewska who ruled Poland, on behalf of or through her husband," wrote Bilinski.[9] Although his is an extravagant view, it was of the kind which stuck in the popular imagination. There was a joke going round Warsaw that Paderewski and Pilsudski would hold conferences while one of them was in the bath—the only method of safeguarding themselves from her intrusions. Some time later, when Dmowski was asked what concessions Paderewski would have to make in order to render their collaboration possible, he answered without any hesitation: "Poison Mrs. Paderewska!"[10]

She refused to abdicate any part of her husband to public life. She was also open to the flattery of sycophants and surrounded herself with what looked like a camarilla of dubious characters. Both Paderewski's secretary, Strakacz, and the American Pole Orlowski were—wrongly, as it happens—seen as her minions, and neither was liked.

She was the victim of much of the frustration felt with the government, and Paderewski resented this aspect of it. "What hurts me most of all is that they do not spare my wife," he said to the deputy Rataj with tears in his eyes. "She is the most wonderful person who has devoted herself entirely to helping those in need. It is cruel. Barbaric. Let them attack me, but let them leave my wife alone."[11] He was still, however, the object of widespread respect, and his wife was therefore fixed on as the scapegoat.

There was certainly need for one, as the government was growing daily more unpopular. The Minister for Home Affairs, Wojciechowski, had resigned, followed by Paderewski's own deputy at the Foreign Ministry, Count Skrzynski. In October, Bilinski withdrew from the government, giving his reasons to the press. They were not calculated to inspire confidence in the government.

Since his government was visibly falling apart, there seemed little point to Paderewski remaining in office, and people expected him to resign at any moment that autumn. Every time there was a crisis, however, he rose to the occasion. He was no great polemical speaker, but he was very good at improvising a fine speech which would defuse the problem and call everyone back to order. Working ever later into the night, smoking cigarette after cigarette, he soldiered on in the belief that the moment demanded it of him. He felt strongly that nobody else could serve the cause as effectively as he at the Peace Conference, which was dragging on month after month. This made life even more difficult for him, as he was continually flitting between Warsaw, Paris and London.

The Treaty of St. Germain, between Austria, the Allies and all the surrounding nations, was signed on 10 September 1919. Poland was given back all the lands taken by the Habsburgs in the Partitions—except of course for the areas in dispute between her and Czechoslovakia. This left, as far as Poland was concerned, only the deferred questions of Danzig and Upper Silesia, as well as the whole eastern frontier, to be dealt with.

The question of a frontier with Russia was ostensibly something to be solved by the two countries involved, but it was complicated by incoherent and indecisive Allied interference in the affairs of Russia. Paderewski had opened negotiations with the Bolsheviks as early as February 1919, but the Allies, particularly the French, supported the White Armies of Denikin and Kolchak, and therefore wanted Poland to make war on the Bolsheviks rather than negotiate with them. Paderewski and the Poles were entirely out of sympathy with the White cause, and in May the Polish Premier told Winston Churchill, the most sanguine partisan of that cause in Britain, that he was not inclined to support it. Churchill insisted that he should, and Paderewski immediately perceived a potential bargaining-point; Great Britain might be induced to pay for Polish participation by adopting a more favourable attitude on Danzig and other matters. Unfortunately, Lloyd George was no more consistent on this issue than on many others, and when Paderewski asked him in London that summer what he expected Poland to do, he answered that he did not know. When Paderewski insisted that the Polish Army must have a definite order to advance or hang back, he answered: "Go ahead and advance, then!" a suggestion forcefully endorsed by Churchill. By the time the Poles did advance, Lloyd George had changed his mind and blamed them for starting a war.[12]

On 10 November the question of eastern Galicia came up once again at a meeting of the Supreme Council in Paris, and while the French and Americans suggested that the Poles be allowed to keep it unconditionally, Lloyd George insisted on his scheme of a mandate, which was provisionally accepted by the others.

News of this reached Warsaw on the following day, and Paderewski was taxed with it in the Sejm on 12 November. He parried with a long speech pervaded with a tone of resignation which reflected his own exhaustion, but there was heckling from the left. The socialist Daszynski called for Paderewski's resignation, trying to soften the blow by referring to him as "a noble man and a devoted citizen" and explaining that "Mr. Paderewski doesn't know how to govern and has no plan; I would offer him all the flowers in Poland if only he were not sitting in the Premier's chair, calmly watching the misfortunes raining down on this country!"[13]

Paderewski called for a vote of confidence in his government, which was passed. Again the storm had been weathered, but the barque of the government was taking water at an alarming rate. It was now obvious to all, even to Paderewski, that he was expected to resign.

On 18 November Hugh Gibson, the American Minister in Warsaw, called at the Castle and found Paderewski writing his letter of resignation. When the Premier explained his motives, Gibson refuted them, feeling that he "somewhat exaggerates the power of the opposition," and, in his own words, "confiscated" the letter. He managed to convince Paderewski that he was seeing things too black, and that if he resigned, the United States would lose confidence in Poland, with disastrous results for the country's economic and diplomatic future.[14]

This was the sort of argument which could be counted on to rally Paderewski. If he was the only person who could save the situation, then he would endure. Gibson called on him virtually every day to give him courage, which he certainly needed. Wacio Gorski had had a dream in which Paderewski was assassinated and told his mother about it; Helena's reaction verged on the hysterical, as she insisted alternately that they should all flee and that they should fight to the end. Paderewski himself felt deserted and betrayed. With his fall now imminent, people began to drift away from him. This was hardly surprising, since, never having belonged to a party, he could count on no party loyalty. The groups which had supported him had to look to their own political future, and there was clearly none for the existing government.

As the sense of uncertainty and anticipation mounted—Gibson described the situation in a report to his government as "a whirling maze of wheels within wheels, with everybody working in half-knowledge and at cross-purposes"[15]—Paderewski felt his presence to be more necessary than ever. When in the last week of November his cabinet resigned, hoping to force his hand, he accepted their resignation and instantly set about trying to form a new government. He talked to various groups and parties, but everyone was non-committal, since certain parties would be prepared to join him only if others did. Participation in a weak Paderewski government at this stage would be fatal to any party.

On 4 December Paderewski finally gave up and sent his own resignation to Pilsudski. On hearing the news, for which some of the parties were presumably not prepared, the Sejm passed a vote of confidence in him, with the Jewish party dramatically tilting the scales at the last minute. On 6 December Pilsudski therefore wrote back, asking him to form a new government. But it was no good; he could not collect a convincing cabinet, so he sent in his resignation once more on 10 December. This time it was accepted.

It was a sad and undignified ending to Paderewski's Premiership, which could have ended two weeks before in a far more elegant manner. It now looked as though he had been forcibly ejected. Much of the blame can be attached to the Americans in general and Gibson in particular. With the best intentions, they had got things hopelessly wrong. One needs only to look at two statements made a little later to see just how wrong. Colonel House declared that "had [Paderewski] been more ambitious and less patriotic and unselfish, he might have continued in power and become an autocrat."[16] Herbert Hoover, who might have been better informed, saw Paderewski's resignation in a more fantastic light. "It was with rare moral courage that he made this momentous decision," he wrote, apparently unaware that Paderewski had fought hard to hang on, "without complaining, refusing to take advantage of the military arm that could have preserved him and his colleagues in office."[17]

Paderewski did complain. He felt that Poland had been "ungrateful," and when some of the parties sent representatives to thank him for his Premiership and his services to the country, he received them almost rudely. When the new government of Skulski sent two delegates to ask him if he would accept the post of Foreign Minister, he indignantly explained that he would not do another thing for a country which had treated him so shabbily.

He did have a point. As the deputy Rataj later admitted:

I was, to a certain extent, instrumental in his downfall. Looking back on it from the perspective of years, I must say that the methods used to bring him down, the brutality shown towards a citizen of great stature and the best intentions, went too far. Paderewski was quite justified in seeing injustice and wrong in it.[18]

After spending a gloomy and bitter Christmas in Warsaw, Paderewski went to Poznan, where he was welcomed with enthusiasm. On New Year's Day he was back in Warsaw, to be greeted with a demonstration organized by various groups of the centre and right and civic bodies as a token of thanks for his services to the country.

A great many people tried to persuade him to accept the post of Foreign Minister in the new government and to stay on in public life, but he would not. He desperately needed a rest, and Helena had to be taken away from Warsaw, which she had come to detest. He was determined eventually to stage a come-back, and therefore did not resign his seat in the Sejm, and he also financed a newspaper which was to be run by Strakacz and Orlowski as a mouthpiece for his views. But in the short term he felt a need to cut loose and to relax, so he left for Switzerland.

CHAPTER XIV

The Elder Statesman

The neat opulence of Switzerland was refreshing after the squalor of war-torn Poland, but the greatest attraction of being back at Riond-Bosson was that Paderewski could forget all about political strife and resume a position to which his right was unquestioned. From now on his entourage referred to him as "the President,"* and if the house had resembled a small court before, it now became a real Versailles.

Paderewski was, more than ever, the *Roi Soleil*. His features had gained in nobility, his bearing in majesty. The golden mane had turned to silver, and he usually dressed in a white or cream suit, white tie and even white shoes; the effect was no longer sunny— it was dazzling. Helena was the perfect Maintenon: weary yet exalted, her spirit pervading the house. Her adulation of the great man set the tone, and this was observed by the courtiers, of whom there was a growing number.

The household and the servants were marshalled, as before, by Paderewski's sister, Antonina, while Helena concentrated on her own little court. This included the secretary she had brought from Warsaw, Helena Liibke, and a selection of widowed or otherwise desolate ladies who came for periods of varying length and some-

* Paderewski's official title while in office had been "President of the Council of Ministers." Since the style of "President" usually corresponds to the Head of State, it has been thought more correct to refer to him as "Premier," which designates precisely the function he fulfilled.

211

times settled. The girls from Poland again descended upon the place to study poultry-rearing, and the house gradually filled up with women—a great congregation with little else to do but plot intrigues and worship Paderewski.

In addition, there were the old regulars, who would stay for indefinite periods and quite settle into the life of the place. One such was Wacio Gorski, who would turn up with his wife, usually when he had run out of money. The ever-devoted Laurence Alma-Tadema would also arrive for long periods, armed with her own victual of herbs and nuts—she had lately become obsessed with her "metabolism." Another occasional and eventually permanent inhabitant was Paderewski's secretary Sylwin Strakacz, often accompanied by his wife and little daughter. He was a curious man who inspired trust and love in the master to whom he was utterly devoted, and fear or jealousy in others.

Riond-Bosson was a weird combination of Paderewski's tastes caricatured and of Helena's, which were often caricatures in themselves. It was compounded with a lack of self-consciousness and a certain naïveté which sometimes laid it open to ridicule. Many found the atmosphere intimidating and were afraid to open their mouths in the divine presence, so revered was it by the household. Fortunately, the divine presence usually dispelled the semi-religious atmosphere itself; as before, Paderewski wanted gaiety and laughter around him, and he had an arsenal of jokes, both verbal and practical—exploding cigars, musical decanters and so on—to help him. In the evenings he would either put on records and hold impromptu dances in the vast hall, or else take all his guests off to the cinema in Lausanne. He adored films and was totally uncritical of what he saw. Although he showed a preference for Westerns, which he called "horse-operas," and Charlie Chaplin films, he would absorb the most inane love-story, becoming so emotionally involved that he was miserable if it ended in tragedy.

The coming and going at Riond-Bosson never ceased. Apart from those who came for longer periods—mostly the same people as before, for he was constant in his friendships—a stream of visitors came from nearby, and they were always royally treated. The celebrations on St. Ignatius' day were more lavish than ever, and the amusements sometimes unexpected. On one occasion the American composer Ernest Schelling, who lived near at hand and was one of Paderewski's closest friends, was in charge of the entertainments. Hearing that Arthur Honegger was to be present, he put on a performance of Honegger's *Pacific 231* suite with an orchestra consisting of a piano, several typewriters, boxes of broken crockery and two garden hoses.[1]

Paderewski's initial holiday at Riond-Bosson did not last very long. In the summer of 1920 the Red Army broke through and advanced rapidly on Warsaw, proclaiming its intention of abolishing the Polish state and spreading world revolution. The bugle call was unmistakable, and Paderewski wrote to Witos, the Prime Minister in the recently formed government of national unity, offering his services. By return he was named Polish delegate to the League of Nations and, more important, to the Conference of Ambassadors, which was the continuation of the Peace Conference.

He set off for Spa in Germany, where the Conference was meeting, but on his arrival he found that there was literally nothing for him to do. The Polish Foreign Minister had recently been there, begging to buy the arms and ammunition which the army so badly needed, and Lloyd George had forced him to sign, in return for the supply of these, an undertaking that Poland would unconditionally accept all future Allied rulings on the outstanding disputes. The Allies promptly decided to give most of Teschen to the Czechs, and all Paderewski could do was protest weakly as he signed away the area.

While the crisis in Poland subsided with Pilsudski's dramatic victory at the gates of Warsaw, Paderewski presided over the final perversion by the Allies of the original idea of creating a strong Poland. Most of Upper Silesia went to Germany, and the whole of south-western East Prussia as well; the narrow stretch of coast which Poland was left was now connected to the rest of the country by a thin strip of land running between the two Germanies; that haunting monstrosity, the Polish Corridor, had been created. Danzig was constituted a Free City, which meant that Poland had to build a port of her own in the interests of security. What might have been in 1939 had Paderewski's suggestions been put into effect is impossible to tell, but what did happen was directly related to the fact that they had been disregarded. The Free City of Danzig was a standing

invitation to German annexation, while the narrowness of the corridor made the seaboard indefensible for the Poles; their lifeline
could be and was cut within a matter of hours. The decisions on
Teschen and Silesia deprived Poland of the two richest parts of the
country and of over a million of her people, and seriously retarded
her economic development. Worst of all, as far as Paderewski was
concerned, the humiliating and aggravating treatment meted out to
them by the Allies in the first two years of their independence had
convinced the majority of Poles that Great Britain, France and
America were not their friends, and this was to have far-reaching
and unfortunate effects on the development of Poland's internal
and external policies.

On 14 December 1920 Paderewski sent in his resignation as Polish
delegate to the Conference. He was terminally disillusioned with the
Allies, and he did not understand the policies of the government
in Warsaw. There seemed little point in carrying on this thankless
task. In the letter of resignation he wrote that he would "sincerely
like to quit everything which involves Polish politics,"[2] but he stayed
on as Poland's delegate to the League of Nations.

This should have been an ideal niche for his personality, his
talents and his kind of idealism, not to mention the fact that Geneva
was conveniently close to Riond-Bosson. But, as he explained in a
letter to Lansing, he derived no pleasure from working there. He
felt the League missed the point of its establishment; as it had no
power, it could at best be a forum for one clique of nations to em-
barrass another.[3] So disillusioned was he with it that on 7 May
1921 he resigned this post, too.

Still he hovered on the brink of Polish politics. He had many
supporters in the country, and the various parties of the right and
centre needed a popular figurehead. The National People's Union
wanted him to stand as their candidate at the next elections, and
there were attempts to build a common platform with the National
Democrats, the Christian Democrats and the National Workers'
Party. At one stage even Dmowski was prepared to consider serving
under Paderewski.[4]

Paderewski was cautious, as he did not want to see a repetition
of his previous experiences. He had never wanted to be a politician

in the usual sense of the word, only to serve his country by using his position and influence. He had certainly helped her cause during the Great War, and there were ways in which he could help her now, if only the right niche could be found for him. If he merely formed a government, he would be dragged once again into party politics, for which he had no interest and no aptitude, and again he would fall ignominiously. The ideal situation would have been one in which he could adopt a Presidential role to a strong government with a definite programme. He could have provided that government with the spiritual authority which he still inspired in Poland and abroad, and he could have played a decisive part in securing for Poland a suitable position on the international scene.

His views on foreign policy showed not only vision but sense as well, as can be gleaned from a set of guidelines he issued, while still in power, to all Polish representatives abroad.[5] He felt that Poland's future prosperity and security were possible only if a working relationship could be developed with Russia, Bolshevik or not. On the one hand, he argued that Poland must enjoy friendly relations with at least one of her major neighbours, and, on the other, he stressed that all the heavy industry in Poland had been geared to markets within the Russian Empire before 1914. It was only by seeking out the same markets that these industries could thrive. Finally, he warned that if Poland turned her back on Russia as she had done in the seventeenth and eighteenth centuries, Russia would be thrown into the arms of Germany, as had happened then with disastrous rsults. He felt that the chaotic state of Russia was, as he wrote to Lansing in February 1922, "a tremendous wound in the body of mankind."[6] At the same time he believed that Poland should make every effort to bind her fate more closely to Great Britain, France and the United States, however much they might have failed her at the Conference.

Whether it would have been possible for Poland to develop a relationship with the Soviet Republic is difficult to tell, but in the early 1920s there was a chance worth trying for. Had Paderewski's ideas been tried and found to work, the consequences for not only Poland but the whole world would have been incalculable. On the other hand, had Poland developed closer ties with the Western

Powers, she might have enjoyed more rapid economic growth, and she would certainly have been less of a pawn in Hitler's and Stalin's games.

Nothing, however, came of Paderewski's political plans. As in so many other European countries, the political scene in Poland of the early 1920s was characterized by bickering among a multitude of small parties and a succession of fragile coalitions. There was no place for someone like Paderewski in such turbulent conditions, and he had the sense to appreciate this. In 1924 he sold his newspaper to Wojciech Korfanty of the Christian Democrats and cut himself off from politics altogether.

By the beginning of the 1920s Paderewski's financial situation had become critical. He had earned nothing since 1917, and his life as a statesman had been ruinously expensive. His investments had not yielded enough during the war for the upkeep of Riond-Bosson and the Rancho San Ignacio at Paso Robles in California, which was, in his own words, "another gold-mine—a mine you pour gold into";[7] oil had been struck on every other estate in the area, but Paderewski's boring yielded not a drop. Somehow he must raise money—and he naturally began to think of where he had come by it before. Although it was only five years since he had last touched a piano, it felt like a long time, and the very thought of approaching one filled him with horror. He had never missed his playing during those years, and had found that "it is more exciting to speak than to play." When he went to a concert to hear a young pianist, he felt "no longing for piano-playing."[8]

One day in May 1922, while he was taking a holiday at Paso Robles after retiring from the League of Nations, Paderewski opened his piano and tried to do some finger exercises. To his surprise, he found his hands in much better shape than when he had stopped playing, so he carried on. Being Paderewski, he did not break himself in gently with a protracted flirtation *vis-à-vis* the instrument; he immediately embarked on a gruelling schedule of twelve hours of ruthless exercising a day. After only three weeks of this he felt very fit and started to prepare a programme. Six weeks later he cabled his erstwhile American manager suggesting a tour.[9] The manager jumped at the idea, as Paderewski was bound to be

a box-office sensation whatever happened—and most people expected the worst.

By the autumn he was ready. "I felt not only very familiar
with my instrument, in spite of those many years spent in complete
separation from the piano, but I was more certain of my means,
more master of my nerves, than ever before," he wrote.[10] This
was just as well, as the first concert, on 22 November 1922 at Carnegie
Hall, promised to be an unnerving moment.

The hall was packed with old admirers praying that he would
come up to their remembered expectations, and others who had
come mainly to see whether the ex-Premier would make a fool of
himself. All the leading pianists in New York at the time came to
see what would happen, including Osip Gabrilowitsch, Jozef Hofmann and Alfred Cortot, while the critics sat wondering what they
might be called upon to describe. When Paderewski appeared on
the platform, the entire audience got to its feet in silence; to them
he had become a quasi-royal personage. Then they sat down and
held their breath.

"I think I played better than ever before," wrote Paderewski[11]
—and so did the audience. When he finished, there was an extraordinary standing ovation, extraordinary even by his standards.
The critic Henry Finck declared that it was the most thrilling moment of his life. Osip Gabrilowitsch turned to him and said: "We
had better all become Premiers, and then come back to music!"[12]
The French pianist Francis Planté promptly dubbed Paderewski
"Nôtre grand chef à tous."[13]

Some of the critics pointed to faults—confusion and lack of clearness in some passages, the old tendency to force the tone of the
instrument, exaggerated pedalling that blurred the notes, broken
chords producing cloudiness and, above all, a runaway *tempo
rubato*—but even the most critical were amazed at the scarcity of
wrong notes. Even they noticed that the tone was richer than ever,
the singing quality of the phrases was delivered more exquisitely,
and a new grandeur had crept into his playing.

"I felt that never had I heard such depth of expression, such
richness of phrasing, or such insight into the whole world of music,"
wrote Fuller Maitland. "That he should have reconquered all the
wonderful technique of the past was amazing enough, but it was a

far greater surprise to find that he was on a higher artistic plane than before."[14] Another critic explained that "the fingers turned out to be as skilful as ever, while his playing had gained yet another quality: a calmness and an unclouded peace of soul which had been through suffering, as well as an unbending will that directed his nerves unhesitatingly."[15] One is, of course, led to suspect a certain degree of self-delusion here—the audience and critics knew what he had been through, admired him for it and read traces of it into his playing. Yet the politics had done something for the artist as well as the man, as Paderewski himself explains: "An added authority had come to me. Yes, it was a new authority. It was in a way more satisfactory than I had expected, because really I was—I would not say a greater artist, but I was a more correct player. It is hard to put it into words, but there was, in a sense, a new kind of mastery."[16]

Paderewski had every reason to rejoice. The triumphant tour which followed this debut netted him half a million dollars, which refilled the coffers and announced further income. More important, a position had been regained, and this would enable him to carry on leading the life most congenial to him. He would be able to continue travelling and meeting people, and he would also be able to repay what he considered to be his own and Poland's war debt to the Allied nations.

The first note of this theme had been struck shortly after his New York concert, in December 1922, when he came across Georges Clemenceau. The French ex-Premier complained that he had never had an opportunity of hearing him play. Paderewski instantly arranged for a piano to be delivered to Clemenceau's hotel room and there he gave a private recital to the old Tiger, who sat in his tatty dressing gown and his little cap, "looking just like a *concierge*."[17]

Over the next ten years Paderewski repeatedly toured the Allied countries giving grand charity concerts for their war casualties. In England in 1925 he raised over £4,000 for Earl Haig's British Legion Appeal; in Italy he played for the Orfani di Guerra; in 1924 he played for the Queen of the Belgians' war charity; in the United States he raised $28,600 for the American Legion Fund, thereby becoming the largest single contributor; in 1927 he played for veterans in Australia; in 1928 he again toured all the Allied countries for war charities. In 1933 he was still giving concerts for Foch's appeal in the Hall of Mirrors at Versailles—that same hall in which he had signed the Treaty fourteen years before. Nor did he forget those he felt had made it all possible. In 1931 he erected a monument to Woodrow Wilson in Poznan, and in the following year, one to Colonel House in Warsaw, both at his own expense.

This touring developed into a sort of royal progress, with governments and people paying respect to his remarkable personality. The example was set in May 1924 when he was playing for the Belgian war charity. While in Brussels, Paderewski stayed with the royal family at the palace of Laeken, and when, at the concert, he came on to the platform, the King and Queen rose in their box. It must have been the first time in history that a monarch rose for a performer in the theatre.

In January of the following year, when he went to Rome, he was automatically received by the Pope, the King and Mussolini, with whom he spent "a delightful evening." When in Washington he would stay at the White House with Calvin Coolidge and later the Hoovers. In London he was received by George V and knighted. The Grand Cross of the British Empire, along with the Grand Cordons of the Légion d'Honneur, the Order of Leopold of Belgium and the Italian Order of Saints Maurice and Lazarus, as well as the two highest Polish orders, made him the most decorated pianist there has ever been. Then came the honorary doctorates. He had already been honoured by the universities of Lwow in 1912, Yale in 1917, Cracow in 1919 and Oxford in 1920; these were now joined by Columbia (1922), Southern California (1923), Poznan (1924), Glasgow (1925), Cambridge (1926) and New York (1933). In 1934 he was asked to become Lord Rector of Glasgow University, which he declined. Honorary citizenships jostled with honorary memberships of every conceivable kind of society and club; banquets were held, speeches were made, biographies were written and his name was included in anthologies of "modern immortals" alongside Einstein, Bernard Shaw, Gandhi, Marie Curie and Edison.

Paderewski had found his niche. He was the universal elder statesman as well as the great star, honoured by heads of state and monarchs, adored by literally millions throughout the world. He stayed with the exalted wherever he went; diners rose when he walked into a restaurant; when he went to the cinema, he was cheered; when travelling in America during the years of Prohibition, his railroad car was anonymously stocked with whiskey. The inhabitants of his home town of Morges kept framed photographs of him on their walls; when he returned from his tours, the streets were draped in bunting to greet him. Even though he was no longer involved with either politics or diplomacy, he continued to be a public figure in every sense. He may no longer have been the greatest pianist, but, as one critic put it, he was still the greatest person who was a pianist.

Riond-Bosson reflected his position in a more and more overpowering way as the trophies of his life piled up. The two grand pianos in the drawing room groaned under the weight of inscribed photographs, which overflowed into the next-door room, originally Alfred's and now the bridge room and a kind of museum. The walls were not to be seen for framed diplomas, scrolls, degrees and addresses of one sort or another. There was a collection of cups, garlands, crowns, shields and a glass cabinet stuffed with smaller marks of recognition or thanks. The ring Queen Victoria had given him a few months before her death was surrounded by inscribed cigarette cases, watches, medals and an assortment of the most unexpected trinkets.

Given this context, it is not surprising to find Paderewski ruminating on the subject of leaving a pianistic legacy to the world. He had taught a few people in the past. Antonina Szumowska, a cousin of Helena's who later married one of the Adamowski brothers and became a highly regarded concert pianist, had been his pupil in the 1890s; another pupil from the same period was the composer and pianist Zygmunt Stojowski; Harold Bauer had been launched as a pianist by Paderewski; and the American Ernest Schelling had also studied under him. But this did not amount to a Paderewski "school."

"I prefer to give ten concerts rather than one lesson," he was wont to say.[18] But he now decided that it was expected of him. In 1928 he therefore gave a summer course to five Polish pianists— Aleksander Brachocki, Zygmunt Dygat, Stanislaw Szpinalski, Henryk Sztompka and Albert Tadlewski—who were joined in the following year by another four. They stayed in Morges and came up to the villa for lessons every few days. Paderewski was autocratic and demanding as he strove to impose his method on them. "There were four stages in his work," explained Dygat; "the first consisted in conquering the technical difficulties, the second of constructing the work, the third of working out the musical detail, and the fourth of forgetting about the first three and giving oneself up to the playing itself, which should sound like the spoken word."[19] It was, in essence, Paderewski's own technique.

He threw himself into this activity as into every other, with abandon, and by all accounts he was a very good teacher. "If he criticizes severely, he also encourages warmly, and arouses an enthusiasm that absorbs one completely," wrote another pupil; "each lesson with him was for me a revelation."[20] But the material was mediocre; only Dygat and Sztompka had talent, but the first was a dilettante and the second gave up the piano. In the late 1930s Paderewski gave some lessons to Witold Malcuzynski, who probably absorbed more of his style than any of the others and became a fine pianist; but no school carried on the Paderewski style.

When asked, in 1919, whether he would ever start playing again, Paderewski had replied: "Never . . . I shall give myself up entirely to composition."[21] Although he did start playing again three years later, he never wrote another bar of music. The war and his political interlude had broken the thread of his musical thought, and when, ten years later, he might have picked it up again, he had lost his bearings completely. Like many people of a certain age who had seen the whole pattern of life shattered by the Great War, he failed to understand emerging trends, seeing in them only an apparently senseless rejection of values he had grown old in. Jazz, for instance, he dismissed as "horrible stuff," and regarded its practitioners as "the Bolsheviks of music."[22] This was perhaps understandable, but what was less so was that even composers who were hardly revolutionaries by the 1920s were beyond his comprehension.

In the 1930s he still believed, for instance, that Ernest Schelling was "one of the most prominent modern composers,"[23] and he was generally slow to take note of anyone in the next generation, or to be particularly impressed when he did. "As for Stravinsky," he wrote, "I have heard a great deal of his work and find it extremely interesting and full of colour,"[24] but it went no further than that. In spite of the fact that Stravinsky lived at Morges, a couple of miles from Riond-Bosson, the two never met. "I was told that when some-one asked him if he wished to meet me," writes Stravinsky, "he answered: 'No thank you; Stravinsky and me we bathe in very different lakes.' "[25]

Paderewski did meet Szymanowski several times and liked him both as a person and as "undoubtedly a man of great talent," but although he included pieces by him in his concert programmes, he admitted that he could not "get into the spirit" of his work as whole.[26] "I have no understanding for Schönberg," wrote Pade-rewski, and the same went for Webern, Hindemith, Alban Berg and others. "Real music must be like a running stream of fresh water that satisfies your thirst. Most modern composers are like soda-water—sparkling at first, but leaving you quite unsatisfied after one or two sips," he continued.[27]

It was not so much that Paderewski was out of his depth, which perhaps he was to some extent, but rather that he was too old and intellectually tired to make the effort to understand younger com-posers. He did not know many of them, while they regarded him as a grand old man of music to whom one dedicated works occa-sionally—as did Goossens, Milhaud and Britten, amongst others —but to whom one did not talk. He had lived too long, musically speaking. When, on 29 March 1937, Szymanowski died in nearby Lausanne, Paderewski hurried over to the funeral and was the first to place a wreath on his coffin. He was already burying the next generation.

Paderewski lived on, apparently indestructible. He did twenty minutes of exercises in the morning, ate well—too well, according to his doctor—drank, smoked and remained active. In 1929 he had to undergo an operation for appendicitis, which at the age of sixty-nine was likely to prove risky. He made his will and his farewells, but came through like a young man and was soon in excellent form again.

Helena was less well. She was ailing and spent, but this was aggravated by advancing senility. She had been growing steadily more difficult and moody, and frighteningly demanding of her various ladies-in-waiting. In the mid-1920s she began to suffer from lapses of memory and to have difficulty in following conversations, in recognizing people and answering even the simplest questions. According to Mrs. Strakacz, "the first symptoms of the progressing illness irritated rather than worried the President." By tacit agreement, nobody mentioned these symptoms, although it soon became clear that they were not just the products of old age or a difficult character. But, as Mrs. Strakacz noted in her diary, "the President somehow cannot reconcile himself to the situation, neither can he bring himself to treat Madame Paderewska as an invalid."[28]

By 1928 she was so ill that for the first time since their marriage he had to go on tour without her; by 1931 she was completely room-bound. She and her nurses took over the whole of the second floor at Riond-Bosson, where Paderewski would visit her daily, spending hours talking to her, completely unable to get through. After a few more years of this existence, on 16 January 1934 she died, aged nearly seventy-eight. Paderewski was shattered by the loss of the companion who had effectively dedicated the last forty-five years of her life to him. He took her body to Paris and buried her next to his son, Alfred, in the cemetery of Montmorency. While he was in Paris he heard of the death, on 18 February, of King Albert of the Belgians. He hurried to the funeral and was afterwards summoned by Queen Elizabeth, whose grief helped to eclipse his own.

Helena's death marked a stage in Paderewski's life. Although she had been little more than a burden to him for the last ten years, her commitment to him had been total, and something of himself passed away with her. He became distinctly gloomier in his general appearance and behaviour. He still enjoyed his little jokes, but he seldom laughed and his eyes wore a sad expression. More than ever now he hated the subject of illness or death in conversation, his dislike of the colour black became more intense, his attitude to the world grimly ambivalent. Although he clung to his faith in the ultimate honesty and goodness of people, he viewed with horror and disgust the direction in which Europe was moving. Most of his friends from Paris days were dead, and he looked round in vain for new Balfours and Houses amongst the rulers of the coming decades.

CHAPTER XV

Fighting to the Last

Ladies in evening dresses clambered on to the stage "like monkeys" to mob the seventy-three-year-old Paderewski when he finished playing. The occasion was a charity concert at the Albert Hall in London, to an audience of nine thousand people. "His *subjugation* of that crowd, compelled to listen and to understand, was one of the most wonderful things I ever saw him do," wrote an admirer who had first heard him in 1891. On the other side of the Atlantic at about the same time, a musician who wanted to shake hands with the pianist "witnessed a combined assault of three overweight women, one of them a teenager, on Paderewski, accompanied by a torrent of loud exclamations."[1] Clearly, age had nothing to do with the magnetism.

Nor did age tell very much on Paderewski's stamina. His tours grew less frequent in the 1930s, but hardly a year passed without him playing in several countries, and the demand never flagged. His agent for America at this time, George Engles, would receive a cable which ran: "What do you think of seventy to seventy-five concerts next winter?" To which he was able to reply after making only two or three telephone calls: "Tour all booked." Engles never had any written contract with Paderewski, but he knew that after months of silence—Paderewski hated unnecessary correspondence—the pianist would be on a certain ship on the appointed date, expecting to find him on the quayside with hotel porters, the Pullman coach booked and waiting—always with the same crew of Copper and Augustus and Charles, the porters, and seven Steinway grands, perfectly tuned, waiting to be tested by Paderewski before being forwarded to the concert halls. "There is no artist more reasonable, reliable and considerate of the local manager's interests," Engles concluded.[2]

Paderewski still suffered from his particular brand of stage-fright, and now that age and position entitled him to be a little difficult, things had to be just right. He would walk off the stage after playing the first piece, for instance, in order to have an EXIT sign switched off at the back of the hall, or to have the piano re-tuned. In Florence in 1932 he stopped in the middle of a piece and repeatedly tapped one key for a few moments, after which he got up and left the stage. A tuner came on and spent twenty minutes re-tuning the instrument. When he had finished, Paderewski walked on, but, after trying the offending key a few times, walked off again. The harassed-looking tuner reappeared and applied himself to the piano once more, after which Paderewski came back and finished his programme. The audience found the whole episode fascinating, which would certainly not have been the case with another pianist.[3]

Arthur Rubinstein remembers going to a recital in Paris at which Paderewski first made his audience wait, then played poorly, and finally gave four encores without very much encouragement. "It remained in my memory as a sad concert," he writes.[4] It was true that Paderewski could be moody or just tired and ill, and sometimes his playing would suffer seriously. In 1934, during a concert tour of Switzerland, he started hitting wrong notes and playing so badly that he had to stop and rest for a year.

He was, however, still an astonishingly fine performer, with a great deal of the old power and depth. No doubt his audiences grew less sophisticated, and increasingly they were made up of people taking their children to see "the great Paderewski—a legend in his time" before he died. He had become an entertainment industry, and something of his art had been lost in the process, but a measure of it was still there.

The Swiss conductor Gustave Doret heard him give a concert for the Debussy memorial in Paris in 1930 and wrote: "I had never heard him so powerful, so energetic, so sensitive, so self-controlled, so delicate, so passionate, in such a prodigious state of equilibrium and loftiness of thought." He went on to explain that it was not a question of virtuosity, but ultimately a kind of spiritually superior interpretation.[5] This was, more than ever, Paderewski's greatest claim to popularity at every level. He could give a performance more sensuously exciting, even intellectually satisfying, than anyone else. As Wiktor Labunski, a musician from a generation utterly out of sympathy with Paderewski's style, wrote after a concert in Nashville, Tennessee: "He was technically not perfect, played many things much too slowly, and there was an aura of 'old-fashionedness' about his whole approach to the keyboard. And then there were magnificent moments of great climaxes, where he moved you to the depths of your heart."[6] Stravinsky, hearing Paderewski play in Paris a couple of years later, was not so much moved as astonished, and was heard to sigh in admiration: *"Quelle discipline!"*[7]

This was bought at the cost of continuous hard work. "I still need four or five hours a day of practising with the concentration of mind that does not admit any intrusion," explained Paderewski. "It is a slavery from which there is no escape."[8] Not that he tried to escape from any part of it. His programmes were still long, lasting about three hours, and he still gave up to ten or twelve encores if the audience asked for them. These were not the usual trifles, but Chopin Ballades, Liszt Hungarian Rhapsodies and, as often as not, an entire Beethoven Sonata. His vitality was staggering. He was highly strung and by no means healthy, and his exhausting life might have left him little more than a wreck in his seventies. Yet he could call on reserves of energy and strength a young man might envy, and he was mentally as agile as ever. He could remember the names and faces of people he had met once in a crowd years before, and he retained the plots and could quote passages of books he had read in the nineteenth century.

It was entirely characteristic that he was able, at the age of seventy-six, to take part in an entirely new venture—cinema. As early as 1922 he had been approached with a view to making a film, but at that time he had refused, thinking it undignified and possibly damaging to his political prospects. In 1935, however, he was again approached, through Strakacz, who thought it a good idea to immortalize his master on cellulose. A script was written in which Paderewski played a grand old pianist sorting out emotional and family problems by being nice and playing the piano. The film was entitled *Moonlight Sonata,* and was directed by Lothar Mendes, who visited Riond-Bosson to finalize the project in the spring of 1936. In July Paderewski went to London to start work on it, taking his doctor with him. The doctor turned out to be a needless precaution, as Paderewski rose to the challenge and, if anything, felt rather better than usual. He astonished one of the collaborators on the film when, during a sumptuous lunch at the old Carlton Hotel in the Haymarket where he was staying, he explained that he ate similar meals every day, drank vintage wines in respectable quantities and often smoked large Havana cigars like the one he was holding. He added that he liked to enjoy a young girl now and again, which was probably bravado.[9]

The film crew had expected a prima donna and were surprised to find Paderewski so patient, indulgent and easy to work with. He made no complaints about the takes he had to repeat dozens of times because someone had forgotten a line or failed to switch on a light. He remembered all his own lines and even prompted the other actors, particularly Marie Tempest, the leading lady. In fact, he enjoyed himself immensely in this new profession, and was, by all accounts, very good at it, instinctively knowing how to move and where to stand.[10] The most tiring moments for him were the scenes in which he had to play the piano. Mendes wanted to record the playing live, but conditions in the studio were so poor that the scenes had to be repeated again and again, until finally the attempt was abandoned and the soundtrack was recorded by Gaisberg in the Abbey Road studio. The recordings were not as good as they might have been, but the final result is impressive and gives some idea of what a Paderewski recital must have been like. For this reason, Henry Wood thought all piano students ought to see the film in the course of their studies.

The film was a box-office success, and this helped the Paderewski finances which, since his investments had never recovered from the Great War, now depended on continuous earnings. But his own success did not blind him to the plight of his less fortunate colleagues caught up in the world economic recession. He finished off his 1932 American tour by playing to sixteen thousand people at Madison Square Garden and raised $37,000 for unemployed American musicians. The following year he gave a similar concert at the Albert Hall in London which raised £4,000 for English musicians.

In June of the same year he gave a concert in Paris for persecuted Jewish intellectuals and refugees from Germany. At the same time he announced that he would not play in that country as long as anti-Semitism was official policy. He had originally been deeply impressed by the apparent benefits achieved for Italy by Mussolini's movement, but his admiration had begun to wane after a long discussion he had with the Duce in 1932. As for German fascism, he regarded it with the deepest horror from the start. If there was one thing he believed to be a historical constant, it was the German urge for domination in Central and Eastern Europe. This was what had lain at the heart of his ideas on Poland's position in Europe, a conception which had been progressively rejected by those in power in Warsaw.

Pilsudski had staged a *coup d'état* in May 1926 which swept away the chaos of small-party bickering into which Poland had slid and imposed monolithic government by the Front of National Unity in its place. Pilsudski became the effective dictator, and it was his ideas which were put into practice; he despised Russia, held the Western Powers to be of no consequence in Polish affairs and gravitated slowly towards friendship with Germany.

Paderewski's dislike for Pilsudski had been growing steadily since his own fall from power. He was convinced that it was Pilsudski who had laid him low, and, as he explained in a letter, that "the megalomania of an unscrupulous demagogue who thinks himself the greatest military genius of all time did not permit me to carry on a good and useful task."[11] He refused to give Pilsudski credit for winning the Battle of Warsaw against the Red Army in 1920, and helped to nourish the myth that the French had been in some way responsible.[12] His loathing for the man and all he stood for continued to grow, and in the will he made in 1930 he concluded traditionally by forgiving everyone who had wronged him— except Pilsudski and his supporters.[13]

This attitude made Paderewski a figure of interest to those wishing to create a coalition of opposition groups, and in particular to General Wladyslaw Sikorski, a former minister and violent opponent of Pilsudski. He felt Paderewski's symbolic leadership was the one thing which could unite a group of parties in opposition, at the same time lending them weight both at home and abroad, and he began to work towards this goal. In the early 1930s the increasingly repressive nature of Pilsudski's dictatorship drove the moderate op-position groupings closer together and a caucus began to form around the figure of Paderewski. It included Wincenty Witos, the peasant leader; Wojciech Korfanty, the leader of the Christian Democrats; Hermann Liebermann of the Polish Socialist Party; General Jozef Haller, the commander of the Polish army in France in 1918; as well as General Sikorski. The National Democrats had shown in-terest, but grew less keen with time. Paderewski had anyway made up his mind on their score, and explained to a friend: "Remember that there is only one other party as repulsive as the [Pilsudski Party], and that is the National Democrats."[14]

In February 1933 Sikorski suggested that they put forward Paderewski as a candidate for the next Presidential elections, but while Korfanty agreed, Witos felt the time was not yet ripe, and the old man was kept in the wings. He was useful for certain things, as when in February 1935 he made a withering denunciation in the international press of the recently signed non-aggression pact be-tween Poland and Germany, which had seriously alarmed France.

While the image of the opposition groups was weak in Poland, they received grateful attention from France, which saw in Sikorski and Paderewski the only hope of bringing Poland back into her essential place in the French hegemony in Eastern Europe.

With the death of Pilsudski in 1935, Poland entered, in Sikorski's words, "a phase of dictatorship without a dictator," and the opposi-tion parties stepped up their activity. In February 1936 Sikorski, Witos and Haller met at Riond-Bosson. Under the aegis of Pade-rewski, they worked out their common ground, and the coalition which emerged from this meeting became known in Poland as the "Morges Front." Paderewski was to be the spiritual father of the movement. Sikorski felt that this would give it a moral authority which would produce an effect in Poland "even if that authority remains high up in the clouds."[15]

Paderewski asserted this authority in the following year, 1937, by issuing a declaration denouncing the dictatorship of the colonels and calling for a new and honest approach in order to bring about a change in the political climate in Poland. "People are taking courage and comfort from [the declaration]," Korfanty wrote to him, "a new spirit seems to be abroad," an impression echoed elsewhere.[16] What was important about the Morges Front was that both at home and abroad an alternative to the ruling clique was seen to have been set up, and the importance of this was to become apparent with the outbreak of war.

Busy as he was with these political schemes, Paderewski kept on at his own work. On the one hand, he was preparing the great new Warsaw edition of the complete works of Chopin, a time-consuming labour of love which kept him occupied for the best part of two years; on the other hand, he carried on giving concerts. By the late 1930s his strength was rapidly waning, and the recitals were shorter than before and usually held only in the afternoon. Gaisberg, who brought him to London in November 1938 to record seven new discs, writes that "he was beginning to show his seventy-eight years. . . . In his playing I found a lack of virility."[17] This is born out by the recordings: there are moments when the tired pianist seems to lose his way.

On 16 February 1939 Paderewski sailed from Le Havre on his twentieth tour of the United States. Doctors and friends thought it rank folly, but he was not one to give up and retire, even at this age. He looked ill and weak, but the moment he ascended the stage a new spirit would take hold of the shrivelled frame and, as Mrs. Strakacz noted, "head high, step firm, he looked capable of playing for hours."[18]

He heard the news of the annexation of Bohemia and Moravia while he was in Chicago and immediately sent a telegram to Benes, his erstwhile colleague in Paris. He was horrified and shamed by the event. But a few weeks later news came of the change of alignment of the Polish government. From Pittsburgh, Paderewski issued a press release in which he congratulated the government for having affirmed its intention of resisting German aggression and standing by Great Britain and France.

On 25 May he was to give a concert at Madison Square Garden to a huge audience. It waited and waited, and eventually was told that the pianist had suffered a heart attack. He had left his private railroad car, parked in Grand Central Station, and, on reaching the taxi, collapsed. He was hurried back to the carriage, and although apparently out of any danger, he suffered a lapse of memory—it became clear at one stage that he thought he was in Paris in 1919. Five days later he sailed for Europe, looking older than ever, but when he returned to Riond-Bosson he started his usual daily practising, as though nothing had happened.

Politics were taking up his thoughts more and more throughout the summer of that year. From Poland, Sikorski was reporting an improvement in the situation and suggesting a visit by Paderewski. He had been back only once since 1920, so a visit would make an impact. But he did not feel strong enough, and he also felt that he could be more useful in his Swiss vantage-point. In July he was in touch with President Roosevelt on the possibility of America stepping in to arbitrate on the German claims to Danzig, but nothing came of this.[19]

On 1 September 1939, when the Germans invaded Poland, fever took over Riond-Bosson. Helena Liibke's radio, an appliance Paderewski hated as much as the telephone, was brought down into the drawing room. A few days later a larger wireless was bought and installed next to Paderewski's armchair. He listened to all the communiqués with stoicism, even while the destruction of Warsaw was being reported.

Meanwhile he pulled every string he could. On 2 September he had a comforting letter from Roosevelt. A couple of days later, on 4 September, he sent a telegram to Gandhi, whom he implored, "as one of the greatest moral authorities of the world," to exert his influence. He was aware that many Indians might be reluctant to fight on the British side during the coming war, and he firmly stated the case for the Allies. A few days later Gandhi replied, lamenting his own "powerlessness to help you and your brave people in any effective or real way," and affirming that "Of course, my whole heart is with the Poles in the unequal struggle in which they are engaged."[20]

One of the worst disappointments to Paderewski was Mussolini's atttiude. On 23 September 1939 the Duce made a speech the gist of which was that, since Poland had been defeated, the war was over. Paderewski could contain himself no longer, and wrote him a long, reproachful letter. "For many years I admired you. I was proud of your friendship, I recognized your merits as the wonderful artisan of Italy's greatness," he wrote. "In spite of the injustice of the attitude you have just adopted towards my country, I do not address you as an enemy. Many may be the reasons which forced you to adopt this attitude, but they are capable of all turning against you, against your nation one day. . . . I still hope that your last word has not been spoken."[21] It must have been embarrassing for practitioners of the politics of blood and iron to receive letters like this, so redolent of another age.

The worst moment at Riond-Bosson came with the news of the Soviet invasion of eastern Poland on 17 September. The game was up as far as defending Poland was concerned. Still they sat and listened to Warsaw radio until finally, on 29 September, it fell silent. Paderewski burst into tears.

On 21 September Sikorski had come to Riond-Bosson for a couple of days to confer with Paderewski, after which he went to Paris, where he and Wladyslaw Raczkiewicz proclaimed the new Polish government-in-exile. On 30 September Paderewski wrote to Raczkiewicz, declaring his support and adding, "While I still have some strength, while I can still be of use in some way in order to help you in your work, you will find me ready and always eager to do my duty."[22]

A few days later a courier arrived at Riond-Bosson bearing an invitation for Paderewski to take symbolic office as President of the National Council. The courier had not seen him for three years and was horrified as he watched the old man come down the great staircase. "Before he reached the bottom I could see that in three years he had changed from the splendid man at the height of his titanic power and vitality into an old man on the brink of senility. . . . I felt a sort of shock."[23] There was an elegant dinner that night, during which Paderewski rose to his feet and, spilling champagne with his shaking hand, proposed a toast to the new government, after which he slumped back into his chair and had to be taken to bed. But on the next day his answer was written out and ready; he accepted, of course.

In December he went to Paris for the inaugural sitting of the National Council. He walked into the meeting supported by two people and spoke with difficulty, but his mind was clear, his words vigorous and the effect deeply moving. A few days later he was off to Switzerland. About a hundred soldiers in tattered Polish uniforms turned up at the Gare de l'Est spontaneously to see him off that night. "Paderewski was already in his compartment," remembered one of them. "He sat motionless, almost petrified. His eyes were closed. We stood in a great semicircle, pressed together in complete silence. This wall of Polish uniforms surrounding the carriage intrigued the travellers drifting about the platform. They would stop, they would stare. Suddenly there was a signal. The grey eyelids lifted for just a moment in the obscurity. A shaky hand was raised towards us. Through the dim station hall, the train moved off into the darkness."[24]

He made several trips to Paris in order to be present at as many meetings of the Council as possible, for he realized that he was in a strong position to soothe any conflicts arising within it, and he certainly used his power effectively in that direction.[25] But his only work was unofficially diplomatic, and although it was bound to be ineffective, it did produce some interesting results. It was, for instance, quite extraordinary to find that Mussolini actually replied to his letter of September 1939, trying to justify his behaviour and affirming his continuing regard for the Poles and for Paderewski.[26] He also corresponded with Pétain, for whom he had always felt respect. After the fall of France and the Vichy compromise, he wrote saying that he understood Pétain's motives and the considerations which had dictated his decision. "I would like to assure you that this fact in no way influences the sentiments and the relationship of unalterable friendship which unite our two countries," he wrote on 21 July.[27] "It is now our turn to go through some terrible moments," answered Pétain, with an assurance of his wish to be of help if he could.[28] Paderewski took him up on this and was able to do a certain amount for Polish military and civilian personnel stranded in Vichy France.

The fall of France put Paderewski himself in a difficult position, as it raised the possibility that sooner or later he could be marooned in Switzerland, and Hitler might try to invade that at some stage. He was also getting restless, for, as he later explained in a letter to

Raczkiewicz, "It was difficult for me to sit idly in Switzerland, and the awareness that I could still, perhaps, make myself useful in some way, gave me no peace."[29]

He was, in fact, again thinking of America. It was certainly the safest place for him, but it was also the obvious field for the sort of activity he craved. He felt that the Polish community there must be brought in behind the Sikorski government, and the Americans must be made aware of the justice of the Allied cause. He was sure that America would once again save Europe, and he felt that she must not be allowed to forget Poland. "President Roosevelt has always been my friend," he said to Mrs. Strakacz, "he won't deny me his help now."[30]

Strakacz was sent to Vichy to negotiate transit to the Spanish frontier. The date of departure, originally set for the beginning of October, was brought forward to 23 September. It looked as though the Laval government was having pressure exerted on it by Germany and it only needed a word to have Paderewski arrested. The date was kept secret and his farewell speech on Swiss radio was not broadcast until the party had reached Spain. "I have sacrificed my life to my country," it ran, "I served it with my whole heart and all of my strength, and you know how wretched it is now, and how it is suffering. It has called on me to serve it. In such circumstances neither age, health, nor the risks of a long journey are worthy of consideration. . . . The house on Lake Geneva stands empty. Shall I ever return to it? God only knows."[31]

The departure on the morning of 23 September 1940 was chaotic. There were two large cars to carry the party, which consisted of Paderewski, his sister, the butler, Strakacz, his wife and daughter. There was little in the way of luggage, since the cars were piled high with cans of gasoline. After much confusion, the convoy moved off. At Annemasse, where they crossed into France, they were joined by another Pole and an agent of the Sûreté Nationale sent by Pétain.

At first everything went smoothly. In the hotels they stopped at, everyone was charming and helpful; at the Spanish frontier the customs officer hummed Paderewski's Minuet as he stamped the passports. On 27 September they slept in Barcelona, and on the next day set off for Madrid. After a time they noticed that they were being followed by another car, and before they reached Saragossa they were stopped by what turned out to be security police, who ordered them back to Barcelona. Strakacz protested vigorously, saying that Paderewski was too tired and old to go back so far. After long arguments the police took them on to Saragossa, where they were placed under arrest in the Gran Hotel. Strakacz cabled American Ambassador Weddell and British Ambassador Sir Samuel Hoare in Madrid, and they waited.

On 2 October they were released and allowed to continue on their way to Madrid. President Roosevelt had sent a telegram to Franco telling him that Paderewski was a personal friend and must be treated with respect. Both the British and the American embassies offered accommodation, but Paderewski preferred to stay in a hotel and to be off as soon as possible. The journey was turning into flight and he did not want to waste any more time. They reached Portugal on 5 October and put up at a hotel in Estoril. There they waited for the next boat, and it was not until 27 October that they could sail, on the S.S. *Excambion*. Halfway across the Atlantic, it was intercepted by a German submarine and boarded, but after searching the ship the Germans allowed it to proceed.

On 6 November 1940, Paderewski's eightieth birthday, it sailed into New York. Crowds swarmed over the quayside, and reporters pressed around the old man. An officer sent by Roosevelt greeted him on the President's behalf and conducted him through immigration. The little group went to the Gotham Hotel, where Paderewski had always stayed since the beginning of the century, but a couple of weeks later they moved to the cheaper Buckingham—money was scarce, and by this stage he could not possibly hope to earn any.

It was good to be back in America. Paderewski was relieved to have left behind the oppressive, doom-laden atmosphere of Europe, and he was touched by the affection he encountered everywhere. On 10 November the three black servants from the touring days, John, Charles and Augustus, came to see him. Equally touching scenes took place at Christmas. Literally thousands of cards and presents poured in from all over the United States, and the hotel room was so full of these and flowers that he could hardly move. On Christmas Eve the manager of a local restaurant sent round a traditional Polish dinner with waiters and an orchestra in national costumes. The extent of Paderewski's popularity as a figure in the United States at this time is impossible to convey.

"I do not come to rest!" he had exclaimed to newsmen on the quayside as he left his ship.[32] Indeed he did not; at his first press conference he made a speech explaining why he had come, and his message was summed up in the last words: "Help Great Britain, save the world!"[33] Almost immediately he sought an interview with Roosevelt and badgered him to intercede with the Vichy government in order to help the Poles stranded in France. On 8 December he was broadcast on the Columbia radio network urging Americans to help Great Britain, explaining that this was not a war over boundaries but an entirely new kind of conflict. While he praised Roosevelt's statesmanship, he asked his audience: "What sacrifice have you really made to help the Allied Democracies resist the barbarous aggression?"[34] He suggested that America should at least grant credits to the British and Polish governments so they could arm themselves.

Early in January 1941 he went to Palm Beach, Florida, in order to escape the cold. He was lent a grand residence by a society friend, and soon found himself the centre of attention of the holidaying rich. There were splendid parties given by Eleanor Roosevelt and others, rather to the annoyance of Paderewski, who could not drag his thoughts away from the horrors of what was happening in Europe. Sikorski, who was on a tour of the United States and Canada, came to spend Easter with him, and together they discussed ways of gaining greater support from America.

Paderewski was restless in Palm Beach, where he could do no real work, and at the beginning of May he was back in New York. He was weakening visibly, but still he kept himself busy, writing letters, preparing memoranda, composing speeches, talking to people. He spoke on the radio several times, both in a private capacity and at the behest of the United States government in aid of its Defense Savings Program. Although his voice was getting hoarse and weak, he could sound remarkably vigorous as he broadcast his battle-cry of "Stop Hitler before he masters the Atlantic!"[35]

New York grew hot in June, and there were days when Paderewski would complain to his valet, "I no longer have the strength!" but he refused to let up on his hectic activity. His entourage—the

Strakacz family, his sister Antonina and the valet—were worried by his condition. He was growing weaker, he found it difficult to eat and he would start choking on his food in an alarming way; but nothing could induce him to take things easy.

On 21 June 1941 he sat up all night with Strakacz listening to the radio bulletins reporting the German invasion of the Soviet Union. "Whom the Gods would destroy they first make mad," he quoted gleefully to his secretary.[36] The next day he was to attend a rally of Polish American veterans of the First World War at Oak Ridge. Since he had not slept the night before, everyone pleaded with him to stay home, but he insisted that these were the people he had sent to war in 1917, his own, almost his very own, nation—he could not let them down.

Not only did he go, he also insisted on making a long speech. "This is no ordinary war," he croaked in his feeble voice. "It is a question of our future, of the future of the whole world!"[37] He was hemmed in by thousands of people trying to get near, to touch him, to kiss his hands, even his clothes. The heat was intense, and he nearly fainted from it. He was finally dragged back to his car. On the way back he stopped at a small house by the wayside and downed an enormous glass of iced water, which was not good for him, and dangerous in his condition.

Back in New York that evening, he felt very ill indeed. Doctors were summoned, and they diagnosed acute indigestion. He did not improve over the next few days and by the end of the week he was flushed and feverish; they diagnosed pneumonia. On Saturday, 28 June, he appeared to be better, but still could eat nothing. The day came and went without bringing any dramatic change in his condition, but his emaciated body looked beyond repair and there could be little doubt that he was dying.

The following morning he seemed healthier, and there was no reason to suppose he might not continue in this state for some time. Strakacz and others of the entourage went out about their business, and nobody noticed that throughout that hot New York Sunday the old man was fighting his last unequal battle—one that was already somewhat irrelevant to the war going on in the world outside. Paderewski, no more than a dry husk now, lay very still in the stuffy, over-decorated hotel room, ministered to in turns by his sister and

Mrs. Strakacz. At three o'clock his tranquillity was disturbed by a choking fit, and he had to be given oxygen. His sister also poured holy water from the shrine of Czestochowa over his throat and called a priest to administer the Last Sacrament.

At five o'clock the supine form came to life once more and astonished those present by asking for champagne. Champagne was brought, and Paderewski drank a glass, after which he fell asleep, never to awake. At one minute to eleven that night, 29 June 1941, he expired.

The manager of the Buckingham Hotel allowed the body to be laid out in the same room after embalming, and during the next two days over seven thousand people filed through to pay their last respects. New York rich waited in the long line with musicians, people off the street and illiterate Poles from the Midwest. The guard of honour kept fainting from the scent of the swathes of flowers sent from all over the United States. Telegrams, too, poured in, from all over the world. Sikorski made a broadcast tribute and awarded Paderewski the highest Polish military decoration; Roosevelt made another, and announced that the body would be laid in Arlington National Cemetery until its return to a free Poland could be arranged.

The body was transferred to St. Patrick's Cathedral without pomp; yet news had spread, and the streets were lined with people come to see "the great Paddyroosky" one last time. Thousands more filed past the coffin in the crypt.

On 3 July Cardinal Spellman celebrated the funeral mass in the cathedral, after which the body was conducted with military escort to Pennsylvania Station, where it was placed on the private car in which Paderewski had made his last tour, with John and Charles in attendance. In Washington the body lay in state at the Polish embassy, where still more people, including the diplomatic corps, came to pay their respects. The Italian Ambassador came to lay a wreath on behalf of Mussolini.

On 5 July Paderewski's body was taken to Arlington Cemetery with full military honours. The Papal Nuncio, Cardinal Cicognani, celebrated mass, after which there was a nineteen-gun salute. The ceremony was as grand as it could have been for anyone who was not actually a head of state, but it lacked both unction and intimacy. The tiny group of the bereaved—Antonina supported by two nuns, the Strakacz family and General Haller, who happened to be in Washington—and the thousands of Poles who had turned up were somehow up-staged, according to the old General, by "the crowd of snapping American photographers and reporters, and the pharisee-like figures of the Rooseveltite benefactors of mankind, already heaving sighs of love for the Bolsheviks.

"And yet," he concludes, "that coffin still constituted a great hope for recovering that which we had lost."[38] The coffin lies there still, awaiting burial in a free Poland. Gazing at it, one is more than ever conscious of the pathetic aspects of Paderewski's life, of his faith in humanity, a faith continually dashed by experience. One can only be grateful that he died before he had to witness his great friend Roosevelt, one of the last recipients of that faith, cancel out at Yalta all President Wilson's work as well as Paderewski's own.

"Paderewski is one of the very few people to whom the word genius can be applied," stated A. J. Balfour, while the French politician and writer Gabriel Hanotaux prophesied that "this Pole will come to be judged by history not only as one of the greatest representatives of his nation, but also of his century."[39] These two statements are outstanding neither for their superlative nature nor for the distinction of those who uttered them. They merely encapsulate views held by a great many people, who all believed that Paderewski would loom large to future generations. They could hardly have been more mistaken.

There are good reasons why he has sunk into near-oblivion. The music he left cannot be compared to that of some of his great contemporaries; his political achievements, such as they were, do not survive; and he never invented anything nor left a profound thought. Even his fabulous earnings evaporated, so that he died a pauper. The biographer may search and pry, but he will unearth no hidden greatness, no unpublished symphony, no secret diplomatic coup with which to vindicate his hero's reputation. All he is left with are the opinions of contemporaries, and it is sometimes tempting to dismiss these as being given lightly or under the spell of the notorious magnetism. But some of them come from people who were neither blind nor foolish, people as different as Lloyd George and Conrad, Balfour and Saint-Saëns, Mussolini and Fauré. These and others regarded Paderewski as an exceptional being and liberally applied the word "genius" to him, and if one is to attempt a final assessment of the man, one must try to understand what they meant.

They were, of course, staggered by the sheer scale of his career and his achievements. He suddenly appeared from nowhere, a dazzling new star in the musical firmament outshining every other and fascinating the gaze of musicians and laymen alike. The compositions he produced cannot be considered great music, but they are certainly not insignificant, and at the time they added an impressive dimension to his artistic stature. This continued to grow instead of gradually waning, as might have been expected after such a meteoric rise. And alongside the artist, the man grew in stature, too, revealing himself to be an intelligent and refined person, a great philanthropist and, finally, a remarkable statesman.

It became obvious to his contemporaries, as it must also be to posterity, that Paderewski was no ordinary man—not in the sense of talent or ability, though these were astonishing, but in terms of motivation and force of personality. They could see that his musical success was not the result of inborn virtuosity, but of some inner fire which they readily took for artistic inspiration. Similarly, he was propelled into public life not by a political, religious or even national party or interest, but by a very personal urge to do good and redress wrong. This medieval, almost crusading sense of mission was striking in the context of the twentieth century, the more so as Paderewski was neither simple nor bigoted, but seemed, indeed, to possess something of the wisdom and serenity of an Eastern sage. On meeting him, people felt themselves to be in the presence of an altogether superior being, and since this was the twentieth century and not the Middle Ages, they dubbed him not a saint but a genius.

With hindsight we can see that he was neither. He was a knight errant, a man who had made his own the traditions of his forefathers and wanted, passionately, to do good in a world which was full of wrongs. He struggled hard to achieve a position, and he conquered—both himself and the obstacles in his path—and this lent him a sense of peace which enhanced his greatest natural gift: his genius for charm, for intercourse, for expression, for life. It added a uniquely cathartic and spiritual quality to his playing, and a moral force to his powers of persuasion. These he used in order to inspire, to comfort and to help, which was from the very start his greatest ambition. He was no genius but ultimately just a good and noble man, and he was both of these on a truly epic scale.

List of Works in Chronological Order

Date of Compo-sition	Opus No.	Title	Dedicatee
1876		*Valse Mignonne*	Gustaw Roguski
	1 no.1	Prelude and Caprice	Antoni Rutkowski
	no.2	Minuet in G minor	” ”
1878		Impromptu in F major	Rudolf Strobl
1879	2 no.1	Gavotte in E minor	Mme. Thérèse Wlassoff
	no.2	Mélodie in C major	” ” ”
	no.3	*Valse Mélancolique* in A major	” ” ”
		Intermezzo in G minor	
		Intermezzo in C minor	
1880	13	Sonata for Piano and Violin	Pablo de Sarasate
1882		Two Canons	
	8	*Chants du Voyageur:*	Mme. Helena Gorska
		1) *Allegro Agitato*	
		2) *Andantino Melancolico*	
		3) *Andantino Gracioso*	
		4) *Andantino Mistico*	
		5) *Allegro Giocoso*	
	11	Variations and Fugue in A minor	Eugène d'Albert
1884	3	*Krakowiak*	
	4	*Elégie*	
	5	Polish Dances:	Paul de Schlözer
		1) *Krakowiak* in E major	
		2) *Mazurek* in C minor	
		3) *Krakowiak* in B flat minor	
		Powodz—Piece for Piano	

Date of Compo-sition	Opus No.	Title	Dedicatee
	9	Polish Dances:	
		1) *Krakowiak* in F major	
		2) *Mazurek* in A minor	
		3) *Mazurek* in A major	
		4) *Mazurek* in B flat major	
		5) *Krakowiak* in A major	
		6) *Polonaise* in B major	
	10	*Album de Mai: Scènes*	Annette Essipov
		Romantiques pour Piano:	
		1) *Au soir*	
		2) *Chant d'amour*	
		3) *Scherzino*	
		4) *Barcarolle*	
		5) *Caprice*	
	12	*Album Tatrzanskie*	
	14	*Humoresques de Concert pour*	
		Piano:	
		I. *A l'Antique: Menuet*	Annette Essipov
		Sarabande	" "
		Caprice	" "
		II. *A la Moderne: Burlesque*	" "
		Intermezzo	
		Polacco	" "
		Cracovienne	
		Fantastique	Alexander Michalowski
1885	6	*Introduzione e Toccata*	Nathalie Janotha
1886	15	*Dans le Désert: Tableau*	
		Musical en Forme de Toccata	Annette Essipov
1887	7	Four Songs to Words by Adam	
		Asnyk: *Gdy Ostatnia Roza*	
		Zwiedla; Siwy Koniu; Szumi	
		Brzezina; Chlopca Mego Mi	
		zabrali	
	16	*Miscellanea pour Piano:*	
		1) *Légende* in A flat major	Mme. Scheurer-Kästner
		2) *Mélodie* in G flat major	Princesse de Brancovan
		3) *Variations* in A major	Mme. Aline Weber-Schlumberger
		4) *Nocturne* in B flat major	Princesse de Brancovan
		5) *Légende* in A major	" "
		6) *Moment Musical*	" "
		7) *Menuet* in A major	" "

244

Date of Composition	Opus No.	Title	Dedicatee
1888	17	Concerto for Piano and Orchestra in A minor	Theodor Leschetitzky
1892		*Moment Musical*	
	18	Six Songs to Words by Adam Mickiewicz: *Polaly sie lzy; Piosnka Dudarza; Moja Pieszczotka; Nad woda wielka i czysta; Tylem wytrwal; Gdybym sie zmienil*	Wladyslaw Mickiewicz
1893	19	Polish Fantasia on Original Themes for Piano and Orchestra	Princesse de Brancovan
	20	*Légende*	
1900		*Manru*—Opera in Three Acts	
1903	21	Piano Sonata in E flat minor	Archduke Charles Stephen of Austria
	22	Twelve Songs to Poems by Catulle Mendès: *Dans la forêt; Ton coeur est d'or pur; Le ciel est très bas; Naguère; Le Jeune pâtre; Elle marche d'un pas distrait; La jeune nonne; Viduité; Lune froide; Querelleuse; L'amour fatal; L'ennemie*	Mme. Marie Trélat
	23	Variations and Fugue in E flat minor	William Adlington
1907	24	Symphony in B minor, "Polonia"	
1917		*Hej Orle Bialy!*—Marching Song for Male Choir and Military Band	

Many of the above works were published in a variety of transcriptions, which are not listed here.

Unfinished works include a cantata for choir and orchestra to words by Tetmajer, a concerto for violin and orchestra, an orchestral suite, and several studies.

Paderewski's Repertoire

Until a few years before his death when he shortened them somewhat, Paderewski's programmes were long and strenuous. A typical recital programme would begin with a longish work by Beethoven, Schumann, Brahms or Mendelssohn, followed by a group of shorter pieces by Bach, Scarlatti, Handel and other composers. After this he would play a sonata—usually one of the great Beethoven sonatas, although he often performed the Chopin and Schumann sonatas. This would be followed by yet another lengthy work before the interval. The second half of the recital would begin with a Chopin group, including longer pieces like the ballades and even a sonata as well as a series of shorter ones. This would be followed by a few popular pieces by Brahms, Schumann, Paderewski, Rubinstein or others, and the recital usually ended with one or two rousing works by Liszt.

The following list of works, culled from the programmes of concerts and recitals, gives as extensive an idea as possible of Paderewski's repertoire:

J. S. Bach	Chromatic Fantasy and Fugue
L. van Beethoven	Concerto in E flat major (op. 73)
	Sonata in C major (op. 2, no. 3)
	”　　” E flat major (op. 27, no. 1)
	”　　” C sharp minor (op. 27, no. 2) "Moonlight"
	”　　” D major (op. 28)
	”　　” D minor (op. 31, no. 2)
	”　　” E flat major (op. 31, no. 3)
	”　　” C major (op. 53) "Waldstein"
	”　　” F major (op. 54)
	”　　” F minor (op. 57) "Appassionata"
	”　　” A major (op. 101)
	”　　” E major (op. 109)

	" " A flat major (op. 110)
	" " C minor (op. 111)
	Trio in B flat major (op. 97)
	32 Variations in C minor
J. Brahms	Capriccio
	Hungarian Dances (nos. 1, 6, 7)
	Intermezzo
	Piano Quartet in A major (op. 26)
	Piano Quintet in F minor (op. 34)
	Variations and Fugue (op. 24)
	Variations on a Theme of Paganini (op. 35)
C. Chevillard	Thème et Variations (op. 5)
F. Chopin	Both Concertos
	The four Ballades
	Barcarolle
	Berceuse
	The four Scherzos
	Sonata in B minor
	Sonata in B flat minor
	Etudes (op. 10 and op. 25)
	Polonaise Brillante (op. 3)
	Grande Polonaise Brillante (op. 22)
	Polonaises: E flat minor of op. 26; A major of op. 40; F sharp minor, op. 44; A flat major, op. 53
	Polonaise-Fantaisie
	Fantaisie (op. 49)
	Impromptu in F sharp major (op. 36)
	Funeral March in C minor (op. 72)
	Preludes (op. 28)
	Nocturnes: op. 15, nos. 1, 2; op. 27, no. 2; op. 32, no. 1; op. 37, nos. 1, 2; op. 48, no. 1; op. 62, nos. 1, 2
	Mazurkas: op. 17, no. 3; op. 24, no. 4; op. 33, no. 4; op. 50, no. 1; op. 56, no. 2; op. 59, nos. 2, 3
	Grande Valse Brillante (op. 18)
	Waltzes: op. 34, nos. 1, 2; op. 42; op. 64, nos. 1, 2
F. Couperin	*La Bandoline*
	Le Carillon de Cythère
F. Cowen	Concertstück
L. C. Daquin	*Le Coucou*
C. Debussy	*Reflets dans l'eau*
	Preludes: *Danseuses de Delphes, Ménestrels, Le Vent dans la Plaine, Voiles*
L. Delibes	Rigaudon
L. Diemer	*Troisième Orientale*
A. V. Duvernoy	Intermedium

247

G. Fauré	Barcarolle
	Romance sans Paroles
J. Field	Selection of nocturnes
A. W. Foote	Caprice
B. Godard	Polonaise
W. Gorski	Berceuse
E. Granados	*Valses Poeticos*
E. Grieg	Concerto in A minor (op. 16)
G. F. Handel	*Harmonious Blacksmith*
	Suite in D minor
J. Haydn	Variations in F minor
A. Henselt	Etude
C. Johnss	Valse
E. Lalo	*Sérénade*
T. Leschetitzky	*Canzonetta Toscana*
	Mazurka
	Menuetto Capriccioso
	Tarantella
F. Liszt	Concerto in E flat major
	Sonata in B flat minor
	Don Juan Fantasy
	Polonaise in E major
	Spanish Rhapsody
	Hungarian Rhapsodies
	Etudes de concert
	Etude Ricordanza
	Valse Impromptu
	Waldesrauschen

Transcriptions of: Bach's Fantasia and Fugue in A minor
Fantasia and Fugue in G minor
Prelude and Fugue in A minor
Chopin's Six Polish Songs
Mendelssohn's Dance of the Elves
Wedding March
Paganini's *Campanella*
Schubert's *Au Bord d'une Source*
Divertissement à
l'Hongroise
Erlkönig
Hungarian March
Hark, Hark, the Lark
Soirée de Vienne
Wagner's *Spinning Song*

H. C. Litolff	Scherzo
D. G. Mason	Caprice

F. Mendelssohn	Songs without Words
	Prelude and Fugue in E minor
	Variations Sérieuses (op. 54)
G. P. Moore	*Etude Pathétique*
M. Moszkowski	Barcarolle
W. A. Mozart	Rondo in A minor
	Sonata in A major
Z. Noskowski	*Krakowiak*
A. Périlhou	Fantasia
	Fugue
G. Pierné	*Sérénade à Colombine*
J. J. Raff	Suite (op. 210)
	Valse Impromptu
A. Ries	Romance
A. Rubinstein	Barcarolle in A minor (op. 93)
	Concertstück
	Piano Concerto in D minor (op. 70)
	Trio in B major
	Barcarolle in A minor (op. 93)
	Barcarolle in F minor (op. 30)
	Prelude in A minor
	Romance
	Etude
	Mazurka in D major
	Valse Caprice (op. 118)
A. Rutkowski	Polonaise
C. Saint-Saëns	Concerto in C minor (op. 44)
	Polonaise for Two Pianos
	Romance
D. Scarlatti	Sonata
	Capriccio
	Pastorale
E. Schelling	Concerto no. 2
	Nocturne
F. Schubert	Impromptus
	Moments Musicaux
	Variations
	Trio (op. 99)
	March
	Menuet
R. Schumann	Piano Concerto
	Sonata in F sharp minor
	Carnaval
	Fantasia in C major
	Etudes Symphoniques

	Fantasiestücke
	Papillons
	Etudes sur Paganini (op. 3, 10)
	Nachtstücke
	Toccata in C major
	Waldszenen (op. 82)
A. Scriabin	Preludes
G. Sgambati	Gavotte (op. 9)
Z. Stojowski	*Chant d'Amour*
	Serenade
K. Szymanowski	Etudes
	Prelude and Fugue
C. Tausig	Valse Caprice after Johann Strauss
F. Thomé	*Chanson du Rouet*
C. M. von Weber	Sonata
	Momento Capriccioso (op. 12)
C. M. Widor	*Zanetto*
H. Wieniawski	Mazurka
A. Zarzycki	Valse
W. Zelenski	Sonata for Violin and Piano

Paderewski often played his own music, particularly before the First World War. In the case of his major works—the Concerto, the Polish Fantasia, the Sonata and the Variations, op. 23—he would give them wide performance for the first couple of years after composition and then drop them from his repertoire. Some of his better short pieces—from the Humoresques, the Miscellanea and the Tatra Album—are to be found in his programmes late into the 1930s, and he also used them liberally for encores.

APPENDIX C

Recordings

1 *PADEREWSKI'S PLAYING*

For a full list of recordings made by Paderewski, see entries under Anderson, H. L., and Fassett, S., in the list of Sources.

A selection of recordings, made between 1911 and 1938, has been reissued on long-playing records by Pavillion Records (U.K.) under the Pearl label (Gemm 136, 140, 150). The complete recorded works 1911–1930 are also available under this label as a five-record set (Pearl IJP 1). Other currently available reissues are to be found on Eurodisc (1976) 27674 XDK.

2 *PADEREWSKI'S COMPOSITIONS*

There are a great many recordings of Paderewski's works on the Polish Muza label, but these are difficult to obtain in Poland, let alone anywhere else. Currently available recordings of Paderewski's music include:

Sonata for Piano and Violin, op. 13:
> —Desmar, U.S.A., 1975 (DSM 1004), Endre Granat, violin, and
> Harold Gray, piano

The Famous Minuet of op. 14:
> —Klavier, 1973 (KS 123), Sergei Rachmaninoff, piano
> —Musical Heritage Society, U.S.A. (MHS 1139, 1971), A. Kann, piano
> (MHS 1730, 1973), A. de Larrocha, piano
> —Connoisseur Society, U.S.A. (C.S 2059, 1974), M. Estrin, piano
> —Saga, 1975 (5400), Edward Moore, piano

The Variations from op. 16:
> —Klavier, 1975 (KS 501), Nicolaisen, piano
> —Pye/Vanguard, 1972 (VSD 71119), Earl Wild, piano

The Piano Concerto:
> —Turnabout, U.K., 1970 (TV 34387S), Felicja Blumenthal, piano, and
> Vienna Symphony Orchestra, Helmuth Froschauer, conductor

—Victor, U.S.A., 1971 (LSC 3190), Earl Wild, piano, and London Symphony Orchestra, Arthur Fiedler, conductor

Polish Fantasia:

—Turnabout, U.K., 1970 (STV 34345), Felicja Blumenthal, piano, and Innsbruck Symphony Orchestra, Robert Wagner, conductor

—Victor, U.S.A., 1971 (LSC 3190), Earl Wild, piano, and London Symphony Orchestra, Arthur Fiedler, conductor

Notes

ABBREVIATIONS IN THE NOTES

AAN   Archiwum Glowne Akt Nowych, Warsaw: Paderewski Archive. See Sources: i. Archival Sources

APP   Archiwum Polityczne Ignacego Paderewskiego. See Sources: iii. Published Sources, under Paderewski, Ignacy Jan.

PM   The Paderewski Memoirs. See Sources: iii. Published Sources, under Paderewski, Ignacy Jan. Unpublished fragments in AAN.

PRO   Public Record Office, London.
See Sources: i. Archival Sources

Chapter 1 A Poor Start

1 Navarro, *A Few More Memories,* pp. 34–5. A great many people have claimed to have been present at this first concert, claims which all too often can be disproved. For the purposes of this opening vignette, however, there seems little point in quibbling about who was at the first Paris concert and who only came to the second.

2 Quoted by Vallerand, "I. J. Paderewski et la tradition humaniste polonaise," p. 211.

3 PM, p. 148.

4 Navarro, pp. 34–5.

5 Landau, *Paderewski,* p. 34.

6 Bobrowski, *Pamietniki Mojego Zycia,* I, 102–3.

7 Conrad, *Some Reminiscences,* pp. 60–1.

8 PM, pp. 30–1.

9 PM, pp. 37, 39.

10 PM, p. 25.

11 PM, p. 36.

12 PM, p. 37.

13 PM, pp. 36, 39.

14 PM, p. 38.

15 PM, p. 44.

Chapter II Warsaw
1 PM, pp. 51–2.
2 PM, p. 55.
3 PM, p. 56.
4 PM, pp. 56–7.
5 PM, p. 61.
6 PM, p. 56.
7 Auer, *My Long Life in Music,* p. 236.
8 PM, p. 59.
9 PM, p. 64.
10 PM, p. 73.

Chapter III The Quest for Virtuosity
1 Bogdanowicz, *Wspomnienia,* I, 227–8.
2 PM, p. 96.
3 PM, pp. 106–7; see also Opienski, *Ignacy Jan Paderewski,* p. 23.
4 Auer, p. 236.
5 PM, p. 74.
6 PM, p. 80.
7 PM, p. 81.
8 Phillips, *Paderewski,* p. 96; Nossig, "The Methods of the Masters," p. 61.
9 PM, p. 81.
10 Grzymala-Siedlecki, *Niepospolici Ludzie,* p. 302.
11 AAN, no. 217, f. 18: "w tej Warszawie w ktorej cie pokochalam"—i.e., before 1885, when the Gorskis moved to Paris; see also Helena Liibke Collection, correspondence between Paderewski and Helena Gorska from 1882; also Modjeska, *Memories and Impressions,* p. 466.
12 Modjeska, *Memories and Impressions,* p. 468.
13 PM, p. 98.
14 *Ibid.*
15 H. T. Finck, *Success in Music,* p. 375.
16 *Ibid.*
17 PM, p. 111.
18 See Newcomb, *Leschetizky as I Knew Him,* pp. 107, 242; Schonberg, *The Great Pianists,* pp. 278–80; Landau, p. 26; Lahee, *Famous Pianists,* p. 220.
19 Quoted in Schonberg, p. 279.
20 PM, p. 99.
21 PM, p. 103.
22 PM, p. 99.
23 Potocka, *Leschetizky,* p. 260.
24 Theodor Leschetizky interview in *Tygodnik Ilustrowany,* Warsaw, 24 January 1899.
25 PM, p. 99.
26 Theodor Leschetitzky interview, *op. cit.*
27 PM, p. 135.

28 PM, p. 108.
29 Quoted in Landau, p. 24.
30 Potocka, p. 262.
31 PM, p. 108.
32 Brook, *Masters of the Keyboard,* p. 109.
33 Review in *Echo Muzyczne i Teatralne,* quoted in Opienski, p. 48.
34 PM, pp. 112–13.
35 Quoted in Fuchss, "Paderewski Compositeur," p. 10.
36 PM, p. 121.
37 PM, p. 126.

Chapter IV The Lion of Paris
1 *Le Monde Artiste,* 18 March 1888; and other reviews quoted in Opienski, pp. 52–3.
2 PM, pp. 131–2.
3 Noailles, *Le Livre de Ma Vie,* pp. 210–12.
4 Bibliothèque Nationale, Montesquiou Papers, N.A. Fr. 15034, ff. 109–10.
5 Helena Gorska to Paderewski, late 1888, AAN 216, no. 35.
6 PM, p. 131.
7 PM, p. 146.
8 Helena Gorska to Paderewski, late 1888, AAN 216, f. 157.
9 PM, p. 133.
10 Quoted in Landau, p. 35; Phillips, p. 170.
11 H. T. Finck, *Success in Music,* p. 312.
12 Hoesick, *Powiesc Mojego Zycia,* pp. 461–2.
13 Noailles, *op. cit.,* p. 218.
14 Speech made at Evian, 25 August 1935, Hoover Institution, Paderewski Collection, Box 3.
15 Rachel de Brancovan to Paderewski, May 1890, AAN 242, f. 43.
16 Rachel de Brancovan to Paderewski, 1 January 1891, AAN 242, f. 49.
17 See AAN 242, 243, 244.
18 PM, p. 147.
19 PM, p. 146.
20 PM, p. 167.

Chapter V The Conquest of London
1 PM, p. 167.
2 *The Musical Times,* July 1890, p. 402.
3 Arthur Rubinstein, *My Young Years,* p. 383.
4 Klein, *Thirty Years of Musical Life in London,* pp. 296–7.
5 *The Musical Times,* June 1890, p. 346.
6 Phillips, p. 131.
7 Scrapbook of English press cuttings, AAN 282.
8 *Ibid.*
9 Phillips, p. 131.

10 *Ibid.*, p. 133.

11 *The Star*, 16 May 1890, article signed "Corno di Bassetto."

12 Wood, *My Life of Music*, p. 50.

13 Klein, *Thirty Years*, p. 298.

14 *Monthly Musical Record*, June 1890, p. 137.

15 *The World*, 18 June 1890.

16 *Ibid.*, 11 June 1890.

17 *Ibid.*, 18 June 1890.

18 *Monthly Musical Record*, July 1890, p. 150.

19 Bauer, *Harold Bauer, His Book*, pp. 23–4.

20 For the various descriptions of the meeting, see Huneker, *Steeplejack*, II, 56; PM, p. 186; G. Henschel, *Musings and Memories of a Musician*, pp. 351–2.

21 PM, p. 186.

22 Burne-Jones, *Memorials of Edward Burne-Jones*, II, 207–8.

23 PM, p. 189.

24 PM, p. 191.

25 Saint-Saëns, *Portraits et Souvenirs*, p. 135.

26 Arthur Rubinstein, *My Young Years*, p. 410.

27 *The World*, 5 November 1890.

28 PM, p. 172.

29 PM, p. 184.

30 PM, p. 180.

31 Helena Gorska to Paderewski, 22 March 1891, AAN 215, f. 13.

32 Helena Gorska to Paderewski, AAN 217, f. 30.

33 Helena Gorska to Paderewski, 22 May 1891, AAN 215, f. 9.

34 Jan Paderewski to Ignacy Paderewski, 26 March 1890, 20 October 1890 and n.d., 1892, AAN 211; also 150 letters from Ignacy Paderewski to Jan Paderewski in Helena Liibke Collection.

35 Klein, *Thirty Years*, p. 299.

36 G. Henschel, pp. 351–2.

37 H. Henschel, *When Soft Voices Die*, p. 72.

38 Hudson, "Chestnuts: A Study in Ivory."

39 PM, pp. 184–5.

40 PM, p. 141.

41 PM, p. 193.

42 Windsor Castle, Journal of Queen Victoria, entry for 2 July 1891—quoted by kind permission of Her Majesty the Queen.

43 PM, p. 193.

44 Scrapbook containing cuttings of English tours, AAN 282.

45 Bernard Shaw in *The World*, 15 July 1891.

46 *Ibid.*, 21 June 1893.

47 Sarrazin, *Imageries de Paderewski*, p. 33.

48 Rachel de Brancovan to Paderewski, ANN 242, f. 158.

49 Helena Gorska to Paderewski, 4 November 1891, AAN 215, f. 18.

50 Hélène Bibesco to Paderewski, May 1891, AAN 236, f. 11.

51 Laurence Alma-Tadema to Paderewski, November 1891; AAN 1151, no. 12.

Chapter VI The New World

1 PM, p. 199.

2 *Ibid.*

3 PM, p. 202.

4 PM, p. 204.

5 *Freund's Music and Drama,* 21 November 1891.

6 *New York Sun,* 18 November 1891.

7 *New York Times,* 18 November 1891; *New York Evening Post,* 18 November 1891.

8 James Huneker, quoted in Phillips, pp. 160–2.

9 *Freund's Music and Drama,* 21 November 1891.

10 PM, pp. 221–3.

11 PM, p. 226.

12 Quoted in Duleba, *Ignacy Jan Paderewski,* p. 59.

13 Helena Gorska to Paderewski, 26 February 1892, AAN 215, f. 53.

14 Ditto, AAN 216, f. 62.

15 Ditto, AAN 217, f. 18.

16 Ditto, AAN 217, f. 133.

17 Ditto, AAN 216, f. 120.

18 Ditto, AAN 216, f. 54.

19 Ditto, AAN 216, f. 128.

20 Fitzgerald, "Paderewski at Home."

21 PM, p. 227.

22 PM, p. 228.

23 PM, p. 229.

24 *Ibid.*

25 Rachel de Brancovan to Paderewski, AAN 242, ff. 84–5.

26 Ditto, AAN 242, ff. 289–90.

27 Helena Gorska to Paderewski, AAN 215, f. 82.

28 Ditto, AAN 215, f. 120.

29 Ditto, AAN 217, no. 35.

30 PM, p. 255.

31 PM, p. 259.

32 Helena Gorska to Paderewski, AAN 216, ff. 2, 12.

33 Ditto, AAN 216, f. 16.

34 Ditto, AAN 217, no. 34.

35 Rachel de Brancovan to Paderewski, AAN 243, f. 122.

36 Ditto, AAN 243, f. 39.

37 Speech made at Evian, 25 August 1935, Hoover Institution, Box 3.

38 Clermont-Tonnerre, *Mémoires,* III, 23.

39 Noailles, pp. 212–13, 218–19.

40 Landau, p. 246.
41 Quoted in Painter, *Marcel Proust,* II, 20.
42 Rachel de Brancovan to Paderewski, AAN 243, f. 39.
43 PM, pp. 268, 272.
44 Quoted in Opienski, p. 144.
45 Krehbiel, *How to Listen to Music,* pp. 154–5.

Chapter VII Paddymania
1 See Robinson Locke Scrapbooks in New York Public Library for headlines; see Schwab, *James Gibbons Huneker,* pp. 63–4, for poem.
2 Quoted in Grobicki, "Paderewski's Concerts in Toronto," p. 80; also Coleman, *Fair Rosalind,* p. 621.
3 Leslie, *The Film of Memory,* p. 209.
4 See scrapbook, AAN 160, f. 91; also Robinson Locke Scrapbooks.
5 Landau, p. 80.
6 Robinson Locke Scrapbooks, Vol. I.
7 Quoted in C. E. Le Massena, "Paderewski"; in Phillips; and in various others.
8 H. T. Finck, *Paderewski and His Art,* p. 11.
9 Quoted in Grobicki, "Paderewski's Concerts," p. 82.
10 Scrapbook, AAN 156, f. 31.
11 Wood, p. 147.
12 *New York Herald,* 26 March 1905.
13 *New York Telegram,* 4 February 1909.
14 A. Dale, quoted in Schonberg, p. 287.
15 Sitwell, *Great Morning,* p. 133.
16 Buffen, *Ignace Paderewski,* p. 5.
17 H. T. Finck, *Paderewski and His Art,* p. 23.
18 William Mason, quoted in Lahee, p. 228.
19 Shaw, *Music in London,* I, 14.
20 Quoted in Lahee, p. 230.
21 William Mason, quoted in H. T. Finck, *Paderewski and His Art,* p. 25; see also A. M. Henderson, "Paderewski as Artist and Teacher," pp. 411–12; Brower, *Piano Mastery,* p. 2; Huneker, *Franz Liszt,* p. 427.
22 W. J. Henderson, *What Is Good Music?,* p. 162.
23 H. T. Finck, *Success in Music,* p. 317.
24 Brower, *Piano Mastery,* p. 6.
25 Szumowska-Adamowska, "How Paderewski Taught Me to Play."
26 "Paderewski on Tempo Rubato," in H. T. Finck, *Success in Music,* p. 457.
27 Bauer, p. 272.
28 "Paderewski on Tempo Rubato," p. 454.
29 H. T. Finck, *Success in Music,* p. 321.
30 *Ibid.,* p. 270.
31 W. J. Henderson, p. 163.

32 Landowska, "Paderewski Orateur," p. 385.
33 Lahee, p. 213.
34 Quoted in Phillips, p. 177.
35 *Ibid.*, p. 189.
36 Brower, *Piano Mastery*, p. 10.
37 Baughan, p. 67.
38 W. J. Henderson, pp. 169–70.
39 Wood, pp. 167–8.
40 Shaw, *Music in London*, II, 97.
41 W. Mason, *Memories of a Musical Life*, pp. 60–1.
42 H. T. Finck, *Paderewski and His Art*, p. 23.
43 H. T. Finck, *Success in Music*, p. 314.
44 Quoted in Philllips, p. 169.
45 Shaw, *Music in London*, I, 208.
46 Chasins, *Speaking of Pianists*, p. 89.
47 Huneker, *Franz Liszt*, p. 428.
48 Montesquiou, *Roseaux Pensants*, p. 266.
49 Bibliothèque Nationale, Montesquiou Papers, N.A. Fr. 15073, f. 14.
50 Huneker, *Steeplejack*, II, 54.
51 Windsor Castle, Journal of Queen Victoria, entry for 2 July 1891—quoted by kind permission of Her Majesty the Queen.
52 Arthur Rubinstein, *My Young Years*, pp. 74–5.
53 Gilder, *Letters*, p. 215.
54 Hudson, p. 36.
55 Chasins, *Speaking of Pianists*, p. 88.
56 Wood, p. 145.
57 *Musical America*, 23 November 1907.
58 Montesquiou, pp. 266–7.
59 Noailles, pp. 218–19.
60 Wood, pp. 146–7.
61 Kirk, *Pablo Casals*, pp. 135–6.
62 PM, p. 280.
63 Makuszynski, *Koncert Paderewskiego*, p. 14.
64 Gaisberg, *Music on Record*, p. 174.
65 *Ibid.*, p. 177.
66 Fuller Maitland, *A Doorkeeper of Music*, p. 199.
67 Friedheim, *Life and Liszt*, p. 215.
68 Chasins, *Speaking of Pianists*, p. 91.
69 Quoted in H. T. Finck, *My Adventures in the Golden Age of Music*, p. 287.
70 Quoted in Phillips, p. 96.

Chapter VIII The Travelling Circus

1 Rachel de Brancovan to Paderewski, AAN 243, ff. 169–70.
2 Arthur Rubinstein, *My Young Years*, p. 74.

3 Navarro, p. 36.
4 Gaisberg, p. 177.
5 PM, p. 298.
6 PM, p. 317.
7 PM, p. 351.
8 PM, pp. 339, 348.
9 PM, p. 372.
10 PM, p. 241.
11 Steed, *Through Thirty Years*, pp. 274ff.
12 Quoted in Landau, p. 250; also PM, p. 184.
13 PM, p. 201.
14 PM, p. 230.
15 PM, p. 268.
16 PM, pp. 279–80.
17 PM, p. 263.
18 PM, pp. 235–6.
19 Gilder, p. 216.
20 PM, p. 213.
21 PM, p. 217.
22 PM, p. 365.
23 PM, pp. 127–8.
24 Arthur Rubinstein, *My Young Years*, p. 77.
25 PM, p. 313.
26 *New York Telegraph*, 4 February 1909.
27 Hadden, *Modern Musicians*, p. 52.
28 Shaw, *Music in London*, III, 14.
29 Robinson Locke Scrapbooks, I, 49.
30 Helena Modrzejewska to Chlapowski, March 1903, in *Korespondencja Heleny Modrzejewskiej*, II, 316–17.
31 PM, p. 308.
32 Quoted in Jarocinski, *Antologia Polskiej Krytyki Muzycznej*, p. 287.
33 *New York Herald*, 31 January 1902.
34 PM, p. 308.
35 Quoted in Jarocinski, p. 290.
36 Chybinski, *W Czasach Straussa i Tetmajera*, p. 44.
37 *New York Sun*, 25 November 1907.
38 PM, p. 326.
39 Gilman, "Paderewski's Symphony."
40 Szymanowski, *Z Listow*, p. 114.
41 Reginald de Koven in *New York World*, 1909; Jules Combarieu, quoted in Landau, p. 70; Marc Blumberg in *Musical Courier*, February 1909.
42 Shaw, *Music in London*, III, 15, 206.
43 PM, II, section VI, AAN 63, p. 69, unpublished; D. G. Mason, "A Conversation on Music with Paderewski"; Gaisberg, p. 178.
44 Labunski, "A Polish Pianist in Russia," p. 263.

45 D. G. Mason.
46 PM, pp. 361, 363.
47 *Musical Courier,* 3 February 1909.
48 PM, p. 367.

Chapter IX The Politician
1 Orlowski, *Paderewski i Odbudowa Polski,* I, 65.
2 APP, I, 28.
3 Laurence Alma-Tadema to Paderewski, AAN 1151, ff. 45–6.
4 Paderewski, *Chopin,* p. 20.
5 APP, I, 32.
6 Alfred Nossig to Helena Paderewska, APP, I, 44–6.
7 APP, I, 33.
8 PM, p. 387.
9 PM, p. 391.

Chapter X The Great War
1 PM, pp. 250–1.
2 PM, II, section V, p. 41, AAN 62, unpublished.
3 Joseph Conrad to Paderewski, 27 March 1915, APP, I, 67.
4 Rudyard Kipling to Paderewski, 27 March 1915, *ibid.*
5 PM, II, section V, p. 42, AAN 62, unpublished.
6 Stevenson, *Lloyd George: A Diary,* p. 38.
7 Newton D. Baker, quoted in Orlowski, *Paderewski,* II, 177.
8 APP, I, 31.
9 PM, II, section V, p. 83, AAN 62, unpublished.
10 Paderewski, *Poland Past and Present.*
11 Borglum, in Kosciuszko Foundation, *Paderewski, His Country and Its Recent Progress,* p. 12.
12 Upton Sinclair to Paderewski, Hoover Institution, Box 3; see also Landau, p. 111.
13 PM, II, section V, p. 64, AAN 62, unpublished.
14 APP, I, 87.
15 APP, I, 89.
16 APP, I, 100ff.
17 PM, II, section V, p. 67, AAN 62, unpublished.
18 Quoted in Phillips, p. 343.
19 APP, I, 91.
20 Wilson, *My Memoir,* p. 135.
21 Quoted in Landau, p. 116; see also Bernstorff, *My Three Years in America,* p. 298.
22 Stirling Memorial Library, Yale, "Diary of Edward M. House," XIII, 19.
23 *Ibid.,* House Ms., folder 10; Phillips, p. 350; APP, III, 135–42.
24 APP, III, 135–42.

25 Polish Institute and Sikorski Museum, London, *Horodyski Papers.*

26 PRO, 800, no. 204.

27 Phillips, p. 355.

28 Quoted in *ibid.,* p. 346.

29 Quoted in Orlowski, *Paderewski,* II, 154.

30 Quoted in Phillips, p. 349.

31 Quoted in Sywak, "I. J. Paderewski," p. 35.

32 APP, I, 169; APP, II, 234.

33 APP, I, 337.

34 Paderewski, *Mowa Mistrza,* p. 7.

35 PM, II, section V, p. 90, ANN 62, unpublished.

36 APP, I, 474.

Chapter XI Premier of Poland

1 PM, II, section V, pp. 95–6, AAN 62, unpublished.

2 *Ibid.,* p. 97.

3 *Ibid.,* p. 100. For the Foreign Office's and Balfour's attitude, see PRO, FO 371, 3282, nos. 190443, 191084, 193407, 206202, 206292.

4 PM, II, section V, p. 101, AAN 62, unpublished.

5 See PRO, FO 371, 3896, no. 753; 3282, no. 213639.

6 Quoted in Popielowna, *I. J. Paderewski,* p. 29.

7 D'Abernon, *The Eighteenth Decisive Battle of the World,* p. 39.

8 Malinowski, *Najnowsza Historia Polski,* II, 172.

9 Komarnicki, *The Rebirth of the Polish Republic,* p. 262; see also V. Kellogg, "Paderewski, Pilsudski and Poland," in *The World's Work,* May 1919.

10 Sywak, p. 126.

11 Hoover, *The Years of Adventure,* p. 356.

12 Sywak, p. 151.

13 Komarnicki, p. 304.

14 D'Abernon, *The Eighteenth Decisive Battle,* p. 40.

Chapter XII The Peacemaker

1 Conrad, *Life and Letters,* II, 216.

2 Proust, *47 Lettres inédites à Walter Berry.*

3 Clemenceau, *Grandeurs et misères d'une victoire,* pp. 124–6.

4 Nicolson, *Peacemaking,* p. 6; Dugdale, *A. J. Balfour,* II, 264.

5 Landau, p. 147.

6 Stevenson, p. 179.

7 Headlam-Morley, *A Memoir of the Paris Peace Conference,* p. 79.

8 *Documents on British Foreign Policy,* ed. E. L. Woodward and Rohan Butler, 1st Series, vol. X, nos. 505, 581.

9 PRO, FO 371, 3897, no. 11899; also Headlam-Morley, p. 70.

10 Lloyd George, *Memoirs of the Peace Conference,* p. 204.

11 APP, II, 83–4.

12 Dillon, *The Peace Conference,* p. 212.

13 PRO, FO 608, 68, no. 8080; 71, no. 6691.

14 PRO, FO 371, 3910, no. 81141.

15 Mordacq, *Le Ministère Clemenceau,* III, 288.

16 PRO, FO 371, 3910, no. 30574.

17 See Hugh Gibson's report, Hoover Institution, Gibson Archive, Box 5; Howard, *Theatre of Life,* vol. II, Appendix C; also Israel Cohen, "My Mission to Poland"; Komarnicki, pp. 310–12; Norman Davies, "Great Britain and the Polish Jews."

18 Nicolson, p. 193.

19 Headlam-Morley, p. 176.

20 House and Seymour, *What Really Happened at Paris,* p. 214; Lloyd George, pp. 888–90.

21 Miller, *My Diary of the Conference of Peace,* IX, 54.

22 Landau, p. 153.

23 Lloyd George, p. 203.

24 Nicolson, p. 354.

25 Lansing, *The Big Four and Others at the Peace Conference,* pp. 204–6.

26 Lloyd George, pp. 646–7; *Documents on British Foreign Policy,* 1st Series, III, 348–55.

27 Dmowski, *Polityka Polska,* II, 37.

28 Lansing, *The Big Four,* p. 20.

Chapter XIII Fall from Grace

1 APP, II, 283–7.

2 Hoover Institution, Gibson Archive, Box 5, no. 8.

3 Drohojowski, *Wspomnienia Dyplomatyczne,* p. 145.

4 Witos, *Moje Wspomnienia,* II, 250.

5 Bilinski, *Wspomnienia i Dokumenty,* II, 205.

6 Rataj, *Pamietniki,* p. 42; also Witos, p. 251.

7 Drohojowski, p. 145.

8 Nicolson, p. 314.

9 Bilinski, II, 205.

10 Grzymala-Siedlecki, *Niepospolici Ludzie,* p. 337.

11 Rataj, p. 42.

12 Gilbert, *Winston S. Churchill,* IV, 288; also Sywak, p. 229.

13 Quoted in Malinowski, II, 379.

14 Hoover Institution, Gibson Archive, Box 5, no. 4.

15 *Ibid.,* no. 8.

16 House, "Paderewski: The Paradox of Europe."

17 Quoted in C. Kellogg, *Paderewski,* p. 180.

18 Rataj, p. 42.

Chapter XIV The Elder Statesman

1 Barblan-Opienska, "Souvenirs sur Paderewski," p. 22.

2 APP, II, 615–19.

3 AAN 1463, no. 29.
4 APP, III, 50–1.
5 APP, II, 254–6.
6 AAN 1463, no. 29.
7 PM, p. 386.
8 PM, II, section V, pp. 126–7, AAN 62, unpublished.
9 *Ibid.*, p. 129.
10 PM, II, section VI, p. 2, AAN 63, unpublished.
11 *Ibid.*, p. 6.
12 H. T. Finck, *My Adventures,* p. 294.
13 Opienski, p. 144.
14 Fuller Maitland, p. 201.
15 Opienski, p. 113.
16 PM, II, section VI, p. 9, AAN 63, unpublished.
17 *Ibid.*, p. 8.
18 PM, p. 90.
19 Bernard Sarrazin, p. 11.
20 Szumowska-Adamowska, *ibid.*
21 Landau, p. 20.
22 A. Strakacz, *Paderewski as I Knew Him,* p. 203.
23 PM, II, section VI, p. 41, AAN 63, unpublished.
24 *Ibid.*, p. 71.
25 Stravinsky, *Expositions and Developments,* p. 79; see another version
of the story, told by Lady Oxford to Rom Landau, in Landau, p. 202.
26 Landau, p. 269.
27 PM, II, section VI, p. 71, AAN 63, unpublished.
28 A. Strakacz, pp. 107–8.

Chapter XV Fighting to the Last

1 Laurence Alma-Tadema to Antonina Wilkonska; Hoover Institution,
Paderewski Archive, Box 4; Labunski, p. 335.
2 Phillips, p. 148.
3 A. Strakacz, p. 145.
4 Arthur Rubinstein, *My Many Years,* p. 263.
5 Doret, *Temps et Contretemps,* pp. 322–3.
6 Labunski, p. 248.
7 Related by Zygmunt Mycielski to the author, Warsaw, 1980.
8 PM, p. 327.
9 Related to the author by Heinrich Fraenkel in a letter dated 6 August
1979.
10 A. Strakacz, pp. 192–200.
11 Hoover Institution, Paderewski Archive, Box 2.
12 Letter to Marshal Foch, *ibid.,* Box 1; letter to Weygand in the possession of M. E. Weygand, Coatamour.
13 Hoover Institution, Paderewski Archive, Box 5.

14 Drohojowski, p. 32.
15 APP, IV, 33–4, 109.
16 APP, IV, 152, 155.
17 Gaisberg, p. 178.
18 A. Strakacz, p. 211.
19 AAN 1647, no. 15.
20 Hoover Institution, Paderewski Archive, Box 6.
21 *Ibid.,* Box 3.
22 APP, IV, 240–1.
23 Wszelaki, "Z Listem do Riond-Bosson."
24 Ligocki, *Dialog z Przeszloscia,* p. 379.
25 Polish Institute and Sikorski Museum, A48, no. 2.
26 A. Strakacz, p. 297.
27 Hoover Institution, Paderewski Archive, Box 3.
28 *Ibid.*
29 Paderewski to Raczkiewicz, 26 October, Polish Institute and Sikorski Museum, A48, no. 5.
30 A. Strakacz, p. 286.
31 Quoted in Opienski, p. 130.
32 A. Strakacz, p. 303.
33 Hoover Institution, Paderewski Archive, Box 4.
34 *Ibid.*
35 Quoted in S. Strakacz.
36 Quoted in A. Strakacz, p. 326.
37 Hoover Institution, Paderewski Archive, Box 1.
38 Haller, *Pamietniki,* pp. 10–11.
39 Balfour, quoted in Landau, p. 201; Hanotaux, *Mon Temps,* III, 354.

Sources

I *ARCHIVAL SOURCES*

Archiwum Glowne Akt Nowych, Warsaw:
    Paderewski Archive.
    Archive of the Polish National Committee.
Hoover Institution, Stanford University:
    Paderewski Collection.
    Hugh Gibson Collection.
Helena Liibke Collection (private), Los Angeles.
Stirling Memorial Library, Yale University:
    House Ms.
Public Record Office, London:
    Foreign Office Papers—Poland; FO 371.
                 —Peace Conference; FO 608.
    Admiralty Papers—Ships' Logs; ADM 53 (H.M.S. *Concord,* 38393).
                 —Baltic Fleet, ADM 137.
Polish Institute and Sikorski Museum, London:
    John Ciechanowski Papers; Kol. 82/3.
    Horodyski Papers.
    Acts of Polish National Committee in Paris 1918–1920.
    Sessions of Council of Ministers; PRM K 102.
Bibliothèque Nationale, Paris:
    Montesquiou Papers.
The Royal Library, Windsor Castle:
    Journal of Queen Victoria.
Chateau de Grandson, Switzerland (Filipinetti Collection):
    Paderewski Papers.
Archives du Ministère des Affaires Etrangères, Quai d'Orsay, Paris:
    Série A. Guerre 1914–1918 Vols. 720–40.
             Paix-Guerre 1918–1920 Vols. 331, 332.

II UNPUBLISHED SOURCES

Borysiewicz, Eleonora, "Mcmoirs." Copy in possession of Dr. E. Paderewska-Chroscicka.

Dygat, Zygmunt, "Wspomnienia o Paderewskim." Private collection.

Labunski, Wiktor, "A Polish Pianist in Russia." Conservatory Library, University of Missouri, Kansas City.

Le Massena, C. E., "Paderewski." Copy in New York Public Library.

Locke, Robinson, "Scrapbooks." New York Public Library.

Sywak, Zofia, "I. J. Paderewski, Prime Minister of Poland." Doctoral thesis. Copy in Pilsudski Institute, New York.

Zaczkowska, Margrit, "Ignaz Jan Paderewski, Leben und Werke." Copy in Polish Museum, Rapperswil, Switzerland.

III PUBLISHED SOURCES

Adlington, W., "Paderewski at Home," in *Pearson's Magazine,* vol. VI, 1898.

Akty i Dokumenty Dotyczace Sprawy Granic Polskich na Konferencji Pokojowej w Paryzu. Paris, 1920.

Aldrich, Richard, *Concert Life in New York, 1902–1923.* New York, 1941.

Anderson, H. L., "Ignace Jan Paderewski—Discography," in *British Institute of Recorded Sound Bulletin,* no. 10, Autumn 1958.

Armstrong, William, "At Paderewski's Villa," in *Saturday Evening Post,* 13 October 1906.

——, "What Good Piano-Playing Calls For," in *Ladies' Home Journal,* February 1907.

Asquith, Earl of Oxford and, *Memories and Reflections.* 2 vols., London, 1928.

Auer, Leopold, *My Long Life in Music.* London, 1924.

Baranowski, Wladyslaw, *Rozmowy z Pilsudskim.* Warsaw, 1938.

Barblan-Opienska, Lydia, "Souvenirs sur Paderewski," in *Revue Musicale de Suisse Romande,* vol. XVII, no. 4, Yverdon, 1964.

Bauer, Harold, *Harold Bauer, His Book.* New York, 1948.

Baughan, Edward A., *Ignace Jan Paderewski.* London, 1908.

Baumgartner, André, *La Vérité sur le Prétendu Drame Paderewski.* Geneva, 1948.

Becket, John, "Paderewski in His Daily Life," in *Ladies' Home Journal,* March 1896.

Beerbohm, Max, ed., *Herbert Beerbohm Tree.* London, 1920.

Bernstorff, Count, *My Three Years in America.* London, 1920.

Bilinski, Leon, *Wspomnienia i Dokumenty.* 2 vols., Warsaw, 1925.

Bobrowski, Tadeusz, *Pamietniki Mojego Zycia.* Warsaw, 1979.

Bochenek, Leon, *W Holdzie I. J. Paderewskiemu.* Poznan, 1935.

Bogdanowicz, Marian Rosco, *Wspomnienia.* Cracow, 1959.

Borglum, Gutzon, *see* Kosciuszko Foundation.

Brook, Donald, *Masters of the Keyboard.* London, 1946.

Brower, Harriette, *Piano Mastery*. New York, 1915.

——, "Some Causes of Paderewski's Leadership in Piano Music," in *The Musician*, September 1926.

Buffen, F., *Ignace Paderewski*. New York, 1891.

Burne-Jones, Lady, *Memorials of Edward Burne-Jones*. 2 vols., London, 1904.

Chantavoine, Jean, "Un Pianiste Homme d'Etat," in *Revue Hebdomadaire*, Vol. IV, Paris, 1919.

Chapin, Adèle le Bourgeois, *Their Trackless Way: A Book of Memories*. London, 1931.

Chasins, Abram, "The Art of Paderewski," in *Saturday Review of Literature*, November 1956.

——, *Speaking of Pianists*. New York, 1958.

Churchill, Lady Randolph (Mrs. George Cornwallis-West), *Reminiscences*. London, 1908.

Chybinski, Adolf, *Utwory na Fortepian Paderewskiego*. Lwow, 1910.

——, *W Czasach Straussa i Tetmajera*. Krakow, 1959.

Cieplinski, Jan, *Ignacy Jan Paderewski*. New York, 1960.

Clemenceau, Georges, *Grandeurs et Misères d'une Victoire*. Paris, 1930.

Clermont-Tonnerre, Duchesse de, *Mémoires*. Paris, 1928–39.

Cohen, Israel, "My Mission to Poland," in *Jewish Social Studies*, Vol. XIII, 1951.

Coleman, Marion Moore, *Fair Rosalind*. Cheshire, Conn., 1969.

Comyns Carr, Mrs. Joseph, *Reminiscences*. London, 1926.

Conrad, Joseph, *Life and Letters*, ed. G. Jean-Aubry. 2 vols., London, 1927.

——, *Some Reminiscences*. London, 1912.

Curie, Eve, *Madame Curie*. London, 1938.

Curle, Richard, *The Last Twelve Years of Joseph Conrad*. London, 1928.

Currier, T. P., "Paderewski—An Example for the Student of Piano-playing," in *The Musician*, May 1890.

Czermanski, Zdzislaw, "O Panu Paderewskim i o Montparnasse," in *Wiadomosci*, 20 September 1959.

D'Abernon, Edgar Vincent, Viscount, *The Eighteenth Decisive Battle of the World*. London, 1931.

——, *Portraits and Appreciations*. London, 1931.

Damrosch, Walter, *My Musical Life*. London, 1924.

Davies, Norman, "Great Britain and the Polish Jews," in *Journal of Contemporary History*, vol. VIII, 1973.

De Koven, Reginald, "Paderewski's Symphony," in *New York World*, 21 February 1909.

Dillon, E. J., *The Peace Conference*. London, 1919.

Dmowski, Roman, *Polityka Polska i Odbudowanie Panstwa*. 2 vols., Hanover, 1947.

Documents on British Foreign Policy, ed. E. L. Woodward and Rohan Butler, 1st Series, vols. 1–12. London, 1947.

Doret, Gustave, *Temps et Contretemps*. Fribourg, 1942.

Draper, Ruth, *The Letters of Ruth Draper*, ed. N. Warren. London, 1979.

Drohojowski, Jan, *Wspomnienia Dyplomatyczne*. Cracow, 1969.

Dugdale, E. C. Blanche, *A. J. Balfour*. London, 1936.

Duleba, Wladyslaw, *Ignacy Jan Paderewski*. Cracow, 1966.

Durand, J., *Quelques Souvenirs d'un Editeur de Musique*. Paris, 1924.

Dziewanowski, M. K., *Joseph Pilsudski: A European Federalist*. Stanford, Calif., 1969.

Fassett, S., "A Paderewski Discography," in *American Music Lover*, August 1941.

Filasiewicz, Stanislaw, *La Question Polonaise pendant la Guerre Mondiale*. Paris, 1920.

Finck, Abbie C., "Paderewski at Home," in *Century Magazine*, vol. LXXXVI, 1913.

Finck, Henry T., *My Adventures in the Golden Age of Music*. New York, 1926.

——, *Paderewski and His Art*. New York, 1895.

——, *Success in Music and How It Is Won* (with a chapter on Tempo Rubato by I. J. Paderewski). London, 1910.

Fitzgerald, W. G., "Paderewski at Home," in *Harper's Weekly*, February 1906.

Fountain, Alvin M., *Roman Dmowski*. New York, 1980.

Frank, Waldo, *Time Exposures*, by "Search-Light." New York, 1926.

Friedheim, Arthur, *Life and Liszt*. New York, 1961.

Fuchss, Werner, "Paderewski Compositeur," in *Annales Paderewski*, no. 2, Morges, 1980.

Fuller Maitland, J. A., *A Doorkeeper of Music*. London, 1929.

Gaisberg, F. W., *Music on Record*. London, 1946.

Gasiorowska, Natalia, *Materialy Archiwalne do Stosunkow Polsko-Radzieckich*. 3 vols., Warsaw, 1957–64.

Gerson, Louis, *Woodrow Wilson and the Rebirth of Poland*. New Haven, Conn., 1953.

Gilbert, Martin, *Winston S. Churchill*. London, 1975.

Gilder, Richard Watson, *Letters*, ed. Rosamond Gilder. New York, 1916.

Gilman, Lawrence, "Paderewski's Symphony," in *Harper's Weekly*, March 1909.

Giron, Simone, *Le Drame Paderewski*. Geneva, 1948.

Glabinski, S., *Wspomnienia Polityczne*. Pelplin, 1939.

Grobicki, Aleksander, "Koncert," in *Kultura*, January–February 1959.

——, "Paderewski's Concerts in Toronto," in V. Turek, *The Polish Past in Canada*. Toronto, 1960.

Grzymala-Siedlecki, Adam, *Niepospolici Ludzie*. Cracow, 1961.

——, *Rozmowy z Samyn Soba*. Cracow, 1972.

——, *Swiat Aktorski Moich Czasow*. Warsaw, 1957.

Hadden, J. C., *Modern Musicians*. London, 1913.

Haller, Jozef, *Pamietniki*. London, 1964.

Halny, Roman, *Ignacy Paderewski*. Warsaw, 1935.

Halski, Czeslaw, *Ignacy Jan Paderewski*. London, 1964.

Hanotaux, Gabriel, *Mon Temps,* vol. III. Paris, 1940.

Haraucourt, Edmond, *Mémoires*. Paris, 1946.

Headlam-Morley, James, *A Memoir of the Paris Peace Conference*. London, 1972.

Henderson, A. M., "Paderewski as Artist and Teacher," in *Musical Times,* August 1956.

——, "A Study of Paderewski's Piano-playing," in *New York Times,* 17 November 1895.

Henderson, W. J., *What Is Good Music?* London, 1898.

Henschel, Sir George, *Musings and Memories of a Musician*. London, 1918.

Henschel, Helen, *When Soft Voices Die*. London, 1949.

Heylbut, Rose, "Stars—What They Are Like," in *Good Housekeeping,* December 1932.

Hoesick, Ferdynand, *Powiesc Mojego Zycia*. Warsaw, 1959.

——, *Szkice i Opowiadania*. Cracow, 1900.

Hoover, Herbert, *The Years of Adventure*. London, 1952.

House, Edward Mandell, "Paderewski: The Paradox of Europe," in *Harper's Magazine,* December 1925.

——, and Charles Seymour, *What Really Happened at Paris*. London, 1921.

Howard, Esme (Lord Howard of Penrith), *Theatre of Life*. London, 1936.

Hudson, G., "Chestnuts: A Study in Ivory," by "Israfel," in *The Dome,* January 1894.

Hullah, Annette, *Theodor Leschetitzky*. London, 1906.

Huneker, James Gibbons, *Franz Liszt*. New York, 1911.

——, *Steeplejack*. 2 vols., New York, 1921.

Janta, Aleksander, "Pamieci Paderewskiego," in *Wiadomosci,* no. 20, 13 May 1963.

Jarocinski, S., ed., *Antologia Polskiej Krytyki Muzycznej XIX i XX Wieku*. Cracow, 1955.

Kanski, Jozef, "Plytowe Dokumenty Sztuki Ignacego Paderewskiego," in *Ruch Muzyczny,* July 1971.

Kellogg, Charlotte, *Paderewski*. New York, 1956.

Kellogg, Vernon, "Paderewski, Pilsudski and Poland," in *The World's Work,* May 1919.

Kirk, H. L., *Pablo Casals*. New York, 1974.

Klein, Hermann, *Musicians and Mummers*. London, 1925.

——, *Thirty Years of Musical Life in London*. New York, 1903.

Komarnicki, Tytus, *The Rebirth of the Polish Republic*. London, 1957.

Kosciuszko Foundation, *Paderewski, His Country and Its Recent Progress*. New York, 1928.

Kozicki, S., *Sprawa Granic Polskich na Konferencji Pokojowej*. Warsaw, 1921.

Krehbiel, H. E., *How to Listen to Music*. New York, 1897.

Krzyzanowski, J. R., "Henryk Sienkiewicz and Ignacy Paderewski," in *The Polish Review*, vol. XV, no. 3, 1970.

Lahee, IIenry C., *Famous Pianists of Today and Yesterday*. Boston, 1901.

Landau, Rom, *Paderewski*. London, 1934.

Landowska, Wanda, "Paderewski Orateur," in *Revue Mondiale*, 15 August 1923.

——, "Recollections of Paderewski," in *Saturday Review of Literature*, June 1951.

Lansing, Robert, *The Big Four and Others at the Peace Conference*. London, 1922.

——, *The Peace Negotiations*. New York, 1921.

Larnac, Jean, *La Comtesse de Noailles*. Paris, 1931.

Lechon, Jan, "Paderewski," in *Wiadomosci*, 11 September 1949.

Leslie, Shane, *The Film of Memory*. London, 1938.

Ligocki, Edward, *Dialog z Przeszloscia*. Warsaw, 1970.

——, *Homage to Paderewski*. Edinburgh, 1941.

Lloyd George, David, *Memoirs of the Peace Conference*. 2 vols., New Haven, Conn., 1939.

Makuszynski, Kornel, *Koncert Paderewskiego*. Lwow, 1936.

Malinowski, Wladyslaw Pobog, *Najnowsza Historia Polski*, vol. II. 2nd ed., London, 1967.

Mamatey, V. S., *The United States and East Central Europe*. Princeton, N.J., 1957.

Martens, F. H., *Paderewski*. New York, 1923.

Martin, Ralph G., *Lady Randolph Churchill*. 2 vols., London, 1969–72.

Masaryk, T. G., *The Making of a State*. London, 1927.

——, *The New Europe*. Washington, D.C., 1918.

Mason, Daniel Greogry, "A Conversation on Music with Paderewski," in *Century Magazine*, November 1908.

Mason, William, *Memories of a Musical Life*. New York, 1901.

——, "Paderewski: A Critical Study," in *Century Magazine*, March 1892.

McMillan, Mary Lee, and Ruth Dorval-Jones, *My Helenka*. Durham, N.C., 1972.

Micewski, A., *Roman Dmowski*. Warsaw, 1971.

Miller, David Hunter, *My Diary of the Conference of Peace*. New York, 1924.

Mlynarski, Feliks, *Wspomnienia*. Warsaw, 1971.

Modjeska (Modrzejewska), Helena, *Korespondencja Heleny Modrzejewskiej i Karola Chlapowskiego*. Warsaw, 1965.

——, *Memories and Impressions*. New York, 1910.

Montesquiou, Robert de, *Roseaux Pensants*. Paris, 1897.

Mordacq, General Jean Jules Henri, *Le Ministère Clemenceau*. Paris, 1931.

Namier, Julia, *Lewis Namier*. London, 1971.

Navarro, Mary Anderson de, *A Few More Memories*. London, 1936.

Newcomb, Ethel, *Leschetizky as I Knew Him*. New York, 1921.

Nicolson, Harold, *Peacemaking*. London, 1933.

Noailles, Comtesse de, *Le Livre de Ma Vie*. Paris, 1932.

Nossig, Alfred, "The Methods of the Masters of Piano-teaching in Europe," in *Century Library of Music,* vol. XVIII. New York, 1902.

——, *Paderewski*. Leipzig, 1901.

Nowakowski, Zygmunt, "Sprzet Podobny do Fortepianu," in *Wiadomosci Polskie,* vol. XXVIII, 1941.

Opienski, Henryk, *Ignacy Jan Paderewski*. Cracow, 1960.

Orlowski, Jozef, *Helena Paderewska*. Chicago, 1929.

——, *Paderewski i Odbudowa Polski*. Chicago, 1939.

Paderewski, Ignacy Jan, *Archiwum Politczne I. J. Paderewskiego*. 4 vols., Warsaw, 1976.

——, "Breadth in Musical Art," in James F. Cook, *Great Pianists on Piano-playing*. Philadelphia, 1917.

——, *Buy a Share in America*. Washington, D.C., 1941.

——, *Chopin* (speech delivered in Lwow, 1910). Rome, 1945.

——, *Discours prononcé à Vevey le 20 Octobre 1924*. Lausanne, 1925.

——, Introduction to Esme Howard, *Music in the Poets*. London, 1927.

——, *Mowa Mistrza I. J. Paderewskiego Wygloszona z Powodu Smierci Henryka Sienkiewicza*. Chicago, 1917.

——, "Mysli, Uwagi, Refleksje," in *Muzyka,* no. 2, 1934.

——, "O Stylu Naradowym w Muzyce," in *Echo Muzyczne i Teatralne,* vol. 1, 1884.

——, *The Paderewski Memoirs*, with Mary Lawton. London, 1939.

——, "Poetic Piano-playing," in *Ladies' Home Journal,* May 1910.

——, *Poland and Peace: An Address*. London, 1933.

——, *Poland Past and Present* (an address delivered 5 February 1916 in the Chicago Auditorium). New York, 1916.

——, "Wizje Przyszlosci," in *Muzyka,* nos. 7–12, 1936.

——, "Wspomnienia," in *Muzyka,* nos. 4–6, 1933.

Painter, George Duncan, *Marcel Proust*. 2 vols. London, 1959–65.

Pawlikowski, Jozef, "A. Wilkonska i I. Paderewski w Moich Wspomnieniach," in *Wiadomosci,* 27 December 1959.

Phillips, Charles, *Paderewski: The Story of a Modern Immortal*. New York, 1934.

Pilsudski, Jozef, *Pisma Zbiorowe*. 12 vols. Warsaw, 1937–8.

Plater-Zyberk, André, *Le Fonds Paderewski de Secours aux Enfants Polonais en Suisse*. Geneva, n.d.

Polinski, Aleksander, "Filharmonia. Pierwszy Koncert," in *Kuryer Warszawski,* no. 307, 1901.

Popielowna, S., *I. J. Paderewski*. Tarnow, 1919.

Porte, J. F., *Chopin: The Composer and His Music*. London, 1935.

Portland, Duke of, *Men and Women and Things*. London, 1937.

Potocka, Countess Angèle, *Leschetizky*. New York, 1903.

Proust, Marcel, *47 Lettres Inédites à Walter Berry*. London, nd.

273

Pruszynski, Ksawery, "Paderewski," in *Wiadomosci Polskie*, no. 28. London, 1941.

Pruszynski, M., "Rozmowa Historyczna z Stanislawem Grabskim," in *Zeszyty Historyczne*, no. 36, Paris, 1976.

Rataj, Maciej, *Pamietniki*. Warsaw, 1965.

Relief Committee for the Victims of War in Poland, *Second and Last Report*. Vevey, 1919.

Rodzinski, Halina, *Our Two Lives*. New York, 1976.

Rubinstein, Anton, *Autobiography*, tr. Aline Delano. Boston, 1980.

Rubinstein, Arthur, *My Many Years*. London, 1980.

———, *My Young Years*. London, 1973.

Saint-Saëns, Camille, *Portraits et Souvenirs*. Paris, n.d.

Sarrazin, Bernard, *Imageries de Paderewski*. Annonay, 1945.

Saxe-Coburg-Gotha, Marie-José, Princess of Belgium, *Albert et Elisabeth de Belgique, Mes Parents*. Paris, 1971.

Schonberg, Harold C., *The Great Pianists*. London, 1969.

Schwab, A. T., *James Gibbons Huneker*. Stanford, Calif., 1963.

Seymour, Charles, ed., *The Intimate Papers of Colonel House*. New York, 1926.

Shaw, Bernard, *London Music in 1888–89 as Heard by Corno di Bassetto*. London, 1937.

———, *Music in London 1890–94*. 3 vols., London, 1932.

Sidorowicz, Boguslaw, *I. J. Paderewski*. Poznan, 1924.

Sitwell, Sir Osbert, *Great Morning*. London, 1949.

Steed, H. Wickham, *Through Thirty Years*, vol. I. London, 1924.

Steinway, Theodore E., *People and Pianos*. New York, 1953.

Stevenson, Frances (Countess Lloyd George), *Lloyd George: A Diary*. London, 1971.

Stoker, Bram, *Personal Reminiscences of Henry Irving*, vol. II., London, 1906.

Strakacz, Aniela, *Paderewski as I Knew Him*. New Brunswick, N.J., 1949.

Strakacz, Sylwin, "Paderewski," in *The Polish Review*, 28 June 1943.

Stravinsky, Igor, *Expositions and Developments*. New York, 1962.

Studnicki, W., *Ludzie Idee Czyny*. Warsaw, 1937.

Sukiennicki, W., "Balfour a Polska," in *Zeszyty Historyczne*, no. 17, Paris, 1970.

———, "Mademoiselle Pilsudskiego," in *Zeszyty Historyczne*, no. 3, Paris, 1963.

Swirski, Czeslaw, "Wyjasnienia," in *Zeszyty Historyczne*, no. 7, Paris, 1965.

Szumowska-Adamowska, Antonina, "How Paderewski Taught Me to Play," interview with William Armstrong, in *Ladies' Home Journal*, May 1905.

Szymanowski, Karol, *Z Listow*. Cracow, 1958.

Temperley, H. W. V., *A History of the Peace Conference of Paris*. 6 vols., London, 1920.

Tretbar, C. F., *Paderewski: A Biographical Sketch*. New York, 1892.

Turczynska, Nina, "Paderewski w Morges," in *Tydzien Polski*, 29 July 1961.

Vallerand, Jean, "I. J. Paderewski et la Tradition Humaniste Polonaise," in *Etudes Slaves,* vol. V, Montreal, 1960–1.

Verne, Mathilde, *Chords of Remembrance.* London, 1936.

Warrender, Lady Maud, *My First Sixty Years.* London, 1933.

Wasilewski, Leon, *Jozef Pilsudski Jakim go Znalem.* Warsaw, 1935.

Wasiutynski, Wojciech, *I. J. Paderewski.*

Waskowski, A., *Znajomi z Tamtych Czasow.* Cracow, 1960.

Wilson, Edith Bolling, *My Memoir.* London, 1939.

Witos, Wincenty, *Moje Wspomnienia.* 3 vols., Paris, 1964–5.

Wood, Sir Henry, *My Life of Music.* London, 1938.

Wroniak, Z., "Geneza Rzadow Paderewskiego," in *Zeszyty Naukowe Uniwersytetu Adama Mickiewicza,* no. 4, Poznan, 1959.

Wszelaki, Jan, "Z Listem do Riond-Bosson," in *Wiadomosci,* 27 September 1959.

Zaleski, August, "Paderewski Byl Federalista," in *Rzeczpospolita Polska,* 15 June 1960.

Zmijewska, Eugenia, *Polak Obywatel.* Kijow, 1917.

Index

ADAM ZAMOYSKI

Adam Zamoyski was born of Polish parents in New York in 1949, but was educated in England, at Downside and Oxford. He has worked for the B.B.C. and the *Financial Times* in London, and has contributed to various papers and periodicals, including *History Today* and the *Times Literary Supplement*. He is the author of a biography of Chopin, as well as a military history of the 1920 Soviet–Polish war. *Paderewski* is his third book.